EIGHTEENTH-CENTURY ENGLISH DRAMA

a comprehensive collection of over 200 representative plays, reproduced in facsimile in fifty-eight volumes with critical introductions by leading scholars

General Editor

PAULA R. BACKSCHEIDER

A GARLAND SERIES

The Plays of
EDWARD MOORE

Edited with an introduction by
J. PAUL HUNTER

GARLAND PUBLISHING, INC.
New York & London
1983

For a complete list of the titles in this series see the final pages of
this volume.

The facsimiles in this volume have been made from copies
in the libraries of Yale University, with the exceptions of
Solomon, which is from the Sibley Music Library of the
Eastman School of Music of the University of Rochester, and
the excerpts from *The World*, which are from the New York
Public Library.

Library of Congress Cataloging in Publication Data

Moore, Edward, 1712–1757.
   The plays of Edward Moore.

   (Eighteenth-century English drama)
   Reprint of works originally published 1743–1756.
   Includes bibliographical references.
      I. Hunter, J. Paul, 1934–   II. Title.   III. Series.
PR3605.M3A19   1983   822'.5   78-66606
ISBN 0-8240-3603-4

The volumes in this series are printed on acid-free,
250-year-life paper.

Printed in the United States of America

CONTENTS

INTRODUCTION

I n his own time, Edward Moore (1712–1757) had a modest reputation as a moralist and social commentator, and he enjoyed the company—if not the full confidence—of many of the major writers and patrons in mid-century. Today, he is all but unknown, the victim of time and the tides of taste rather than of conscious or unconscious neglect. There is no use pretending that our time is deprived because his works remain unread; those works served a temporal purpose and the world moved on. Yet Moore is an interesting historical case, for he seems one of the least likely people in the early eighteenth century to have sought a literary career (let alone a career in the theatre), and he nevertheless developed a body of literary work—and a way of life—that is altogether representative of his time. If one wished to study social and cultural patterns of the mid-eighteenth century—or if one wanted to identify a typical Englishman of 1750—one could hardly do better than read the works, or consider the case, of Edward Moore.

He was largely self-educated, widely read without being truly learned, well connected without any social pretensions of his own, and skilled in the kind of cool observation that made him a spectator and rambler rather than a courtier or an isolate, a beadsman or a sybarite. He was a committed (but transplanted) Londoner whose roots were still planted firmly in the green and pleasant countryside of a century earlier; he was a man displaced from the common labors of the hands and from the elemental process of survival in a world where work and life had been intimately, tensely connected, and yet a figure ill at home in the newer world of commerce, industry, professionalism, and abstraction. He was devout (but not so religious as his parents), enlightened (but not so sophisticated as Continental counterparts he never met), successful at his trade yet never celebrated or even passingly well-to-do. He was conventional in behavior, common-sensical in his ideas and commitments, sentimental in his tastes, conventionally moral in his judgments. Although never fully settled in any way of life, he nevertheless seemed beyond restlessness; although an admirer of intensity, he never fully engaged it as its celebrant or prophet. His life, like his writing, looks nostalgically to a past that had become irrelevant but still lingered into his own time, and he provides little analysis of his own time or prediction of where the future will go. Moore is a literary and cultural puzzle much as the age in which he lived and wrote is a puzzle: it is tempting to find extensions of times gone by or hints of uncharted ages to come, but hard to locate a firm center. He exemplifies the "literary loneliness" of his age and typifies its aloofness from a flow of time that it did not understand and would have preferred to ignore.[1]

I

Moore did not set out to be a man of letters, and the fact that he became a fabulist, poet, playwright, and journalist tells us more about practical possibilities in the rapidly expanding print economy of mid-century than it tells us about Moore's motivation and talent. Precisely why Moore turned to writing when he failed as a linen-draper we do not know; it may simply have been the least unattractive of possibilities open to him in his world and time. There is nothing in his published work to suggest burning literary ambition, but there is also nothing to suggest significant aspirations in any other career. He left school fairly young (but we do not know exactly when) to apprentice himself to a wholesale linen-draper in London, later became a factor to a merchant in Ireland, then returned to London as a partner in the linen trade.[2] Moore must have been about thirty when the partnership was dissolved, and the world was not exactly all before him. Moore's writings suggest very little disappointment and no bitterness about his business failure, but his best play (*The Gamester*, 1753) takes much of its energy from a prevailing concern with the ability to achieve a minimal and respectable level of sustenance. The tragedy of the titular hero consists in his inability to be satisfied with what he has, and his poor stewardship leads to poverty, ruin, and disgrace; but the values of the play ultimately have to do with the capacity to be content with a humble lot, justly earned. "What a World is this!" the hero soliloquizes on his way to disaster. "The Slave that digs for Gold, receives his daily Pittance, and sleeps contented. . . . O Shame! Shame!—Had Fortune given me but a little, that little had been still my own. But Plenty leads to Waste; and shallow Streams maintain their Currents, while swelling Rivers beat down their Banks, and leave their Channels empty" (II, i).

Family tradition might seem to have pointed toward a career as a dissenting clergyman, and Moore's writings consistently show a religious and moral concern appropriate to his upbringing, but they do not suggest that degree of religious zeal (or the obsession with any particular "calling") that it would probably have taken for Moore to follow—in the age of Law, Whitefield, and Wesley—in the steps of his father and grandfather as dissenting clergymen. At least one of his brothers, John, his elder by four years, did extend the family tradition, but the record left by Edward Moore of his own mind suggests interest rather than intensity in religious issues and moral concerns. And despite their firm didactic thrust,

Moore's works suggest a mind and will easily contented with modest attainments both material and moral. There seems to have been nothing driven or obsessional in Moore's temperament; he was a man of solid character rather than a rugged explorer of the human spirit. We may never know why he left so young the two dissenting academies (one run by his uncle) where he spent his childhood and early youth, but the traces he left of himself in the themes and concerns and moods of his writing suggest a conventional decision, even passive acquiescence, rather than determined choice. The decision not to extend his education toward a career as, for example, a schoolmaster or lawyer may or may not have been influenced by scholarly aptitudes and interests, but in becoming a London apprentice in a respectable, developing trade Moore flowed with the times—from country to city, from zealous religious dissent to honest commerce, from eager intellectual curiosity to practical, utilitarian concerns. Moore grew up in a world defined by Defoe, prophetic of George Eliot.

The rigorous, but brief, years in a dissenting academy provided Moore an education neither more nor less adequate than that of most people who, in the 1740's and 1750's, made their livings by their pens. When he turned to writing as a career about 1742 or 1743, he must have done so with a fairly full awareness of what his contemporaries were reading, whether or not he himself was widely read in the popular literature of the moment. Moore's efforts in all the genres of prose and poetry that he tried show an ease of address that argues a ready awareness of what predecessors and competitors are doing. If Moore is almost never allusive in the Augustan manner, he is seldom self-consciously novel or singular either. All his works fit rather easily into a genre or subgenre popular (or at least readily recognizable) in his own time, even if they seem odd to a modern eye. The modesty about literary tradition expressed by Moore in the first number of *The*

World—the periodical of his later years—is genuine but nevertheless misleading,[3] for if Moore did not often carry traces of classical learning into his writings and if he did not frequently cite his contemporaries, he still drew confidently upon the native fund (hardly yet noticed by most university-educated writers) that sustained most writers in the English tradition after Pope.

II

Moore's only modern biographer judiciously notes the parallel between Moore's literary career and that of John Gay, who shared with Moore a dissenting family background, a rural boyhood in the West of England, and failure in business as a mercer.[4] Gay's *Fables* (1727–1729; 1738) were certainly the model—whether or not they were the ultimate inspiration—for Moore's first major publication, *Fables for the Female Sex* (1744), and whether or not Moore consciously moved to the theatre in emulation of Gay, his writing career represents a distinct (and probably self-conscious) departure from the "Vergilian progression" that had led classically inspired writers from Spenser to Pope through pastoral and georgic to epic in quest of complexity and posterity.

Moore did write a variety of conventional verses and songs that demonstrate a modest capability in emulating poets from Carew and Herrick to Suckling and Prior. Some follow traditional forms such as the pastoral dialogue, and some bear Ovidian traces or other minor features that suggest an awareness of the classical tradition. But although the poems do not feature startling originality or bold imaginative strokes, their commitment is clearly to a native and vernacular tradition. No one has ever claimed that Moore was a significant poet or even an accomplished versifier; about the most that can be said

qualitatively of his verse is that it is competent, but the fact
that he bothered to write poems—occasional poems, *vers de
société*, lyrics of several kinds—suggests at once a sophisticated,
playful quality in Moore and a conviction (however unconscious) that literature in his own time was undergoing a trans-
formation that suggested both a new audience and a new
authorial class—as well as a loosened sense of form and tradition. It is not much of a tribute to his contemporaries that
Moore dared hope, in the late 40's, for the laureateship in case
of Cibber's death; there are strong indications that Moore's
then-friend Lyttelton would have proposed Moore for the bays
if the opportunity had arisen.[5] But there is a little more to be
said for Moore's claims than that he had the proper Whig
opinions and connections: Moore was in tune with the changing sense of tradition, and if those changes were not altogether
for the better in his own time, they still represent the altered
literary and cultural assumptions necessary to the development
of the novel, of a variety of prose nonfictional forms, and
ultimately of the poetry of later ages. Present-day readers will
find Moore's miscellaneous poems readily available in the facsimile edition of the 1756 collected *Poems, Fables, and Plays*,
issued by Gregg International Publications in 1969.

Moore's *Fables for the Female Sex* (also available in the Gregg
edition) represents his highest poetical accomplishment; it was
reprinted frequently throughout the eighteenth century and
into the nineteenth, often entire and sometimes combined in
thicker volumes with Gay's *Fables*. Modern readers tend to find
the morals too intrusive and the verse somewhat labored, but
the main barrier to appreciation seems to be changes in taste
that have taken verse fables from us as a viable literary form.
The fortunes that elevated Moore to modest fame (his first play
was identified as "By Mr. Moore, Author of *Fables for the Female
Sex*") because he read the tastes of his time correctly turned
against him after nearly three quarters of a century of atten-

tion; Moore's talent for measuring and meeting popular expectations has turned out to be, in poetry as in drama, both his greatest distinction and his ultimate limitation.

III

Of the works included in this volume, *Solomon. A Serenata, In Score, Taken from the Canticles* is the slightest from a strictly literary point of view but one of the most interesting from the perspective of its total artistic accomplishment. It is, to be sure, at best quasi-dramatic; only one of its sections, a dream sequence, is fully dramatic in its appeal, but its potential as a performance piece persuaded me to include it in this volume—that, plus the fact that it has apparently not been reprinted in its entirety since 1749. Excerpts from it have been reprinted frequently in collections of songs, and many of these excerpts continue to be played and sung frequently, but the total work, conceived as a longish performance by Moore and the famous composer Dr. William Boyce, has languished in rare book rooms.

It was, of course, Boyce's reputation that gained the work its contemporary attention, and at least four editions appeared between 1743 (or possibly 1742) and 1749.[6] Moore's name did not appear on the title page for his contribution of the libretto; it is, however, his first published work, and even read as a poem apart from the music it is not totally negligible. What is perhaps most striking about Moore's libretto is its vivid sensuousness and sensuality. A modern reader may be surprised that a man of Moore's Puritan background would savor so fully, and without allegorical trappings, the open eroticism of the *Song of Songs*, but Moore's contemporaries, less squeamish even if less worldly than we are, would not have been mystified or even surprised. Moore remains true to the spirit of the original and often close to the phrasing as well; it is no more odd that a man of Moore's background is attracted to the eroticism of the Solomon legend than that Matthew Prior found Solomon a subject for a lengthy philosophical poem: Both men would have argued that their choice of subject was traditional, orthodox, and reverent. But the fact that Moore would feel free—true as he was to the spirit of his religious heritage—to adapt the *Song of Songs* for public performance accurately suggests how much expectations (and philosophical assumptions about the nature of representation and performance) had changed since Cromwell's followers had darkened the theatres a century earlier. No doubt Moore was not nursed on stage plays during his childhood in Berkshire, Somerset, and Dorset, and had his rural clergyman father lived to see Moore's own plays performed, he very likely would not have approved, but Edward Moore evidently felt no deep contradiction in the fact that his didactic impulse, displayed early in *Fables for the Female Sex*, found its most successful outlet on the stage. Moore had neither abandoned his religious heritage in turning to the stage, nor does he seem to have felt compromised by using the theatre to promote deeply held moral convictions.

Moore's first play, *The Foundling*, opened at Drury Lane on 13 February 1748 with David Garrick, Charles Macklin, Spranger Barry, Peg Woffington, and Susannah Cibber in the cast; it was an immediate success, playing to largely appreciative audiences for eleven nights and receiving favorable notice in the press. Most contemporary comment centered on the play's characters, and the judgment of Moore's ability with characterization was almost wholly favorable except for severe and sustained criticism of the character of Faddle, a fop and would-be wit whom the audience evidently found tedious, "low," and unlikely as a lover for the attractive Rosetta. Sensitive to the objections, Moore cut the part radically after the first night; in the Dedication to the published version, Moore says that "The Disapprobation which the Character of *Faddle* met with the first Night, made it necessary for me to shorten it in almost every Scene" (pp. iv–v). The first edition printed, however, the uncut version ("But tho' Success has attended the Alteration, I have ventur'd to publish it in its original Dress," p. v), and Moore evidently remained partial himself to the full version; even in the collected edition of 1756 he printed most of the play unchanged from the first edition, although implying in the Dedication that he is presenting a much abbreviated Faddle. He does excise one passage of about a page and a half (from the bottom of page 24 in the version printed here up to Faddle's long speech on page 26) in which Faddle recounts how his drinking buddies had toasted Rosetta—and also Fidelia, the "foundling" heroine. That passage is hardly more gross or less witty than the rest of the scenes involving Faddle, and Moore's decision to delete it quietly (he makes no reference to the omission) while leaving the rest of the original version intact suggests a modest bending to criticism alongside a prevailing preference for his own taste in low farce. It may have been the extended references to heavy drinking or the almost (but not quite) indelicate compliments to Rosetta and Fidelia that changed Moore's mind in this single instance. It would be interesting to know whether this passage was included on the night when Henry Fielding saw the play. Tradition has it that Fielding took his subtitle for *Tom Jones* from Moore after seeing the play performed,[7] and the toasting passage omitted from the later printed version bears a general resemblance to the toasting scene in *Tom Jones* in which Northerton and Tom Jones fight over Northerton's claim to have known Sophia, although in Moore the toasting is merely recounted, not staged.

The Foundling is a sentimental comedy in the tradition of Steele's *Conscious Lovers* (1722), and contemporaries immediately noticed the close resemblance, both in spirit and in plot, between the two plays. Moore's play is derivative, both particularly to Steele and more generally to plays old and new that were repeatedly performed in the 40's, but the nature of its debts to other plays and playwrights suggests the efforts of a theatrical newcomer trying to learn his craft rather than any slavish imitation or unseemly theft. As in his poems, Moore made himself very much aware of the tradition and the competition; it was consistently his way of learning his craft, and if he never really rose above the general level of dramatic fare in his time or carved out a distinctive, individual style of his own, he reminds us of the strategic imitation characteristic of apprenticeship in his time. Almost all the best English writers in the two centuries before Moore had developed their own distinctive craft by first imitating the masters, and Moore— although he never transformed the strategies of imitation into a distinctive voice or form of his own—was solidly, consciously, and comfortably in the tradition. The difference was that his models were, in drama as in poetry, primarily domestic and relatively recent; Moore may well have known Plautus and Terence, but the models significant to his own art were English and contemporary—at least in the sense that they were being performed contemporaneously, although some of them originated in an older age.

It has not, I think, been noticed how significant Shakespeare seems to have been for Moore. His plays ring with Shakespearean echoes that suggest a long and comfortable acquaintance. It is not that Moore consciously alludes to Shakespeare very much or that his effects depend upon a recognition of Shakespearean structures or phrases, but rather that an admiration for Shakespeare and an alertness to Shakespearean strategies seem to have been prominently in Moore's mind as he wrote. Often one gets the sense that Moore falls into a quiet but discernible pattern of both phrase and charac-

ter conception that derives from a close and sympathetic reading (and probably seeing) of Shakespeare's works. It is as if
Shakespeare's presence hovers over Moore as a model of how
people are to act, feel, and speak. There is in Moore no sense
of anxiety of influence, no sense of wrestling a guardian angel
or paternal figure into submission or of transforming inherited
identity into some new individual self, but rather a sense of a
peaceful, knowledgeable presence into which Moore would
like to—and sometimes almost does—disappear.

Sometimes Moore almost seems to imagine himself in
Shakespeare's world of words once he has set his own plot and
characters into motion. He is fond of the Elizabethan soliloquy
as a device of avowal and self-exposure, the conversations of his
leading characters are full of extended metaphors that faintly
echo Shakespeare's cosmic resonance, and his heroines often
seem to wish to speak (and imagine) in ways characteristic of
Shakespeare's romances. Moore's character conception is
hardly Shakespearean, and only occasionally does he raise pas-
sionate attention to the plight of his creations, but even in their
most bourgeois plights they seem to aspire to Shakespearean
language to provide them with a sense that they belong on the
stage and in a lengthy tradition. Whether they call on a
Shakespearean formula ("Be cool, my Life!"[8]), ponder a familiar topos ("I never built a Castle in my Sleep, that wou'd not
last 'till Doomsday—Give me a Dream, and I am Mistress of
the Creation—I can do what I will with every Man in it"[9]), or
engage in direct allusion ("Let not Excess of Wonder over-
power you, *Fidelia*—For I have a Tale to tell, that will exceed
Belief"[10]), they seem to long for a text and context better than
Moore can give them. Moore seems to yearn for a verbal
tradition in which he can lose his identity (rather than in
which to find himself), and he reaches widely for formulas and
echoes to achieve a stock theatrical response, as when he has a
seducer mouth Roman/Renaissance carpe diem platitudes:

"'Tis now the Summer of your Youth; Time has not cropt the Roses from your Cheek, tho' Sorrow long has wash'd 'em— Then use your Beauty wisely."[11] For Moore, the Elizabethan age seems to have been the verbal ideal, and if his subjects and themes are distinctively mid-eighteenth century, his language harks back, like that of the bardolaters just after him, to earlier times. Moore had a pretty good ear, and for him the language of the theatre seems to have been the words he heard Shakespearean actors deliver.

Reading Moore's plays with Shakespeare constantly in mind does not make them any better, but it does sometimes give them a sense of ease, liveliness, and familiarity that Moore seems not to have achieved in his nondramatic prose or poetry. Moore's own language seldom seems very rich, and his sentences, one by one, in prose and poetry, usually seem flat and rather lifeless. His style is functional—it serves—but it seems to lead to (or reflect) nothing significant beyond itself. But sometimes the speeches in his plays are better than that, and (if I am right that he achieves this quality because of a kind of aura that lasts in his mind from reading, seeing, and hearing Shakespeare) the performances of his work, done by actors who played Shakespeare very frequently, may well have achieved theatrically a richer sense of conception and implication than Moore's plays, seen as his own wholes, actually justify. Not that the Shakespearean influence was altogether positive: often Moore seems simply to slide into a formula that he associates with Shakespeare, and the result may be somewhat ludicrous in the characterizations that emerge. *The Foundling*'s villain, Villiard, for example, takes on, through verbal echoes, Shylockian associations that are neither appropriate nor convincing, and in *The Gamester*, the villain Stukely is sometimes heightened, and sometimes not, by a verbal and conceptual closeness to Iago. Resonance by association is not the surest way to art.

The plot of *The Foundling* is slight, conventional, and fairly incredible. It involves two love relationships, one between the Young Belmont and Fidelia, the other between Colonel Raymond and Rosetta. Faddle is the supposed complication in the latter relationship, although no one but Colonel Raymond seems to believe that Rosetta actually has any interest in Faddle, and it is no wonder that first-nighters felt insulted at being asked to accept Rosetta as worthy and at the same time believe she is interested in Faddle. The complications in the relationship of Young Belmont and Fidelia are twofold. First, Belmont is a stereotypical rake, initially interested only in seduction, and, second, Fidelia's uncertain parentage leaves not only her marital possibilities but her identity and heritage somewhat in doubt. Belmont has brought Fidelia to live in the family home, making everyone believe that she is the sister of a dead friend from college. Actually, he has stolen her away from her evil guardian, Villiard; somehow her virtue has remained intact, and ultimately she brings Belmont to the altar, though not before the discovery that she is really the long-lost (and, up until now, forgotten) sister of Colonel Raymond. The recognition scene at the end of the play is, it seems to me, even more than usually improbable in this popular variety of romantic plot; Moore makes no real effort to make it credible, and the play ends on the usual note celebrating romantic, familial, and cosmic order.

The Foundling played fifteen nights in its first season and was revived fairly often for many years, until just after the turn of the century. In the 1790's, it was still playing fairly often in America, and there are both French and German translations. It is, however, hardly a significant dramatic effort; it is a pleasing entertainment, no more. The fact that it remained popular for so long is a tribute to the fine acting traditions of Garrick's time and after, and the fact of its popularity does not, in fact, speak well of the playwriting talents of Moore's contemporaries.

Moore's second play, *Gil Blas*, apparently was occasioned by

Smollett's translation of Le Sage in 1749. It opened at Drury Lane on 2 February 1751 and failed to excite much enthusiasm, although hanging on for nine nights; it was never revived. There is little of Moore the moralist in *Gil Blas*, and apparently the audience was disappointed in expectations that, according to the *Gentlemen's Magazine* (February 1751), had been very high. "[I]t is doing [the author] some honour to say [the audience] were *disappointed*," says the author of the *Gentlemen's Magazine* piece, who went on to berate the play for its lack of "moral sentiment."[12] But there is much more to be disappointed in here than the lack of moral sentiment.

The play derives from the early chapters of the fourth book of Le Sage's *Gil Blas*, the episode in which the hero goes into the service of Don Vincente de Guzman and thus comes to attend his only daughter, Aurora. Moore apparently did not feel obliged to follow Le Sage too closely, but the details of plot are not very important anyway in either the romance or the play. Most of the effects in Moore's play depend upon misunderstandings (Gil Blas thinks that Aurora is in love with him but then discovers that the lover she was talking about in code is actually someone else) and disguises, often disguises that involve men posing as women or women as men, and the sexual comedy of misunderstandings and disguises becomes a farce of cross-sexual duplicity based on disguises within disguises; it is dramatic irony gone mad. Moore does manage some fairly witty lines and a few situational smiles, but it is no wonder that, coming just after *The Foundling*, *Gil Blas* had been published as "By Mr. Moore," whereas the play that followed *Gil Blas* (*The Gamester*) was published anonymously. There was considerable speculation about the authorship of *The Gamester* even before it opened, and the continuing prevalence of rumors that seem far from the mark (that the author was a woman, for example, or that the Rev. Joseph Spence was the author) suggests that someone—possibly Moore himself, possibly Garrick—was deliberately misleading the public so that Moore's name would not be associated with the play until the public had judged it on its own merits.

The Gamester opened at Drury Lane on 7 February 1753 with Garrick in the title role of Beverley and ran for ten nights. Contemporary reaction was favorable but not enthusiastic, and it was not until later in the century that *The Gamester* became a theatrical staple. Once established, however, *The Gamester* held its popularity for three quarters of a century, and there are all sorts of translations, adaptations, and imitations.[13] *The Gamester* has many of the best (and worst) features of nineteenth-century melodrama, and it is not difficult to imagine why audiences found it affecting, even when lesser actors than Garrick played the key role.

The Gamester is relentless in its attack on gambling, and Moore uses every trick in his power to turn audience sympathies on that central issue. Beverley is portrayed as hopelessly within the grasp of a force he does not understand; he abhors his vice and is full of self-hatred, but finds himself unable to stop his continuing plunges to try to recoup his modest fortune, salvage his family's welfare, and save himself. The uncompromising villain, Stukely, repeatedly drives him on, pretending to be his friend and making small loans to guarantee that Beverley continues to venture. Stukely repeatedly steps forward to remind us of his own villainy, telling us plainly that his only motive is to ruin Beverley, or that he covets Mrs. Beverley, or that he loves evil for its own sake—ultimately even plotting murder to achieve his wicked ends. He hovers over Beverley and over nearly every scene like a bad dream; sometimes he talks like an anthology of Iago imitations, but his relentless presence and ceaseless drive into scene after scene of his own making not only push his plot and Moore's play forward but also produce a tense sense of impending doom that lingers and appalls. Beverley is thus always a victim, yet he claims (and actually seems to retain) full responsibility for his own fate so that, although the prevailing mood of the play is certainly pathos, there are tragic overtones as well. Beverley is over-drawn as well as overwrought throughout, yet he is somehow almost believable; Beverley clearly takes some of his features from Fielding's Booth in *Amelia*, but a case could be made for his being a superior fictional creation.

The play deals in extreme emotional excesses throughout, and some of the lines seem utterly impossible (Mrs. Beverley, for example, says: "I have my Jewels left yet. I'll sell 'em to supply our Wants; and when all's gone these Hands shall toil for our Support. The Poor should be industrious . . . ," I, i). But the play also contains some very moving moments. The gimmicks are blatant and sometimes clumsily wrought, as when Beverley (after losing all near the end of the play) tries to evoke sympathy through his suddenly produced infant son, whose existence until now had only been mentioned once in passing, even though much of the play had been about the disintegration of the family in the wake of Beverley's incurable vice. Much pathos is wrung, too, from the faithful sister of Beverley, whose inheritance is ventured and her lover nearly killed because of her compassion.

The ultimate "source" for Moore's play is probably, as Caskey has argued,[14] the pseudo-Shakespearean *Yorkshire Trag-edy*, and once again Moore depends heavily on the dramatic tradition for his effects, although here Moore comes closest to turning the tradition into something of his own. But the crucial decisions are again made by Moore's reading of what the contemporary public wanted and expected.

By any standard, *The Gamester* is sentimental in the ex-treme, and by prevailing standards now it is just plain corny. And yet its intensity is somehow affecting. It may be that, as contemporary rumor had it, Garrick wrote some of the play's best speeches, but Moore's achievement here, if far short of

greatness, is not negligible. If Moore's best comedy, *The Foundling*, has seemed to most critics far inferior to the stock eighteenth-century example of bourgeois comedy, *The Conscious
Lovers*, on which it is based, *The Gamester* at least rivals its
contemporary model, *The London Merchant*, usually considered
the chief example of eighteenth-century bourgeois tragedy. It
seems to me better theatre, and it richly deserves to be available to readers who wish to understand the force of moral
sentiment in the later eighteenth century.

IV

A month before the first performance of *The Gamester*, Moore
began the periodical project that absorbed his energy during
the remaining four years of his life—*The World. By Adam Fitz-
Adam*. Actually the project belonged to the publisher Dodsley,
and several of Moore's friends had cooperated to set up
Moore's editorship in order to provide him a modest, comfortable living. *The World* delivered to the public 209 weekly papers, 61 of them written by Moore, with most of the others
written by those who donated their talents in Moore's support.
I am sorry to have to say that many of *The World*'s best papers
are not by Moore, but the general level of the periodical was
fairly high, and Moore's own contribution was always competent, if never dazzling. *The World* was quite popular from the
start, usually printing between two thousand and three thousand copies, and sets of it were frequently reissued later in the
century.[15] Many of the best papers were by Lord Chesterfield,
Richard Owen Cambridge, and Horace Walpole, but some
thirty authors contributed to the pages of *The World*.
    Like many another eighteenth-century periodical, *The
World* chiefly contained commentary on the passing fashionable

scene. Manners and contemporary social customs were its major subject for comment, and one can get from its pages a tolerably accurate sense of what it was like to be alive and trendy in the 1750's. Its prose was often ironic, sometimes caustic; it specialized in mild "social" satire, although occasionally rising to considerable concentration, as in its repeated attacks on gambling. Moore was not a man of many ideas, and when he found one that he liked he stuck to it, turned it several ways, and channeled what intensity he had toward it. *The World* was generally well received, although Dr. Johnson's modest opinion of it[16] is perhaps the most accurate reflection of its middle place in eighteenth-century journalism.

Perhaps the most surprising thing about *The World*, given Moore's own career, is its relative lack of interest in drama and the theatre. Of the sixty-one papers by Moore, only four have anything remotely to do with plays, performances, or behavior in the theatre, and none of these says anything significant about the nature of dramatic art. I have included those papers here, along with three others that suggest Moore's interest (never very intense) in other literary issues and social habits.

The World ended on 30 December 1756, and Moore's own demise came less than two months later, surprisingly and quite suddenly, in the midst of his plans for a new periodical to succeed *The World*. His widow, Jane Hamilton Moore, whom he had married in 1750, lived until 1804; his only child, a son, died in 1773 after a brief career at sea. If Moore counted on immortality through his writing (and it is unlikely that he did), he came closest to achieving it in some of the characters, most notably Beverley, whom he fleshed out upon the stage. He cannot be said to have made any major original contribution to the history of drama, but his work, while derivative and conventional, is usually interesting, competent, and (almost profoundly) representative of the theatre of his time.

In the Prologue to *The Foundling*, Moore characterized his own work this way:

> He forms a *Model* of a virtuous *Sort*,
> And gives you more of *Moral* than of *Sport* (ll. 9–10)

It is a just appraisal and could stand as his appropriately plain epitaph.

J. Paul Hunter
University of Rochester

Notes

1. For a fine discussion of the mid-century sensibility familiar to Moore, see John Sitter, *Literary Loneliness in Mid-Eighteenth Century England* (Ithaca and London: Cornell University Press, 1982).

2. The standard biography of Moore is that of John Homer Caskey, *The Life and Works of Edward Moore* (New Haven: Yale University Press, 1927), still the readiest source of most information about Moore and largely reliable for biographical information. *The London Stage* should, however, be consulted for more accurate information about the performance of the plays.

3. Moore claimed he would seldom use Latin mottoes for his *World* essays, although he used, for No. 1, the following motto from Lucretius:

> Nil dulcius est, bene quam munita tenere
> Edita doctrina sapientum templa serena;
> Despicere unde queas alios, passimque videre
> Errare, atque viam palanteis quaerere vitae.
> Certare ingenio, contendere nobilitate,

NOTES

Nocteis atque dies niti praestante labore
Ad summas emergere opes, rerumque potiri.
4. See Caskey, pp. 9, 21–24.

5. Caskey reprints (p. 54) a letter from Fielding to Lyttelton suggesting that the latter "destined" Moore for the laureateship.

6. The facsimile reprinted here is from an edition dated 1743, which may be the first edition, although an undated edition entitled *Solomon; a Serenata for the Voice, Harpsichord, and Violin* may be earlier. The work was not, however, performed until 1743.

7. See Wilbur Cross, *The History of Henry Fielding*, 3 vols. (New Haven: Yale University Press, 1918), II, 107.

8. *The Gamester*, p. 29.

9. *The Foundling*, p. 7.

10. *The Foundling*, p. 63.

11. *The Gamester*, p. 48.

12. Quoted by Caskey, p. 73. Caskey records as well several other hostile reactions to *Gil Blas*.

13. A number of them are conveniently listed by Caskey, pp. 175–77.

14. Pp. 100–06.

15. One of the reprints—the Dodsley edition of 1761—contains the publisher's list of the authors of most of the papers.

16. See Boswell's *Life of Johnson*, Hill ed., 1887, I, 410.

SOLOMON

SOLOMON.

A

SERENATA,

In SCORE,

Taken from the CANTICLES.

Set to MUSICK

By Mr. WILLIAM BOYCE,

Compofer to HIS MAJESTY.

LONDON:

Printed and Sold for the Author, by J. WALSH, in
Catharine-Street in the *Strand.*

M. DCC. XLIII.

A

L I S T

OF THE

S U B S C R I B E R S.

A.

*T*HE *Rev. Mr.* Abbot, *Gentleman of his Majesty's Chapel Royal, and Minor Canon of* St. Paul's *Cathedral,* &c.
Miss Aylworth, *of* Chelsea.
Mr. John Awbrey, *of* New *College, in* Oxford.
Mr. John Alcock, *Organist of* St. Laurence, *in* Reading.
The Apollo *Academy.*

B.

The Hon. *the Lady* Harriot Beard.
The Lady Bampfield.
Dr. Battie.
Mrs. Burk.
Miss Catharine Bovey.
Miss Brydges.
Miss Bouch.
Thomas Bower, *Esq;*
Mr. William Barns, *Merchant, in* Bristol.
Mr. Beauvoir, *of* St. John's *College, in* Cambridge.
Mr. Edward Boyce, *of* Pembroke-hall, *in* Cambridge.
Mr. Belchier, *Surgeon.*
Mr. Joshua Baker.
Mr. George Burton.
Mr. Beard.
Mr. Brown.
Mr. Joseph Baudin.
Mr. John Barret.
Mr. Thomas Bence, *of* Exeter.
Mr. John Barker, *Organist of* Holy Trinity *Church, in* Coventry.

C.

The Right Hon. Thomas Carter, *Esq; Master of the* Rolls *in* Ireland.
Sir William Codrington, *Bart.*
The Rev. Mr. Carleton, *Subdean of his Majesty's Chapels Royal,* &c.
Miss Molly Codrington.
Miss Molly Caswall.
Mrs. Crane.
Mrs. Clive.
John Codrington, *Esq;*
Byam Crump, *Esq;*
John Crew, *Esq;*
Charles Cutts, *Esq;*
Samuel Cox, *Esq;*
Thomas Cooper, *Esq; of* Dublin.
Patrick Cockburn, *Esq; of* Dublin.

Richard

A LIST of the SUBSCRIBERS.

Richard Cox, *Esq*;
The Rev. Mr. Camplin, *of* Chrift-Church College, *in* Oxford.
Mr. Joshua Cox.
Mr. Thomas Clarke.
Mr. David Cheriton, *Gentleman of his Majesty's Chapel Royal, and Vicar Choral of* Westminster-Abbey.
Mr. Richard Church, *Organist of* Chrift-Church, *in* Oxford.
Mr. John Church, *Vicar Choral of* St. Patrick's, *and* Chrift-Church, *in* Dublin, *and Vicar Choral of* St. Patrick's, *in* Ardmagh.
Mr. Thomas Chilcot, *Organist, in* Bath.
The *Musical Society in* Canterbury.
The *Musical Society in* Chichefter.
The *Musical Society in* Coventry.
The *Charitable Musical Society, in* Fishamble-ftreet, Dublin.

D.

His Grace the Lord *Archbishop of* Dublin.
The Rev. Sir John Dolben, *Bart.*
Sir Francis Dafhwood, *Bart.*
The Hon. *Lieutenant General* Dalzel.
Miss Dobbs, *of* Dublin.
John Davis, *Esq; of* Watlington, *in* Norfolk.
Charles Dunbar, *Esq*;
George Dodfon, *Esq*;
Timothy Dewel, *Esq; of* Hemftead, *near* Gloucefter.
William Dean, *Esq; of* Dublin.
The Rev. Mr. De Chair, *Minor Canon of* St. Paul's *Cathedral,* &c.
Mr. Henry Dunsford, *of* Exeter.
Mr. Michael Dorfett, *of* Pembroke-hall, *in* Cambridge.
Mr. David Digard, *Organist, of* Oxford *Chapel;* Ludgate *and* Limehoufe *Churches.*
Mr. William Denby, *junior.*

E.

Auguftine Earle, *Esq*;
Mr. Charles Eldridge, *of* New Windfor.
Mr. Thomas Edwards, *of* Greenwich.

F.

Miss Betty Fifher, *of* Briftol.
William Freeman, *Esq*;
Marmaduke Fothergill, *Esq; of* York, *Two Books.*
Samuel Fofter, *Esq; of* Windfor.
The Rev. Mr. Fitzherbert, *Prieft-Vicar of* Exeter *Cathedral.*
Mr. John Philip Fuhr, *Merchant, in* Briftol.
Mr. Richard Fuller, *Banker.*
Mr. Michael Chriftian Feftin.
Mr. Robert Frith.

Mr. Charles Froud, *Organist of* St. Giles's, Cripplegate.

G.

The Rev. Dr. Green, *Prebendary of* Worcefter, *and Rector of* St. George's, Ormond-ftreet.
Dr. Maurice Greene.
Miss Mary Gilbert.
Miss Sarah Gibbon.
Miss Elizabeth Gibbon.
Miss Rebecca Godwin.
James Gibbon, *Esq; Two Books.*
Waterhoufe Gibbon, *Esq*;
Richard Glynn, *Esq*;
Mr. Greenbank, *of* Worcefter.
Mr. Prince Gregory, *Gentleman of his Majesty's Chapel Royal,* &c.
Mr. Grover.
Mr. Thomas Gladwin, *Organist of* St. George's *Chapel, near* Grofvenor Square, *Two Books.*
Mr. Barnaby Gunn, *Organist of* Birmingham.
Mr. John Gerard, *Organist of the Cathedral at* St. Afaph.
Mr. William Godfrey, *Organist of* Lambeth *Church.*
The *Musical Society at the* Globe *in* Fleet-ftreet.
The *Musical Society at the* Greyhound *in the* Strand.
The *Musical Society in* Gloucefter.

H.

Sir Jofeph Hankey, *Knight, Alderman of* London.
Miss Amie Harcourt, *of* Briftol.
Miss Hornby.
George Frederick Handel, *Esq*;
Henry Hudfon, *Esq*;
Benjamin Hall, *Esq*;
James Hunter, *Esq*;
The Rev. Mr. Hooper, *Prieft-Vicar of* Exeter *Cathedral.*
The Rev. Mr. Hughes, *Minor Canon of* Worcefter *Cathedral.*
Mr. Hart, *Banker.*
Mr. Thomas Hudfon, *of* Lincoln's-Inn-Fields.
Mr. William Hayes, *Professor of Musick in the University of* Oxford, &c.
Mr. Heffetine, *Organist of the Cathedral at* Durham.
Mr. Richard Hains.
Mr. Charles Holder.
Mr. John Hadlow, *Vicar Choral of* Weftminfter-Abbey.
Mr. Samuel Howard, *Organist of* St. Bride's *in* Fleet-ftreet.
Mr. Samuel Hawkes, *Organist of* Dulwich College *in* Surry.

Mr.

A LIST of the SUBSCRIBERS.

Mr. Matthew Huffey, *Organist of* St. Alban's *in* Woodstreet.
Mr. —— Hudson, *Organist of* St. George's Ratcliff Highway.
Mr. —— H.
Mr. John Hitchcock, *Harpsichord-maker.*

I.

Mrs. Ann Jones, *of* Stepney.
Miss Elizabeth Jelf.
John Irwin, *Esq; of* Dublin.
Mr. Thomas Jersey, *of* Oxford.
Mr. Thomas Jesser.
Mr. Jordan, *Organ-builder.*
Mr. George Jones.
Mr. David Jones, *Vicar Choral of* Westminster-Abbey.
Mr. Jeacock.
Mr. John Johnson, *Six Books.*

K.

Miss Kingscote.
Mr. Knowles.
Mr. Kent, *Organist of* Winchester *Cathedral and College.*
Mr. John Keeble.
Mr. T. K.

L.

Sir Bybie Lake, *Bart.*
Stephen Lightfoot, M. D.
Mrs. Lynch.
Miss Catharine Maria Long.
Miss Charlotte Long.
Miss Anne Lavington.
Bybie Lake, *Esq;*
Stephen Legrand, *Esq;*
Charles Lawrence, *Esq;*
The Rev. Mr. Lloyd, *Gentleman of his Majesty's Chapel Royal, and Minor Canon of* St. Paul's *Cathedral,* &c.
Mr. Lally.
Mr. John Lloyd.
Mr. Lloyd, *of the* Post-Office.
Mr. Lockman.
Mr. Nicolas Ladd, *of* Windsor *Choir.*
Mr. Edward Lee, *Lay-Vicar of* Exeter *Cathedral.*
Mr. Thomas Lowe.

M.

The Rev. Dean Maturin, *of* Dublin.
Dr. Meyrick.
Mrs. Maitland.
Mrs. Marten, *of* Windsor.
Miss Molyneux.
Miss Susanna Myster.
—— Moore, *Esq;*
Withrington Morris, *Esq;*

—— Morris, *Esq; Fellow Commoner of* Trinity-hall, *in* Cambridge.
Bendal Marten, *Esq;*
Mr. Edward Moore.
Mr. Maclean, *of* Exeter.
Mr. James Morley, *Organist of the Cathedral at* Bristol.
Mr. William Middlebrook, *Organist of the Cathedral at* Lincoln.
Mr. Joseph Mahoon, *Harpsichord-maker to his Majesty.*

N.

Mrs. Nuthall.
Mrs. Neate.
Mrs. Hannah Norfa.
John Nichols, *Esq; of* Court-Lodge, *in* Sussex.
Mr. James Neale, *of* Pembroke-hall, *in* Cambridge.
Mr. James Nares, *Organist of the Cathedral at* York.
Mr. Thomas Newton.
Mr. Edward Nichson.

O.

The Right Hon. the Countess of Orrery.
Miss Oliver.
The Musical Society at Oxford.

P.

Sir John Pryce, *Bart.*
The Hon. John Ponsonby, *Esq; of* Dublin.
Dr. Pepusch.
Mrs. Powney.
Miss Parkin, *of* Exeter.
Miss Letitia Powel, *of* Pembroke.
—— Pitt, *Esq;*
—— Pryce, *Esq;*
Joseph Porter, *Esq;*
Peter Prideaux, *Esq; of* King's *College in* Cambridge.
William Mackworth Prade, *Esq;*
John Putland, *Esq; of* Little Chelsea.
Arthur Pomroy, *Esq; of* Dublin.
Thomas Pickering, *Esq;*
The Rev. Mr. Pinkney, *Gentleman of his Majesty's Chapel Royal, and Minor Canon of* St. Paul's *Cathedral.*
The Rev. Mr. Pearce, *Minor Canon of* St. Paul's *Cathedral.*
Mr. Joseph Phillips, *Two Books.*
Mr. Thomas Pink.
Mr. Phillips, *Surgeon.*
Mr. John Pearce, *of* Falmouth, *in* Cornwall.
Mr. George Jones Palmer.
Mr. Henry Purcell, *Organist of* St. Clement's Lombard-street.
The Philharmonic *Society in* Dublin, *Three Books.*

R.

A LIST of the SUBSCRIBERS.

R.

The Right Hon. the Earl of Radnor.
Mrs. Redhead.
Chrift. Roberts, *Efq*;
Henry Raper, *Efq*;
George Raper, *Efq*;
John Rochfort, *Efq; of* Dublin.
Mr. George Twifelton Rifdale.
Mr. Francis Rowe, *Gentleman of his Majefty's Chapel Royal, and Vicar Choral of St. Paul's Cathedral, &c.*
Mr. Randal, *Organift of* King's College Chapel *in* Cambridge.
Mr. Nelme Rogers.

S.

The Right Hon. *Lady* Frances Seymour.
The Right Hon. *Lady* Charlotte Seymour.
The Right Hon. the Earl of Sandwich.
Mrs. Skellern, *of* Dublin.
Mifs Henrietta Shaw.
Mifs Francifca Stagg.
Mifs Sophia Scott.
The Rev. Mr. John Smith, *Gentleman of his Majefty's Chapel Royal, and Minor Canon of* Cathedral Church at Worcefter, *&c.*
The Mr. Stonehoufe, *of New College in* Oxford.
Mr. John Stanley, *Organift of the* Temple, *and* St. Andrew's Holborn.
Mr. Martin Smith, *Organift of the Cathedral at* Gloucefter.
Mr. John Silvefter, *Organift of the Cathedral at* Exeter.
Mr. John Snow, *Organift of* St. John's College *in* Oxford.
Mr. William Savage, *Organift of* Finchley.
Mr. William Spencer, *Organift of* Biddeford.
Mr. Smith, *Organift of* Plymouth.
Mr. William Smith, *Organift of* Chrift-Church *in* Cork, Ireland.
Mr. John Simpfon.

T.

The Right Hon. *Lady Vifcountefs* Tyrone, *in* Ireland.
Mrs. Elizabeth Tollet.
Mrs. Teale.
Mifs Tighe.
Mifs Charity Treby.
William Thomas, *Efq*;
Robert Tape, *Efq*;
Reily Towers, *Efq; of* Dublin.
Jonathan Tiers, *Efq*;

The Rev. Mr. Tindal.
The Rev. Mr. Tatterfall, *Rector of* Bletchington, *in* Suffex.
The Rev. Mr. Tims, *Minor Canon of* St. Paul's Cathedral.
The Rev. Mr. John Talman, *Minor Canon of* Salisbury Cathedral.
Mr. John Travers, *Organift of his Majefty's Chapel Royal, and* St. Paul's, Covent-Garden.
Mr. Edward Thompfon, *Organift of the Cathedral at* Salisbury.
Mr. William Tireman, *Organift of* Trinity College *in* Cambridge.
The Mufical Society at Tewksbury.

V.

Mrs. Vernon.
—— Vaughan, *Efq*;
Mr. James Vincent, *Organift of the* Temple, *and* St. Luke's Old-ftreet.

W.

The Hon. Edward Walpole, *Efq*;
Mrs. Wickham.
Mifs Walker.
Mifs Maria Wright.
Richard Warner, *Efq*;
James Woolfton, *Efq*;
Ifaac Ware, *Efq; Three Books.*
The Rev. Mr. Worrall, *Vicar Choral, and Mafter of the Boys of* Chrift-Church, *and* St. Patrick's, *in* Dublin.
Mr. John Walfh, *Twelve Books.*
Mr. John Warrall.
Mr. Jofeph Wight.
Mr. Samuel Weely, *Gentleman of his Majefty's Chapel Royal, and Vicar Choral of* St. Paul's Cathedral.
Mr. Samuel Weely, *junior.*
Mr. Thomas Weely, *of* Lincoln.
Mr. Richard Ward, *Organift of* St. Antholin's Watling-ftreet, *and* St. Bartholomew's the Great.
Mr. George Walfh, *Organift in* Dublin.
The Mufical Society at Worcefter.

Y.

Mr. John Young, *Organift of* Chrift-Hofpital, Chrift-Church *in* Newgate-ftreet, *and* St. Matthew's Friday-ftreet.

Z.

Mr. Zinke.

OVERTURE

Allegro

Allegro

Young and Old their Voi _ _ ces raife and wake the Echos with his Praife _ _ _ _ _

while Young and Old their

and wake the Echos with his Praife   wake the Echos with his Praife _ _ _ _ _ and wake the Echos

and wake

Violoncelli   Tutti

Voi _ _ ces raife   and wake the   Echos with   his   Praife _ _ _ _ _   and wake the

with   his   Praife _ _ _ _ _   and wake the

Echos with his Praife   wake the E _ _ chos with his Praife _ _ _ _ _

Violonc:

and wake the Echos and wake the Echos and wake the Echos with his Praiſe wake the

and wake the Echos and wake the Echos and wake the Echos with his Praiſe wake the

and wake the Echos and wake the Echos and wake the Echos with his Praiſe wake the

and wake the Echos and wake the Echos and wake the Echos with his Praiſe wake the

E...chos with his Praiſe.

E...chos with his Praiſe.

E...chos with his Praiſe.

E...chos with his Praiſe.

Allegro

throng of Zion's Daughters Swell, Swell the Song: and wake the Echos with his Praise, wake

throng of Zion's Daughters Swell, Swell the Song: and wake the Echos with his Praise, - - -

While Young and Old their Voices raise, and

While Young and Old their Voices raise, and

Allegro

the E——chos with his praise - - - - - - - - - - - - - - - - wake

- - - and wake the Echos wake the Echos with his Praise - - - - - -

wake the Echos with — his Praise — - - - - - their Voices raise, and

wake the Echos with his Praise - - - - - while Young and Old their Voices raise, and

the E—chos with his Praise. wake the Echos with his Praise. wake the Echos

wake the Echos with his Praise. wake the Echos with his Praise. with his Praise—

wake the Echos with his Praise. wake the Echos with his Praise. wake the Echos

wake the Echos with his Praise. wake the Echos

Violoncelli

tutti

76   7 4   7   7 4   5 6   7 6   7   7   7   5 6   7 6 4   ⁕

with his Praise. and wake the Echos with his Praise. wake

While Young and Old their Voi—ces raise, and

with his Praise.

with his Praise.

6 4   ⁕

wake the Echos with his Praise. While

wake the Echos, the Echos with his Praise. While

wake the Echos with his Praise. While

wake the Echos with his Praise. While

Young and Old, Young and Old, Young and Old their

Young and Old, Young and Old, Young and Old their

Young and Old, Young and Old, Young and Old their

Young and Old, Young and Old, Young and Old their

Young and Old, Young and Old, Young and Old their

Voices raiſe, their Voices raiſe, and wake the Echos, and wake the Echos,

Voices raiſe, their Voices raiſe, and wake the Echos, and wake the Echos,

Voices raiſe, their Voices raiſe, and wake the Echos, and wake the Echos,

Voices raiſe, their Voices raiſe, and wake the Echos, and wake the Echos,

Adagio

and wake the Echos with his Praiſe. wake the Echos with his Praiſe.

and wake the Echos with his Praiſe. wake the Echos with his Praiſe.

and wake the Echos with his Praiſe. wake the Echos with his Praiſe.

and wake the Echos with his Praiſe. wake the Echos with his Praiſe.

Adagio

She Recit.

FROM the Mountains, lo! he comes, Breathing from his Lips Perfumes; Whil

piano

Zephyrs on his Garments Play, and Sweets thro' all the Air convey.

Vio. Unison

Vivace

Tell me, lovely Shepherd, where where Tell me, where thou feed'st at Noc

for. pia.

pia. for. pia.

for. pia. for.

pia.

fleecy Care: Direct me to the Sweet Retreat, That guards thee from the Midday Heat,

for. pia.

pia.

Left by the Flocks I Lonely Stray Without a Guide, and lose

pia.

they shall guide thee to the Shade.   Fairest of the Virgin

Throng Dost thou seek thy Swain's Abode? See yon fertile Vale a-long the new worn Path the

tasto solo

Flocks have trod. Pur _ sue the Prints their Feet have made And they shall guide thee

24

to the Shade. And they shall guide thee to the Shade.

F° tasto solo

tasto solo

SHE. Recit.

As the Rich Apple on whose Boughs Ripe Fruit with streaky Beauty glows, Excells the

Trees that shade the Grove, so Shines a-mong his Sex my Love.

28

P°

foli

Flowers on her Cheeks are blowing And her Voice with Mu -fic thrills thrills

6   P° 6   6 4   6 6   4 5 1 6

tutti P°

thrills her Voice her Voice with Mufic - thrills . . . . Flowers

6   7   5   6 4   6

on her Cheeks are blowing And her Voice with Mufic   thrills . Flowers on her Cheeks are blowing

6   4   6 6   6 5 4 3   6 #   6 4

P°

P°

And her Voice with Mufic   thrills

6 5   6 4 3   P°   6 7 6   6 6 4   6 4 6 7 b   2

Zephyrs o'er the spi - - ces fly - ing Wafting sweets from every Tree Sickning sense with

Odours cloying Breathe not half so sweet as she. sickning sense with Odours

cloying, Breathe not half so sweet as she ALLEGRO

D. Capo al segno S.

me! my own more dear: A - lafs! A - lafs! A - lafs! My

own, a - lafs! was not my Care: my own, a - lafs! was not my Care: My

own, a - lafs! was not my Care:

Invading Love the Fen - ces

Tutti Viol. 1º. Fº

Viol. 2do. Fº

Fº

broke, And tore the Clufters from the Stock: With eager Grafp the Fruit De - - -
pia

Trom:1º

Trom:2º

Haut:1º

Haut.2º

Viol:1º

Viol:2º

Presto Allegro

tasto solo

O   fill   fill   fill   fill with cooling   Juice the   Bowl:

Afswage the Fever in my Soul! the Fever

in my Soul! With Copious Draughts my Thirſt remove

tafto folo

Thirſt remove . . . . And ſooth the Heart that's ſick of

foli   tutti F⁰

Love ſooth the Heart that's ſick of Love,

fill   fill   fill   fill with Cooling   Juice the Bowl:

Heart that's sick of Love. sooth the Heart — — — that's sick of Love.

With Copious Draughts My Thirst remove My

tafto folo

9 8 4 3

6 9 8 4 3

9 8   4 3   9 8   6

The end of the First Part

52

. . way, come a - way, come a - way, The chearfull Spring begins to Day:

Bleak Winters gone, with all her Train of Chilling Frosts, and cropping

Amidst the Verdure of the Mead The Primrose lifts her Velvet Head:

Rain: Tisto Solo   German Flutes   Vio.Virio.º

Pianisso.

The warbling Birds the Woods a - mong; Salute the Seafon with a Song: Sa -

Fair One! come a - - way. come a - - way. come a - - way. Arise, O Fair One! come a - - way.

Fair One! come a - - way. come a - - way. come a - - way. Arise, O Fair One! come a - - way.

Fair One! come a - - way. come a - - way. come a - way. Arise, O Fair One! come a - - way.

Fair One! come a - - way. come a - - way. come a - way. Arise, O Fair One! come a - - way.

come a - - way. come a - - way. Arise, O Fair One! come a - - way.

come a - - way. come a - - way. Arise, O Fair One! come a - - way.

come a - - way. come a - - way. Arise, O Fair One! come a - - way.

come a - - way. come a - - way. Arise, O Fair One! come a - - way.

the Sul _try Hours away.   We'll love ____ the Sultry Hours away.   the

love ____   the Sultry Hours away.   We'll love ____   the Sultry Hours a_

For.

For.

For.

For.

Sultry Hours away.   We'll love ____   the Sultry Hours away.

_way.   the Sultry Hours away.   We'll love _ the Sultry Hours away.   For.

Fortiss°

Fortiss°   Pia

Fortiss°

Together,   Together,

Together,   Together,   To_

Together let us range the Fields, Impearled with the morn — — ing

— gether let us range the Fields, Impearled with the morn — ing Dew;

Dew; Or the Apples clustering Bough: There in close embower'd

Or view the Fruits the Vineyard veilds, There in close embower'd

Shades, Impervious to the Noon-tide Ray, By tinkling Rills, on Rosy

Shades, Impervious to the Noon-tide Ray, By tinkling Rills, on Rosy Beds,

63

We'll love . . . . . the Sultry Hours a-

For. Pia. For. Pianiss°

-way. We'll love . . . . . the Sultry Hours away.

Tasto Solo

Recitative.

HE.

How lovely art thou to the Sight, For Pleasure form'd, and Sweet Delight! Tall as the

Palm-Tree is thy Shape, Thy Breasts are like the clust'ring Grape.

She. Recitative.

O that a Sister's Specious Name Conceal'd from prying Eyes my Flame: Uncensur'd then I'd own my Love, And Chastest Virgins shou'd approve: Then fearless to my Mother's Bed, My Seeming Brother wou'd I lead: Soft Transports shou'd the Hours employ, And the Deceit shou'd crown the Joy.

Adagio

Sisters I adjure you, I adjure you by the Fawns,That bound across the flowery Lawns, Ye Virgins, Ye Virgins, Ye Virgins, that ye light----ly move, Nor with your Whispers wake----my Love.

Violoncello Adagio

Vio.1mo

Pianissimo

Vio.2do

Pianissimo

Pianissimo

He. Recitative.

My Fair's a Garden of Delight, Enclos'd, and hid from vulgar Sight; Where Streams from bubbling Fountains Stray, And Flowers enrich the Verdant Way.

Softly rife   O fouthern Breeze

And kind-ly fan the bloom-ing Trees;

Up-on my spi-cy Gar-den

blow,   That sweets from ev'ry Part from ev'ry Part may flow.

That sweets from ev'ry Part from ev'ry Part may flow.

That sweets from ev'ry Part from ev'ry Part may flow.

Soft-ly rife O fouththern

71

Breeze! . . . . And kind—ly fan the blooming

Trees. Up--on my

spi..cy Garden blow. That sweets from ev'ry Part from ev'ry

Part may flow - - - - - - -

Up-on my fpi-cy Garden blow, That fweets from ev'ry Part from ev'ry

Part may flow That fweets from ev'ry Part from ev'ry Part may Flow.

That sweets from ev'ry Part, from ev'ry Part may flow

That sweets from ev'ry Part, from ev'ry Part may flow   That

That sweets from ev'——ry Part may flow.   That

That sweets from ev'——ry Part may flow.

organo   senza org.

That sweets from ev'ry Part from ev'—ry Part may flow.

sweets from ev'ry Part That sweets from ev'ry Part from ev'ry Part may flow.

sweets from ev'ry Part That sweets from ev'——ry Part may flow.

That sweets from ev'——ry Part may flow

org.   senza org.

75

Part from ev'ry Part may flow.

ev' — ry Part may flow.

Part from ev' — ry Part may flow.

ev' — ry Part may flow.

Pianiss *Sinz: Org.*

The end of the Second Part.

78

Dolce

Dolce

Dolce

Dolce

dropping to thy Breaſt, And lull me lull me in thy Arms to Reſt. lull me in thy

Taſto Solo

Arms ——————— lull me lull me in thy Arms ——— in thy Arms to Reſt.

Where!

Where is my lovely Wand'rer Flown!

Vivace ma non Troppo

Ye Bloom—ing Virgins,

Ye Bloom—ing Virgins, as you rove, If

Vivace ma non Troppo

84

Vio. 1mo Pia.

Vio. 2do Pia.

Pia.

He. Recit.

Sweet Nymph, whom ruddier Charms adorn, Than open with the rosy Morn; Fair as the

Pia.

Moon's unclouded Light, And as the Sun in Splendor bright; Thy Beauties dazzle from afar,

5   6   ✗   6   ✗

For.   Largoe Piano

For.   Pia.

For.   Pia.

She

Like glitt'ring Arms that gild the War.   O take me!   take me!

For.   6

✗   Largoe Piano   6   5

Chorus

95

poor a Bribe to purchafe Love. The Treafures of — the World will prove, Too poor

Too poor a Bribe to purchafe Love. The Treafures of the World will prove, will

The Treafures of the World will prove Too poor a Bribe to

Bribe to purchafe Love. Too poor a Bribe to pur — chafe Love.

to purchafe Love.

prove Too poor a Bribe to purchafe Love.

The Treafures of the

The Treafures of the World will prove Too poor a Bribe to purchafe Love. Too

purchafe Love.

Violoncello

trace the Globe to try If pow'rfull Gold thy Joys can buy: to try If pow'rfull Gold thy

trace the Globe to try If pow'rfull Gold thy Joys can buy: to try If pow'rfull Gold thy

trace the Globe to try If pow'rfull Gold thy Joys can buy: to try If pow'rfull Gold thy

trace the Globe to try If pow'rfull Gold thy Joys can buy: to try If pow'rfull Gold thy

Joys can buy:

Too poor a Bribe to purchase

Joys can buy: The Treasures of the World will prove Too poor a Bribe to purchase

Joys can buy:

The

Joys can buy: 2 6 6

Violoncelli

Bribe to purchase Love.

Love. The Treasures of the World will prove   The Treasures of the World — will

Love.   The Trea ___ fures of the World   will   prove

Treasures of the World — will prove   of the World will   prove The Treasures of the World will

The Treasures of the World will prove   of the World   will

2   Tutti Bassi   6   4   6   6   7

prove   Too poor a Bribe   Too poor   a Bribe to purchase

Too poor   a   Bribe   Too poor   a   Bribe   Too poor a Bribe to purchase

prove   Too poor a   Bribe to purchase Love.   Too poor a   Bribe   Too poor a   Bribe to purchase

prove   Too poor   a   Bribe   Too poor   a   Bribe to purchase

Violoncelli   Tutti   Violoncelli.   Tutti

101.

THE
FOUNDLING

THE

FOUNDLING.

A

COMEDY.

By Mr. MOORE,
AUTHOR of FABLES for the FEMALE SEX.

LONDON:
Printed for R. FRANCKLIN, in *Russel-street*,
Covent-Garden. 1748.

[Price One Shilling an Six Pence.]

To Her G R A C E, the

Duchess of *BEDFORD*.

M A D A M,

T H E Permiſſion Your G R A C E honours me with, of preſenting the *Foundling* to Your Protection, is the higheſt Gratification of my Pride, and my beſt Security for the Indulgence of the Town. It is in Writing, as in Life: An Introduction to the World by a Great Name is a Sanction, even where Merit is wanting, and can adorn it, where it is. And tho' my Pretenſions are inconſiderable, my Fears are leſſen'd, while I can boaſt the Ducheſs of BEDFORD for my Patroneſs.

I

I have no Intention to alarm Your Grace with the common Flattery of Dedications. The Mind, that deferves Praife, is above receiving it. Your own Confcioufnefs, tho' in Your humbleft Hours, will afford truer Satisfaction, than the beft written Panegyrick. But while Your Grace forbids me Praife, I am at Liberty to indulge my Wifhes for Your Happinefs and Honour. In Thofe, I may be allow'd to name the Duke of Bedford with his Duchefs, and to rejoice with every *Englifhman*, that the higheft Dignities are the Reward of the higheft Merit.

If I defcend, to fay a little of myfelf, I fhall hope for Your Grace's Pardon. This is my firft Attempt in Dramatic Poetry. Whether I deferve the Favour, the Town has fhewn me, is fubmitted to Your Grace's Candour, and the Judgment of my Readers. The Difapprobation, which the Character

of

of *Faddle* met with the firſt Night, made it neceſſary for me to ſhorten it in almoſt every Scene, where it was not immediately connected with the *Fable.* But tho' Succeſs has attended the Alteration, I have ventur'd to pub- liſh it in its original Dreſs; ſubmitting it ſtill to Your GRACE and the Public, from whom I have no Appeal to my own Partiality. But I am detaining Your GRACE too long, and ſhall only add, that I am,

M A D A M,

Your GRACE'S

moſt oblig'd, and

moſt obedient Servant,

EDW. MOORE.

Dramatis Perſonæ.

MEN.

Sir Roger Belmont,	*Mr*. Yates.
Sir Charles Raymond,	*Mr*. Barry.
Young Belmont,	*Mr*. Garrick.
Colonel Raymond,	*Mr*. Havard.
Villiard,	*Mr*. Sparks.
Faddle,	*Mr*. Macklin.

WOMEN.

Roſetta,	*Mrs*. Woffington.
Fidelia,	*Mrs*. Cibber.

SCENE.

Sir Roger Belmont's *Houſe in* LONDON.

PRO-

PROLOGUE.

Written by Mr. Brooke.

Spoken by Mrs. Pritchard.

UNpractic'd in the Drama's artful Page,
 And new to all the Dangers of the Stage,
Where Judgment sits to save, or damn his Play,
Our Poet trembles for his first Essay.
 He, like all Authors, a conforming Race!
Writes to the Taste, and Genius of the Place;
Intent to fix, and emulous to please
The Happy Sense of these politer Days,
He forms a Model of a virtuous Sort,
And gives you more of Moral than of Sport;
He rather aims to draw the melting Sigh,
Or steal the pitying Tear from Beauty's Eye;
To touch the Strings, that humanize our Kind,
Man's sweetest Strain, the Musick of the Mind.
 Ladies, he bids me tell you, that from You,
His first, his fav'rite Character he drew;
A young, a lovely, unexperienc'd Maid,
In honest Truth, and Innocence array'd;
Of Fortune destitute, with Wrongs oppress'd,
By Fraud attempted, and by Love distress'd;
Yet guarded still; and every Suff'ring past,
Her Virtue meets the sure Reward at last.

From

From such Examples shall the Sex be taught,
How Virtue fixes whom their Eyes have caught;
How Honour beautifies the fairest Face,
Improves the Mein, and dignifies the Grace.
  And hence the Libertine, who builds a Name
On the base Ruins of a Woman's Fame,
Shall own, the best of human Blessings lie
In the chaste Honours of the nuptial Tie;
There lives the home-felt Sweet, the near Delight,
There Peace reposes, and there Joys unite;
And female Virtue was by Heav'n design'd
To charm, to polish, and to bless Mankind,

THE

The FOUNDLING.

A

COMEDY.

ACT I.   SCENE I.

An Apartment in Sir ROGER BELMONT'S *Houſe.*

Enter YOUNG BELMONT, *and* Col. RAYMOND.

BELMONT. **M**Y dear Colonel, you are as unletter'd in Love as I am in War—— What, a Woman, a fine Woman, a Coquet, and my Siſter!——and to be won by whining!——Mercy on us! that a well-built Fellow, with common Senſe, ſhou'd take Pains to unman himſelf, to tempt a warm

B   Girl

Girl of two-and-twenty to come to Bed to him!——
I fay again, and again, Colonel, my Sifter's a Woman.

Col. And the very individual Woman that I want,
Charles.

Bel. And of all Women in the World, the leaft
fit for thee——An *April* Day is lefs changeable than
her Humour——She laughs behind her Fan at what
fhe fhou'd not underftand; calls Humility, Meannefs,
and Blufhing, the Want of Education. In all Affairs
with a Man, fhe goes by Contraries; if you tell her a
merry Story, fhe fighs —— if a ferious one, fhe laughs;
——for yes, fhe fays no, and for no, yes; and is
Miftrefs of fuch obedient Features, that her Looks are
always ready to confirm what her Tongue utters.

Col. Fine painting, upon my Word, and no Flattery!

Bel. This is the Lady—— Now for the Lover.
——A Fellow, made up of Credulity and Sufpicion;
believing where he fhou'd doubt, and doubting where
he fhou'd believe; jealous without Caufe, and fatisfy'd
without Proof—— A great Boy, that has loft his Way;
——and blubbering thro' every Road, but the right,
to find his Home again; ha! ha! ha!

Col. Mighty florid, indeed, Sir!

Bel. Come, come, Colonel—— Love, that can
exalt the Brute to the Man, has fet you upon all-fours.
——Women are indeed delicious Creatures!——but
not what you think 'em——The firft Wifh of every
Mother's Daughter is Power—the fecond, Mifchief—
The Way to her Heart is by Indifference, or Abufe;
——For whoever owns her Beauty, will feel her Ty-
ranny —— but if he calls her ugly, or a Fool, fhe'll fet
her Cap at him, and take Pains for his good Opinion.

Col. And fo, Submiffion and Flattery are out of
your Syftem?

Bel. For Submiffion and Flattery, I fubftitute Impudence and Contradiction—— Thefe two, well ma-
nag'd, my Dear, will do more with Beauty in an Hour,

than

than fine Speeches in a Year——Your fine Woman expects Adoration; and receives it as common Incense, which every Fool offers —— while the rude Fellow, who tells her Truth, claims all her Attention——Difficulty endears Conqueft—— To Him only fhe appears what fhe fhou'd be to all; and while fhe labours with her natural Charms to fecure Him——fhe's loft herfelf.

Col. Why, faith, *Charles*, there may be fome Mufick in thefe wild Notes ——but I am fo far gone in the old Ballad, that I can fing no other Words to any Tune.

Bel. Ha! ha!——Thou poor, mournful Nightingale in a Cage, fing on then —— and I'll whiftle an upper Part with thee, to give a little Life to the Meafure.

Col. That will be kind ——for Heaven knows, I have Need of Affiftance—— Prithee tell me——doft think *Rofetta* wants Underftanding?

Bel. N——o, faith, I think not.

Col. Good-humour?

Bel. Hum!——She's generally pleas'd.

Col What then can reconcile her Behaviour to me, and her Fondnefs for fuch a Reptile as *Faddle?* A Fellow, made up of Knavery and Noife ——with Scandal for Wit, and Impudence for Raillery; and fo needy!——that the very Devil might buy him for a fingle Guinea ——I fay, *Charles*, what can tempt her even to an Acquaintance with this Fellow?

Bel. Why, the very Underftanding and good-Humour, you fpeak of——A Woman's Underftanding is Defign, and her good-Humour——Mifchief——Her Advances to one Fool are made only to teize another.—

Col. Sir, your moft humble Servant.

Bel. And her good-Humour is kept alive by the Succefs of her Plots.

Col. But why fo conftant to her Fool?

Bel. Becaufe her Fool's the fitteft for her Purpofe.——He has more Tricks than her Monkey, more Prate than her Parrot, more Servility than her Lap-Dog,

more

more Lies than her Woman, and more Wit than her —— Colonel. And, faith, all thefe Things confider'd, I can't blame my Sifter for her Conftancy.

Col. Thou art a wild Fellow, and in earneft about nothing but thy own Pleafures——and fo we'll change the Subject.——What fays *Fidelia*?

Bel. Why there now!——That a Man can't inftruct another, but he muft be told, by way of Thanks, how much he ftands in Need of Affiftance himfelf!——

Col. Any new Difficulties?

Bel. Mountains, Colonel, a few Mountains in my Way——But if I want Faith to remove 'em I hope I fhall have Strength to climb 'em——and that will do my Bufinefs.

Col. She's a Woman, *Charles!*

Bel. By her Outfide one wou'd guefs fo —— but look a little farther, and, except the Stubbornnefs of her Temper, fhe has nothing feminine about her —— She has Wit without Pertnefs, Beauty without Confcioufnefs, Pride without Infolence, and Defire without Wantonnefs.——In fhort, fhe has every Thing ——

Col. That you wou'd wifh to ruin in her.——Why, what a Devil are you, *Charles*, to fpeak fo feelingly of Virtues, which you only admire to deftroy!

Bel. A very pretty Comforter, truly!

Col. Come, Come, *Charles*, if fhe is as well born as you pretend, what hinders you from cherifhing thefe Qualities in a Wife, which you wou'd ruin in a Miftrefs?——Marry her, marry her.

Bel. And hang myfelf in her Garters next Morning, to give her Virtues the Reward of Widowhood! Faith, I muft read *Pamela* twice over firft.——But fuppofe her not born as I pretend; but the Outcaft of a Beggar, and oblig'd to Chance for a little Education!

Col. Why then her Mind is dignify'd by her Obfcurity; and you will have the Merit of raifing her to a Rank, which fhe was meant to adorn.——And

where's

where's the mighty Matter in all this!——You want
no Addition to your Fortune, and have only to facrifice a little unneceffary Pride to neceffary Happinefs.

Bel. Very heroical, upon my Word! And fo,
my dear Colonel, one Way, or other, I muft be marry'd, it feems!

Col. If *Fidelia* can be honeft, my Life on't, you
are of my Mind within this Fortnight.—— But prithee,
——fince I am not to believe your former Account of
her——who is this delicious Girl, that muft and will
get the better of your Pride?

Bel. A Sifter of the Graces, without mortal Father, or Mother.—— She dropt from the Clouds in her
Cradle, was lull'd by the Winds, chriften'd by the
Rains, fofter'd by a Hag, fold for a Whore, fentenc'd
to a Rape, and refcu'd by a Rogue——to be ravifh'd
by her own Confent.——There's Myftery and Hiero-
glyphic for you!——and every Syllable, my Dear, a
Truth beyond Apochrypha!

Col. And what am I to underftand by all this?

Bel. Faith, juft as much as your Underftanding can
carry.——A Man in Love is not to be trufted with a
Secret.

Col. And pray, moft difcreet Sir, is *Rofetta* acquainted with her real Hiftory?

Bel. Not a Circumftance.——She has been amus'd
like you, and ftill believes her to be the Sifter of a dead
Friend of mine at College, bequeath'd to my Guardianfhip.——But the Devil I find owes me a Grudge for
former Virtues —— for this Sifter of mine, who doats
upon *Fidelia*, and believes every Thing I have told her
of her Family and Fortune, has very fairly turn'd the
Tables upon me.——She talks of Equality of Birth,
forfooth —— of Virtue, Prudence and good Senfe;
and bids me blefs my Stars for throwing in my Way
the only Woman in the World, that has good Qualities
enough to reclaim my bad ones —— and make me,
what fhe fays every Man ought to be —— a good Hufband!   *Col.*

Col. Was ever poor, innocent Fellow in such Distress!——But what says the old Gentleman, your
Father?

Bel. Why, faith, the Certainty of a little Money
wou'd set him at Work the same Way.—— But I'll
have one Trial of Skill with 'em yet.——As I brought
her in by one Lie, I'll take her out by another ——
I'll swear she's a Whore ——that I may get an Opportunity to make her one.

Col. Most religiously resolv'd, upon my Word!

Bel. Between you and me, Colonel, has not your
old Gentleman, sir *Charles*, a liquorish Look-out for
Fidelia himself?

Col. No, upon my Honour. —— I believe his As-
siduities there, are more to prevent the Designs of another, than to forward any of his own.

Bel. As who shou'd say, because I have no Teeth
for a Crust, I'll muzzle the young Dog that has.——
A Pox of every Thing that's old, but a Woman!——
for 'tis but varying her Vocation a little, and you may
make her as useful at fifty-five, as fifteen. —— But
what say you to a little Chat with the Girls this Morning?——I believe we shall find 'em in the next Room.

Col. Not immediately—— I have an Appointment
at *White's*.

Bel. For half an Hour, I am your Man there too.
—— D'ye return so soon?

Col. Sooner, if you will.

Bel. With all my Heart.——*Allons.*

Exeunt.

S C E N E II. *Another Apartment.*

Enter Rosetta *and* Fidelia, *meeting.*

Roset. O, my Dear! I was just coming to see if
you were dress'd. You look as if you had had pleasant
Dreams last Night. *Fid.*

Fid. Whatever my Dreams were, they can't difturb the Morning's Happinefs, of meeting my dear
Rofetta fo gay and charming.

Rofet. My fweet Creature!——But what were
your Dreams?

Fid. O, Nothing —— A Confufion of gay Caftles,
built by Hope, and thrown down by Difappointment.

Rofet. O barbarous!—— well, for my Part, I never
built a Caftle in my Sleep, that wou'd not laft 'till Doomsday——Give me a Dream, and I am Miftrefs of the
Creation——I can do what I will with every Man in
it——And Power, Power! my Dear, fleeping or waking,
is a charming Thing!

Fid. Now, in my Opinion, a Woman has no Bufinefs
with Power—— Power admits no Equal, and difmiffes
Friendfhip for Flattery.——Befides, it keeps the Men
at a Diftance, and that is not always what we wifh.

Rofet. But then, my Dear, they'll come when we
call 'em, and do what we bid 'em, and go when we
fend 'em——There's fomething pretty in that, fure——
And for Flattery,——take my Word for't, 'tis the
higheft Proof of a Man's Efteem——'Tis only allowing
one what one has not, becaufe the Fellow admires what
one has——And fhe, that can keep That, need not be af-
fraid of believing fhe has more.

Fid. Ay, if fhe can keep that——But the Danger
is, in giving up the Subftance for the Shadow——Come
come, my Dear, we are weak by Nature; and 'tis but
knowing that we are fo, to be always upon our Guard.
——Fear may make a Woman ftrong; but Confidence
undoes her.

Rofet. Ha! ha!——How different Circumftances
direct different Opinions!—— You are in love with a
Rake of a Fellow, who makes You afraid of your felf
— —And I hold in Chains a mighty Colonel, who's a-
fraid of me—And fo, my Dear, we both go upon right
Principles——Your Weaknefs keeps You upon your
Guard, and my Power leaves Me without Danger.

Fid.

Fid. And yet you muſt forgive me, if I tell you, that you love this Colonel.

Roſet. Who told you ſo, my dear Creature?

Fid. I know it by the Pains you take to vex him—Beſides, I have ſeen you look as if you did.

Roſet. Look Child!—— why don't I look like other People?

Fid. Ay, like other People in Love——Oh, my Dear, I have ſeen juſt ſuch Looks in the Glaſs, when my Heart has beat at my very Lips.

Roſet. Thou art the moſt provoking Creature!

Fid. You muſt pardon me, *Roſetta.*——I have a Heart but little inclin'd to Gaiety; and am rather wondering, that when Happineſs is in a Woman's Power, ſhe ſhou'd neglect it for Trifles——or how it ſhou'd ever enter her Thoughts, that the Rigour of a Miſtreſs can endear the Submiſſion of a Wife.

Roſet. As certain, my Dear, as the Repentance of a Sinner out-weighs in Opinion the Life of a Saint.——But, to come to ſerious Confeſſion, I have, beſides a Woman's Inclination to Miſchief, another Reaſon for keeping off a little—— I am afraid of being thought mercenary.

Fid. Hey Day!——why, are not you his Equal every Way?

Roſet. That's not it—I have told you, that before his Father's Return from Exile — You know his unhappy Attatchments to a ſucceſsleſs Party——This Colonel (brought up in our Family, and favour'd by Sir Roger and my Brother) laid violent Seige to me for a whole Year.—— Now, tho' I own I never diſliked him —— in all that Time, either thro' Pride, Folly, or a little Miſchief, I never gave him the leaſt Hint, by which he cou'd gueſs at my Inclinations.

Fid. Right Woman, upon my Word!

Roſet. 'Tis now about three Months, ſince the King in his Goodneſs recall'd Sir Charles; and, by reſtoring the Eſtate, made the Colonel Heir to a Fortune, more than equal to my Expectations——And now, to confeſs all, the

the Airs that Folly gave me before, Reafon bids me continue —— for to furrender my Heart at once to this
new-made Commander, wou'd look as if the poor Colonel had wanted a Bribe for the Governor.—— Befides,
he has affronted my Pride, in daring to imagine I cou'd
defcend fo low, as to be fond of that Creature, *Faddle.*
—— a Fellow, form'd only to make one laugh——a
Cordial for the Spleen, to be bought by every body;
and juft as neceffary in a Family as a Monkey—For
which Infolence, I muft and will be reveng'd.

Fid. Well, I confefs this looks a little like Reafon.
—But are you fure, all this while, the Colonel, in
Defpair, won't raife the Seige, and draw off his For-
ces to another Place?

Rofet. Pfhah!—I have a better Opinion of the Men,
Child—Do but ply 'em with Ill-ufage, and they are
the gentleft Creatures in the World—Like other Beafts
of Prey, you muft tame 'em by Hunger—but if once
you feed 'em high, they are apt to run wild, and forget their Keepers.

Fid. And are all Men fo, *Rofetta?*

Rofet. By the Gravity of that Queftion, I'll be
whipt now, if you don't expect me to fay fomething
civil of my Brother—Take Care of him, *Fidelia,*
for Hunger can't tame him, nor Fullnefs make him
wilder—To leave you to his Guardianfhip, was fetting
the Fox to keep the Chicken.

Fid. Wild as he is, my Heart can never beat to
another—And then I have Obligations, that wou'd
amaze you.

Rofet. Obligations!—Let me die, if I wou'd not
marry my Colonel's Papa, and put it out of his Power
to oblige, or difoblige me.

Fid. Still you will banter me with Sir *Charles*—
Upon my Life, he has no more Defigns upon me than
you have—I know no Reafon for his Friendfhip, but his
general Humanity, or perhaps the Particularity of my
Circumftances.

C   *Rofet.*

Rofet. Why, as you fay, Youth and Beauty are particular Circumftances to move Humanity—Ha! ha! ha!—O, my Dear, Time's a great Tell-tale, and will difcover all—What a fweet Mamma fhall I have, when I marry the Colonel!

SCENE III.

Enter YOUNG BELMONT, *and the* COLONEL.

Bel When you marry the Colonel, Sifter!—A Match, a Match, Child!—Here he is, juft in the Nick—And, Faith, as Men go, very excellent Stuff for a Husband.

Col. Thofe were lucky Words, Madam.

Rofet. Perhaps not fo lucky, if you knew all, Sir. —Now, or never, for a little Lying, *Fidelia*, if you love me. [*Apart to* Fidelia.

Fid. I'll warrant you, my Dear—You muft know, Sir, *(to* Belmont *)* that your Sifter has taken it into her Head, that the Colonel's Father is my Lover.

Rofet. What is fhe going to fay now? [*Afide.*

Fid. And as fhe looks upon herfelf to be as good as marry'd to the Colonel——

Rofet. Who I!——I!——

Fid. She has been fettling fome Family Affairs with her new Mamma here—And upon my Word, fhe's a fweet Contriver.

Rofet. And you think I won't be even with you for this, *Fidelia?*

Bel. Sifter!

Col. And was it fo, Madam?—And may I hope?

Rofet. Was it fo Madam?—And may I hope? *(mocking him)*—No, Sir, it was not fo—and you may not hope— Do you call this Wit, *Fidelia?*

Fid My dear Creature, you muft allow me to laugh a little—Ha! ha! ha!

Rofet.

Rofet. 'Tis mighty well, Madam—Oh for a little Devil at my Elbow now, to help out Invention. [*Afide.*

Bel. Ha! ha! ha!—Won't it come, Sifter?

Rofet. As foon as your Manners, Brother—You and your grave Friend there, have been genteelly employ'd indeed, in liftening at the Door of a Lady's Chamber——And then, becaufe you heard nothing for your Purpofe, to turn my own Words to a Meaning, I fhould hate myfelf for dreaming of.

Bel. Why, indeed, Child, we might have perplex'd you a little, if *Fidelia* had not fo artfully brought you off.

Rofet. Greatly oblig'd to her, really!
[*Walking in Diforder.*

Col. I never knew till now, *Rofetta*, that I cou'd find a Pleafure in your Uneafinefs.

Rofet. And you think, Sir, that I fhall eafily forgive this Infolence?——But you may be miftaken, Sir.

Bel. Poor Thing, how it pants!——Come, it fhall have a Husband!—We muft about it immediately, Colonel, for fhe's all over in a Flame.

Rofet. You grow impertinent, Brother——Is there no Relief? [*Afide.*

Bel. Shall I lift up the Safh for a little Air, Child?

Enter SERVANT.

Rofet. So, *John!*——Have you deliver'd the Cards, I gave you?

Serv. Yes, Madam——and Mr. *Faddle* defires his Compliments to your Ladyfhip, and Madam *Fidelia.*

Rofet. Mr. *Faddle*, *John!*——Where did you fee him?

Serv. He met me in the Street, Madam, and made me ftep into a Coffee-houfe with him, 'till he wrote this, Madam. [*Delivers a Letter, and Exit.*

Rofet. O, the kind Creature!——Here's a Letter from Mr. *Faddle, Fidelia!*——Fortune I thank thee for this little Refpite. [*Afide, and reading the Letter.*

Col. Does fhe fuffer the Fool to write to her too?

Fid.

Fid. What, pining, Colonel, in the Midſt of Victory?

Col. To receive his Letters, Madam!——I ſhall run mad.

Bel. So!—Away Prop, and down Scaffold—All's over, I ſee.

Roſet. O, *Fidelia!*——You ſhall hear it.——You ſhall all hear it——And there's ſomething in't about the Colonel too.

Col. About me, Madam? [*Peeviſhly.*

Roſet. Nay, Colonel, I am not at all angry now.——Methinks this Letter has made me quite another Creature.——To be ſure Mr. *Faddle* has the moſt gallant Way of writing!—But his own Words will ſpeak beſt for him.

[*Reads.*]

" *Dear Creature,*

" SINCE I ſaw you *Yeſterday, Time has hung*
" *upon me like a Winter in the Country—and*
" *unleſs you appear at Rehearſal of the new Opera*
" *this Morning, my Sun will be in total Eclipſe for*
" *two Hours.—Lady* Fanny *made us laugh laſt Night,*
" *at* What's my Thought like, *by comparing your Co-*
" *lonel to a great Box o' the Ear—Becauſe it was very*
" *rude, ſhe ſaid, and what no body car'd for—I have*
" *a thouſand Things to ſay—but the Clamour of a*
" *Coffee-houſe is an Interruption to the Sentiments of*
" *Love and Veneration, with which I am*

" *Madam,*

" *moſt unſpeakably yours,*

" WILL. FADDLE."

—Is not it very polite, Colonel?

Col. Extreamly, Madam!—Only a little out as to the Box o' the Ear—For you ſhall ſee him take it, Madam, as careleſsly as a Pinch of Snuff.

Roſet. Fie, Colonel! You would not quarrel before a Lady, I hope—*Fidelia*, you muſt oblige me with your

your Company to Rehearfal—I'll go put on my Capu-
chin, and ftep into the Coach, this Moment.

Fid. I am no Friend to public Places; but I'll attend you, Madam.

Rofet. You'll come, Colonel?

Col. To be fure, Madam.

Bel. Sifter!—Oh, you're a good Creature!
　　　　　　　　[*Exit Rofetta, laughing affectedly.*

Fid. Shall we have your Company, Sir.　[*to* Bel.

Bel. We could find a Way to employ Time better,
Child—But I am your Shadow, and muft move with
you every where.　　　　　　　　[*Exit* Fidelia.
—Ha! ha! ha!—How like a beaten General do'ft thou
look now!—while the Enemy is upon the March, to
proclaim *Te Deum* for a compleat Victory!

Col. I am but a Man, *Charles,* and find myfelf no
Match for the Devil and a Woman.

Bel. Courage, Boy!—and the Flefh and the Devil
may be fubdu'd—Ha! ha! ha!—Such a Colonel!
　　　　　　　　　　　　　　　　[*Exit.*

Col. Why, this it is to be in Love!—Well!—Let
me but flip my Leading-Strings!—and if ever I am a
Woman's Baby again!—

　　To cheat our Wifhes Nature meant the Sex,
　　And form'd 'em, lefs to pleafe us, than perplex.
　　　　　　　　　　　　　　　　[*Exit.*

ACT

ACT II.   *Scene Continues.*

Enter Sir Roger Belmont, *and Sir* Charles Raymond.

Sir *Ro.*   A Voracious young Dog!—Muſt I feed Ortolans to pamper his Gluttony!

Sir *Char.*   Be under no Apprehenſions, Sir *Roger*; Mr. *Belmont*'s Exceſſes are mitigated by the Levity of Youth, and a too early Indulgence. In his Moments of thinking, I know him generous and noble—And for *Fidelia*!—I think, I can be anſwerable for her Conduct, both in Regard to what ſhe owes herſelf, and you.

Sir *Ro.*   Why, look you, Sir *Charles*—the Girl's a ſweet Girl, and a good Girl—and Beauty's a fine Thing, and Virtue's a fine Thing—But as for Marriage!—Why—a—Man may buy fine Things too dear. —A little Money, Sir *Charles*, wou'd ſet off her Beauty, and find her Virtue Employment—But the young Rogue does not ſay a Word of that, of late.

Sir *Char.*   Nor of Marriage, I am ſure—His Love of Liberty will prevent your Fears one Way, and, I hope, *Fidelia's* Honour, another.

Sir *Ro.*   Muſt not have her ruin'd tho!

Sir *Char.*   Fear it not, Sir *Roger*—And when next you ſee your Son, be a little particular in your Enquiries about her Family and Circumſtances—If ſhe is what her Behaviour ſpeaks her, and he pretends, a Lady of Birth and Fortune—Why, Secrets are unneceſſary—If ſhe declines an Explanation, look upon the whole as a Contrivance, to cover Purpoſes, which we muſt guard againſt.

Sir *Ro.*

Sir *Ro.* Why you don't think the Rogue has had her, hah, Sir *Charles?*

Sir *Char.* No, upon my Honour—I hold her Innocence to be without Stain—But to deal freely with my Friend, I look upon her Story, as strange and improbable. —An Orphan, of Beauty, Family and Fortune; committed by a dying Brother to the sole Care of a licentious young Fellow!—You must pardon me, Sir *Roger.*

Sir *Ro.* Pray go on Sir.

Sir *Char.* Brought in at Midnight too!—And then a young Creature, so educated, and so irresistibly amiable, to be in all Appearance, without Alliance, Friend, or Acquaintance in the wide World!—a Link, torn off from the general Chain!—I say, Sir *Roger,* this is strange.

Sir *Ro.* By my Troth, and so it is!

Sir *Char.* I know not why I am so interested in this Lady's Concerns; but Yesterday, I indulg'd my Curiosity with her, perhaps, beyond the Bounds of Good-manners—I gave a Loose to my Suspicion, and added Oaths of Secresy to my Enquiries. But her Answers only serv'd to multiply my Doubts—And still as I persisted, I saw her Cheeks cover'd with Blushes, and her Eyes swimming in Tears—But, my Life upon't, they were the Blushes, and the Tears of Innocence!

Sir *Ro.* We must, and will be satisfy'd, Sir *Charles.*

Sir *Char.* For who knows, while we are delaying, but some unhappy Mother, perhaps of Rank too, may be wringing her Hands in Bitterness of Misery for this lost Daughter.—Girls, who have kept their Virtue, Sir *Roger,* have done mad Things for a Man they Love.

Sir *Ro.* And so indeed they have—I remember when I was a young Fellow my self—But is not that my *Charles* coming thro' the Hall yonder?

Sir *Char.* Ay, Sir *Roger.* Attack him now—But let your Enquiries have more the Shew of accidental Chat than Design; for too much Earnestness may beget Suspicion—And so, Sir, I leave you to your Discretion.

(*Exit.*
Sir

Sir *Ro.* You fhall fee me again before Dinner—
A Pox of thefe young, rakehelly Rogues!—a Girl's
worth twenty of 'em—if one cou'd but manage her.

SCENE II.

Enter *Young* BELMONT, *repeating.*

Bel.   *No Warning of th' approaching Flame,*
             Swiftly, like fudden Death, it came;
             Like Mariners, by Lightning kill'd,
             I burnt the Moment——

My dear Sir, I have not feen you to Day before!

Sir *Ro.* What, ftudying Poetry, Boy, to help out
the Year's Allowance?

Bel. Faith, Sir, Times are hard—and unlefs you
come down with a frefh Hundred now and then, I may
go near to difgrace your Family—and turn Poet.

Sir *Ro.* And fo want Friends all thy Life after!—
But now we talk of Money, *Charles,* what art thou
doing with *Fidelia's* Money?—I am thinking, that a
round Sum thrown into the Stocks now, might turn to
pretty tollerable Account.

Bel. The Stocks, Sir?

Sir *Ro.* Ay, Boy. My Broker will be here after
Dinner, and he fhall have a little Chat with thee, about
laying out a few of her Thoufands.

Bel. I hope, he'll tell us where we fhall get thefe
Thoufands.   [*Afide.*

Sir *Ro.* Thou doft not anfwer me, *Charles*—Art
dumb, Boy?

Bel. Why, to be fure, Sir, as to that—*Fidelia*—
I can't fay, but that fhe may—However, that is, you
know, Sir—If as to Poffibility—Will your Broker be
here after Dinner, Sir?

Sir *Ro.* Take a little Time, *Charles*—For at prefent, thou doft not make thy felf fo clearly underftood.

Bel. Quite right, to be fure, Sir—Nothing cou'd,
                                                    beyond

beyond all Doubt, be more judicious, or more advan-
tageous—Her Intereft, Sir—why as to that—a pretty
Fortune—but—did you know her Brother, Sir?

Sir *Ro.* Who I, Child?—No.

Bel. Faith, nor I neither. (*Afide*)—Not know
Jack, Sir?—The Rogue wou'd have made you laugh.
—Did I never read you any of his Epigrams?—But
then he had fuch an Itch for Play!—Why he wou'd fet
you a whole Fortune at a Caft—And fuch a Mimmic
too!—but no OEconomy in the World—Why, it coft
him a cool fix thoufand, to ftand for Member once—O,
I cou'd tell you fuch Stories of that Election, Sir—

Sir *Ro.* Prithee, what Borough did he ftand for?

Bel. Lord, Sir!—He was flung all to nothing—
My Lord What-d'ye-call-um's Son carry'd it fifteen to
one, at half the Expence—In fhort Sir, by his Extravagance, Affairs are fo perplex'd, fo very intricate,
that upon my Word, Sir, I declare it, I don't know
what to think of 'em—A Pox of thefe Queftions.[*Afide.*

Sir *Ro.* But fhe has Friends and Relations, *Charles!*
—I fancy, if I knew who They were, fomething might
be done.

Bel. Yes, yes, Sir, fhe has Friends, and Relations—I fee, Sir, you know nothing of her Affairs—
Such a String of 'em!—The only wife Thing her
Brother ever did, was making Me her Guardian, to
take her out of the Reach of thofe Wretches—I fhall
never forget his laft Words—Whatever you do, my
dear *Charles*, fays he, taking me by the Hand, keep
that Girl from her Relations—Why, I wou'd not for
a thoufand Pounds, Sir, that any of them fhou'd know
where fhe is.

Sir *Ro.* Why, we have been a little cautious,
Charles—But where does the Eftate lie?

Bel. Lord, Sir!—an Eftate and no Eftate—I wonder a Man of your Knowledge wou'd ask the Queftion.
—An Earthquake may fwallow it, for any Thing I
care.

D.   Sir *Ro.*

Sir Ro. But where does it lie, *Charles ?*—In what County, I say?

B l. And then there's the six thousand Pounds, that her Father left her—

Sir Ro. What, that gone too, *Charles?*

Bel. Just as good, I believe—Every Shilling on't in a Lawyer's Hands.

Sir Ro. But she is not afraid to see Him too, *Charles?* —Where does He live?

Bel. Live, Sir !—Do you think such a Fellow ought to live? Why he has trumpt up a Contract of Marriage with this Girl, Sir, under the Penalty of her whole Fortune—-There's a Piece of Work for you!

Sir Ro. But has he no Name, *Charles?*—What is he call'd, I say?

Bel. You can't call him by any Name, that's too bad for him—But if I don't draw his Gown over his Ears—why say, I am a bad Guardian, Sir—that's all.

Sir Ro. If this should be apocryphal now?

Bel. Sir?

Sir Ro. A Fetch! a Fib, *Charles!*—to conceal some honest Man's Daughter, that you have stolen, Child!

Bel. And brought into a sober Family, to have the entire Possession of, without Lett, or Molestation?— Why, what a Deal of Money have You lavish'd away, Sir, upon the Education of a Fool?

Sir Ro. There is but that one Circumstance to bring thee off—For to be sure, her Affairs might have been as well settled in private Lodgings—And besides, *Charles*, a World of troublesome Questions, and lying Answers might have been sav'd—But take Care, Boy; —for I may be in the Secret before thou art aware on't—A great Rogue, *Charles!*   [*Exit.*

Bel. So!—The Mine's sprung, I see—and *Fidelia* has betray'd me—And yet, upon cooler Thoughts, she durst not break her Word with me—For tho' She's a Woman, the Devil has no Part in her—Now will I be be hang'd, if my loving Sifter is not at the Bottom of all this—But if I don't out-plot her!—Let me fee!—Ay—*Faddle* fhall be call'd in—For the Fool loves Mifchief like an old Maid; and will out-lie an Attorney.

SCENE III.

Enter ROSETTA.

Rofet. What, mufing, Brother!—Now wou'd I fain know, which of all the Virtues has been the Subject of your Contemplations?

Bel. Patience, Patience, Child—For he that has Connection with a Woman, let her be Wife, Miftrefs, or Sifter, muft have Patience.

Rofet. The moft ufeful Virtue in the World, Brother! —and *Fidelia* fhall be your Tutorefs—I'll hold fix to four, that fhe leads you into the Practice on't with more Dexterity, than the beft Philofopher in *England* She fhall teach it, and yet keep the Heart without Hope, Brother.

Bel. Why that's a contrary Method to yours, Sifter; —for you give Hope, where you mean to try Patience moft—And I take it, that you are the abler Miftrefs in the Art—Why every Coxcomb in Town has been your Scholar, Child.

Rofet. Not to learn Patience—There's your Miftake now—For it has been my conftant Practice, to put my Scholars Out of all Patience—What are you thinking of, Brother?

Bel. Why, I was thinking, Child, that 'twou'd be a Queftion to puzzle a Conjurer, what a Coquet was made for?

Rofet. Am I one, Brother?

Bel. O, Fie, Sifter!

Rofet. Lord! I, that am no Conjurer, can tell you that.—A Coquet!—Oh!—Why, a Coquet is a Sort of beautiful Defert in Wax-work, that tempts the

Fool to an Entertainment, merely to baulk his Appetite.—And will any one tell me, that Nature had no Hand in the making a Coquet, when she answers such wise and necessary Purposes?—Now, pray Sir, tell me what a Rake was made for?

Bel.. Am I one, Sister?

Rosit. O, Fie, Brother!

Bel. Nay, Child, if a Coquet be so useful in the System of Morals, a Rake must be the most horrid Thing in Nature—He was born for her Destruction, Child—She loses her Being at the very Sight of him—and drops plum into his Arms, like a charm'd Bird into the Mouth of a Rattle-Snake.

Roset. Bless us all!—What a Mercy it is, that we are Brother and Sister!

Bel. Be thankful for't Night and Morning upon your Knees, Huffy—for I should certainly have been the Ruin of you—But come, *Rosetta*—'Tis allow'd then, that we are Rake and Coquet—And now, do you know, that the essential Difference between us lies only in two Words—Petticoat and Breeches?

Roset. Ay, make that out, and you'll do something.

Bel. Pleasure, Child, is the Business of both—And the same Principles, that make Me a Rake, wou'd make You—no better than you shou'd be—were it not for that Tax upon the Petticoat, call'd Scandal. Your Wishes are restrain'd by Fear—Mine, authoris'd by Custom—And while you are forc'd to sit down with the starv'd Comfort of making Men Fools—I am upon the Wing to make Girls—Women, Child.

Roset. Now, as I hope to be marry'd, I wou'd not be a Rake for the whole World—unless I were a Man; —and then I do verily believe, I should turn out just such another.

Bel. That's my dear Sister! Give me your Hand, Child—Why now thou art the honestest Girl in St. *James*'s Parish—And I'll trust thee for the future with all my Secrets—I am going to *Fidelia*, Child.

Roset.

Roſet. What a Pity 'tis, Brother, that ſhe is not ſuch a Coquet as I am?

Bel. Not ſo neither, my ſweet Siſter—For, Faith, the Conqueſt wou'd be too eaſy to keep a Man conſtant.

Roſet. Civil Creature!

Bel. But here comes the Colonel—Now to our ſeveral Vocations—You to Fooling, and I to Buſineſs—At Dinner we'll meet, and compare Notes, Child.

Roſet. For a Pot of Coffee, I ſucceed beſt.

Bel. Faith, I'm afraid ſo. [*Exit.*

SCENE IV.

Enter the COLONEL.

Col. To meet you alone, Madam, is a Happineſs—

Roſet. Pray, Colonel, are you a Rake? Methinks I wou'd fain have you a Rake.

Col. Why ſo, Madam?—'Tis a Character I never was fond of.

Roſet. Becauſe I am tir'd of being a Coquet—and my Brother ſays, that a Rake can transform one, in the Flirt of a Fan.

Col. I wou'd be any Thing, Madam, to be better in your Opinion.

Roſet. If you were a Rake now, what wou'd you ſay to me?

Col. Nothing, Madam—I wou'd——
[*Snatches her Hand, and Kiſſes it.*

Roſet. Bleſs me!—is the Man mad!—I only ask'd what you wou'd ſay to me?

Col. I wou'd ſay, Madam, that you are my Life, my Soul, my Angel!—That all my Hopes of Happineſs are built upon your Kindneſs!

Roſet. Very well!—Keep it up!

Col. That your Smiles are brighter than Virtue, and your Chains ſweeter than Liberty!

Roſet. Upon my Word!

Col. O, *Roſetta!*—How can you trifle ſo with a Heart that loves you?

Roſet. Very well!—Pathetic too! *Col.*

Col. Nay, nay, this is carrying the Jest too far—If you knew the Situation of my Mind, you wou'd not torture me thus.

Rofet. Situation of the Mind!—Very geographical! —Go on!

Col. Pfhah!—This is not in your Nature.

Rofet. Sufpicion!—pretty enough!

Col. You know I have not deferv'd this.

Rofet. Anger too! –Go on!

Col. No, Madam,—*Faddle* can divert you this Way at an eafier Price.

Rofet. And Jealoufy!—All the Viciffitudes of Love! —Incomparable!

Col. You will force me to tell you, Madam, that I can bear to be your Jeft no longer.

Rofet. Or thus——

> *Am I the Jeft of her I love?*
> *Forbid it all the Gods above!*

—It may be render'd either Way—But I am for the Rhyme—I love Poetry vaftly—Don't you love Poetry, *Colonel?*

Col. This is beyond all Patience, Madam.

[Very angrily.

Rofet. Blefs me!—Why, you have not been in Earneft, *Colonel?*—Lord, Lord, how a filly Woman may be miftaken!

Col. Shall I ask you one ferious Queftion, Madam?

Rofet. Why, I find my felf fomewhat whimfical this Morning—and I don't care if I do take a little Stuff— but don't let it be bitter.

Col. Am I to be your Fool always, Madam, or, like other Fools, to be made a Husband of, when my Time's out?

Rofet. Lord, you Men Creatures do ask the ftrangeft Queftions!—Why how can I poffibly fay now, what I fhall do ten Years hence?

Col. I am anfwer'd, Madam. *[Walking in diforder.*

Enter SERVANT.

Serv. Mr. *Faddle*, Madam. *[Exit.*

SCENE V.

Enter FADDLE.

Fad. O, my dear, foft Toad!—And the Colonel, by all that's fcarlet?—Now Pox catch me, if Nature ever form'd fo compleat a Couple—fince the firft Pair in Paradife.

Rofet. 'Tis well you are come, *Faddle*——Give me fomething to laugh at, or I fhall die with the Spleen.

Col. Ay, Sir, make the Lady laugh this Moment, or I fhall break your Bones, Rafcal.

Fad. Lord, Colonel!—What!—what!—hah!—

Col. Make her laugh this Inftant, I fay, or I'll make you cry—Not make her laugh, when fhe bids you!—Why, Sirrah!—I have made her laugh this half Hour, without bidding.

Rofet. Ha! ha! ha!

Fad. Why there, there, there, Colonel!—She does, fhe does, fhe does! ——

SCENE VI.

Enter YOUNG BELMONT, *and* FIDELIA.

Bel. Why how now, *Faddle!*—What has been the Matter, prithee?

Col. A Rafcal!—Not make a Lady laugh!

Fad. What *Charles*, and my little *Fiddy* too! —Stand by me a little—for this robuft Colonel has relax'd my very Sinews, and quite tremulated my whole Syftem.—I cou'd not have collected myfelf, without your Prefence.

Fid. And was he angry with you, *Faddle?*

Fad. To a Degree, my Dear—But I have forgot it—I bear no Malice to any one in the World, Child.

Rofet. Do you know, *Faddle*, that I have a Quarrel with you too?

Fad. You, Child!—Heh! heh!—What, I am inconftant, I fuppofe—and have been the Ruin of a few Families this Winter, hah, Child?—Murder
will

will out, tho' it's done in the Center—But come, *Vivace*! Let the Storm loofe—and you fhall fee me weather it, like the Ofier in the Fable—It may bend, but not break me.

Rofet. Nay, it fhall come in a Breeze—I'll whifper it. [*Whifpers Faddle*]

Bel. Colonel!

Col. Now cou'd I cut my Throat, for being vext at this Puppy—And yet the Devil Jealoufy will have it fo. [*Apart to Belmont.*]

Fad. Oh, what a Creature have you nam'd, Child!—Heh! heh! heh!—May Grace renounce me, and Darknefs feal my Eye-lids, if I wou'd not as foon make Love to a Milliner's Doll.

Bel. Prithee, what Miftrefs has fhe found out for thee, *Faddle?*

Fad. By all that's odious, *Charles*—Mifs *Gargle,* the 'Pothecary's Daughter—The Toad is fond of me, that's poffitive—But fuch a Mefs of Water-gruel!—Ugh!—To all Purpofes of Joy, fhe's an Armful of dry Shavings!—And then fhe's fo jealous of one!—Lord, fays fhe, Mr. *Faddle,* you are eternally at Sir *Roger's*—One can't fet Eyes upon you in a whole Day—Hch! hch!—And then the Tears do fo trickle down thofe white-wafh Cheeks of her's—that if fhe cou'd but warm me to the leaft Fit of the Heart-burn, I believe I fhou'd be tempted to take her—by Way of Chalk and Water.— Heh! hch! hch!

Bel.
Rofet. } Ha! ha! ha!
Fid.

Rofet. Isn't he a pleafant Creature, Colonel?

Col. Certainly, Madam—of infinite Wit, with Abundance of Modefty.

Fad. Pugh!—Pox of Modefty, Colonel!—But do you know, you flim Toad you, [*To Rofet.*] what a Battle I had laft Night, in a certain Company, about you, and that ugly Gipfy there?

Fid. Meaning me, Sir? *Fa},*

Fad. Pert, and pretty!—You muſt know, there was Jack Taffety, Billy Cruel, Lord Harry Gymp and I, at Jack's Lodgings, all in tip-top Spirits, over a Pint of Burgundy—A Pox of all Drinking tho'—I ſhall never get it out of my Head—Well, we were toaſting a Round of Beauties, you muſt know—The Girl of your Heart, *Faddle*, ſays my Lord?— *Roſetta Belmont*, my Lord, ſays I—And, Faith, down you went, you delicate Devil you, in almoſt half a Glaſs—Rot your Toaſt, ſays my Lord, —I was fond of her laſt Winter—She's a Wit, ſays Jack—And a Scold, by all that's noiſy, ſays Billy— Isn't ſhe a little freckled, ſays my Lord?—Damna- tionly padded, ſays Jack—And painted like a Dutch Doll, by Jupiter, ſays Billy—She's very unſuſcepti- ble, ſays my Lord—No more Warmth than a Snow- ball, ſays Jack—A mere Cold-bath to a Lover, Curſe catch me, ſays Billy—Heh! heh! heh!—ſays I, that's becauſe you want Heat to warm her, my Dears—To me now, ſhe's all over Cumbuſtibles—I can electrify her by a Look—Touch but her Lip, and ſnap ſhe goes off in a Flaſh of Fire.

Roſet. O, the Wretch!—what a Picture has he drawn of me! [*to* Fidelia.

Fid. You muſt be curious, my Dear.

Bel. Ha! ha!—But you forget *Fidelia, Faddle.*

Fad. Oh!—And there's the new Face, ſays Billy— *Fidelia,* I think they call her—If ſhe was an Apurte- nance of mine, ſays my Lord, I'd hang her upon a Peg in my Wardrobe, among my caſt Clothes— With thoſe demure Looks of hers, ſays Jack, I'd ſend her to my Aunt in Worceſterſhire, to ſet her Face by, when ſhe went to Church—Or what think you, ſays Billy, of keeping her in a Show-glaſs, by Way of—Gentlemen and Ladies, walk in, and ſee the Curioſity of Curioſities— the perfect Pamela in High Life!—Obſerve, Gentlemen, the Bluſhing of her Cheeks, the Turning up of her Eyes, and her

E Tongue,

Tongue, that fays nothing but Fie! Fie!—Ha! ha!
ha!—Incomparable!—faid all three—Pugh, Pox,
fays I—not fo bad as that neither—The little Toad
has not feen much of the Town indeed—But fhe'll
do in Time—And a Glafs of Preniac may ferve one's
Turn, you know, when Champain is not to be had
[*Bowing to Rofetta.*

All. Ha! ha! ha!

Bel. Why, thou did'ft give it 'em, Faith, Bully.

Fid. I think, *Rofetta*, we were mighty lucky in an
Advocate.

Rofet. Prodigious!

Fad. Poor Toads!—Oh!—I had forgot—You left
the Rehearfal of the New Opera this Morning in the
moft unlucky Time!—The very Moment you were
gone, foufe came into the Pit, my Friend the Alderman
and his fat Wife, trick'd out in Sunfhine—You muft
know, I drank Chocolate with 'em in the Morning,
and heard all the Ceremony of their Proceedings—Sir
Barnaby, fays my Lady, fays fhe—I fhall wear my Pink
and Silver, and my beft Jewels—and, d'ye hear?—Do
you get Betty to tack on your Drefdens, and let Pom-
pey comb out the white Tie, and bring down the
blue Coat lin'd with Buff, and the brown filk Breeches,
and the gold-headed Cane—I think as you always
wear your Coat button'd, that green Waiftcoat may
do—But 'tis fo befmear'd, that I vow it's a filthy
Sight with your Night-gown open—And as you go
in the Coach with me, you may get your white
Stockings air'd—But you are determin'd never to
oblige me with a Pair of Roll-ups upon thefe Occafions, notwithftanding all I have faid—We are to
mix with Quality this Morning, Mr. *Faddle*, and it
may be proper to let 'em know as how, there are
People in the City, who live of the *Weftminfter* Side
of *Wapping*—Your Ladyfhip's perfectly in the Right,
Madam, fays I—(*Stifling a Laugh*) and for fear of
a Horfe

a Horfe-laugh in her Face, flap-dafh, I made a Leg, and brufh'd off like Lightning.

All. Ha! ha! ha!

Enter Servant, *and whifpers* Rofetta.

Rofet. Come, Gentlemen, Dinner waits—We fhall have all your Companies, I hope.

Bel. You know, you dine with me at the King's-Arms, *Faddle.*   [*Apart to Fad.*

Fad. Do I?—I am forry, my dear Creature, that a particular Appointment robs me of the Honour.
   [*to Rofetta.*

Rofet. Pfhah! you are always engag'd, I think—Come, *Fidelia.*   [*Exe. Rofet. & Fide.*

Col. Why then, thank Heaven there's fome Re-fpite!   [*Exit.*

Bel. Hark you, *Faddle*—I hope you are not in the leaft ignorant, that upon particular Occafions, you can be a very great Rafcal?

Fad. Who I, *Charles?*—Pugh!—Pox!—Is this the Dinner I am to have?

Bel. Courage, Boy!—And becaufe I think fo well of thee—there—[*Gives him a Purfe*]—'Twill buy thee a new lac'd Coat, and a Feather.

Fad. Why ay, this is fomething, *Charles*—But what am I to do, hah?—I won't fight—upon my Soul, I won't fight.

Bel. Thou can'ft lie a little.

Fad. A great deal *Charles*—Or I have fpent my Time among Women of Quality to little Purpofe.

Bel. I'll tell thee then—This fweet Girl, this An-gel, this ftubborn *Fidelia*, fticks fo at my Heart, that I muft either get the better of her, or run mad.

Fad. And fo thou woud'ft have me aiding and abetting, hah, *Charles?*—Muft not be tuck'd up for a Rape neither.

Bel. Peace, Fool!—About three Months ago, by a very extraordinary Adventure, this Lady dropt into

E 2   my

my Arms—It happen'd that our Hearts took Fire at first Sight—But as the Devil wou'd have it, in the Hurry of my first Thoughts, not knowing where to place her, I was tempted, for Security, to bring her to this haunted House here—where, between the Jealousy of Sir *Charles*, the Gravity of the Colonel, the Curiosity of a Sister, and the awkward Care of a Father, she must become a Vestal, or I—a Husband.

Fad. And so, by Way of a little simple Fornication, you want to remove her to private Lodgings, hah, *Charles!*

Bel. But how, how, how!—thou dear Rascal?

Fad. Let me see!—Hum!—And so, you are not her Guardian, *Charles?*

Bel. Nor she the Woman she pretends, Boy—I tell thee, she was mine by Fortune—I tilted for her at Midnight—But the Devil tempted me, I say, to bring her hither—The Family was in Bed; which gave me Time for Contrivance—I prevail'd upon her to call me her Guardian—that by pretending Authority over her, I might remove her at Pleasure—But here too I was deceiv'd—My Sister's Fondness for her has render'd every Plot of mine to part 'em impracticable—And without thy wicked Assistance, we must both die in our Virginity.

Fad. Hum! That wou'd be a Pity, *Charles*—But let me see!—Ay!—I have it—Within these three Hours, we'll contrive to set the House in such a Flame, that the Devil himself may take her—if he stands at the Street-Door—To Dinner, to Dinner, Boy! 'Tis here, here, here, *Charles!*

Bel. If thou dost!

Fad. And if I don't!—Why no more Purses *Charles*—I tell thee, 'tis here, here Boy! To Dinner, to Dinner!

[*Exeunt.*

ACT

ACT III.
SCENE *continues.*
Enter ROSETTA *and* FIDELIA.

FIDELIA.

'TIS all your own doing, my Dear. You firſt teize him into Madneſs, and then wonder to hear his Chains rattle.

Roſet. And yet how one of my heavenly Smiles ſober'd him again!

Fid. If I were a Man, you ſhou'd uſe me ſo but once, *Roſetta.*

Roſet. Pſhah!—If you were a Man, you wou'd do, as Men do, Child—Ha! ha! ha!—They are Creatures of robuſt Conſtitutions, and will bear a great deal—Beſides, for my Part, I can't ſee what a reaſonable Fellow, ought to expect before Marriage, but ill Uſage—You can't imagine, my Dear, how it ſweetens Kindneſs afterwards—'Tis bringing a poor, ſtarv'd Creature to a warm Fire, after a whole Night's wand'ring thro' Froſt and Snow.

Fid. But, to carry on the Image, my Dear— won't he be apt to curſe the Tongue that miſguided him; and take up with the firſt Fire he meets with, rather than periſh in the Cold?—I cou'd ſing you a Song *Roſetta,* that one wou'd ſwear was made o'Purpoſe for you,

Roſet. O, pray let me hear it.

SONG.
FIDELIA.
I.

FOR a Shape, and a Bloom, and an Air, and a Mein, Myrtilla *was brighteſt of all the gay Green* ; But artfully wild, and affectedly coy, Thoſe her Beauties invited, her Pride wou'd deſtroy.

I. By

II.

By the Flocks, as she stray'd with the Nymphs of the Vale,
Not a Shepherd but woo'd her to hear his soft Tale;
Tho' fatal the Passion, she laugh'd at the Swain,
And return'd with Neglect, what she heard with Disdain.

III.

But Beauty has Wings, and too hastily flies,
And Love, unrewarded, soon sickens and dies.
The Nymph cur'd by Time, of her Folly and Pride,
Now sighs in her Turn for the Bliss she deny'd.

IV.

No longer she frolicks it wide o'er the Plain,
To kill with her Coyness the languishing Swain;
So humbled her Pride is, so soften'd her Mind,
That, tho' courted by none, she to all wou'd be kind.

How d'ye like it, my Dear?

Roset, Pshah!—there's a Song indeed!—You shou'd
sing of Men's Perjuries, my Dear—of kind Nymphs,
and cloy'd Shepherds—For take my Word for't—
there's no Charm like Cruelty to keep the Men con-
stant; nor no Deformity like Kindness to make 'em
loath you.

Enter Servant.

Serv. A Letter for your Ladyship, Madam. [*Exit.*
Roset. For me? I don't remember the Hand. (*Opens*
and reads the Letter to herself.)
Fid. I have little Inclination to be chearful, tho' I
sing Songs, and prattle thro' the whole Day—*Bel-*
mont! Belmont! [*Afide.*] You seem strangely concern'd, Madam!—I hope no ill News!
Roset. The worst in the World, *Fidelia,* if it be
true.
Fid. Pray Heaven it be false then!—But must it
be a Secret?—I hope my dear *Rosetta* knows, that
whatever affects her Quiet, can't leave mine un-
disturb'd.
                                                    Roset.

Rofet. Who's there?

Enter Servant.

How did you receive this Letter?

Serv. From a Porter, Madam.

Rofet. Is he without?

Serv. No, Madam, he faid it requir'd no Anfwer.

Rofet. Had you any Knowledge of him?

Serv. Not that I remember, Madam.

Rofet. Shou'd you know him again?

Serv. Certainly, Madam.

Rofet. Where did my Brother fay he din'd to Day?

Serv. At the King's-Arms, Madam.

Rofet. And Mr. *Faddle* with him?

Serv. They went out together, Madam.

Rofet. Run this Moment, and fay I defire to fpeak with both of 'em immediately, upon an extraordinary Affair.

Serv. Yes, Madam.   [*Exit.*

Fid. What can this mean, *Rofetta?*—Am I unfit to be trufted?

Rofet. Tell me, *Fidelia*—But no Matter—Why fhou'd I difturb you?—I have been too grave.

Fid. Still more and more perplexing!— But my Enquiries are at an End—I fhall learn to be lefs troublefome, as you are lefs kind, *Rofetta.*

Rofet. Prithee don't talk fo, *Fidelia*—I can never be lefs kind.

Fid. Indeed, I won't deferve you fhou'd.

Rofet. I know it, *Fidelia*—But tell me then—Is there a Circumftance in your Life, that wou'd call a Blufh to your Cheeks, if 'twere laid as open to the World's Knowledge, as to your own?

Fid. If from the Letter you afk me that ftrange Queftion, Madam, furely I fhou'd fee it.

Rofet. I think not, *Fidelia* – For upon fecond Thoughts, 'tis a Trifle, not worth your Notice.

Fid. Why were you fo much alarm'd then?

Rofet.

Rofet. I confefs, it ftartled me at firft—But 'tis a lying Letter, and fhou'd not trouble you.

Fid. Then it relates to me Madam?

Rofet. No Matter, *Fidelia.*

Fid. I have loft my Friend then—I beg'd, at firft, to be a Sharer in *Rofetta's* Griefs—But now I find they are all my own, and fhe denies my Right to 'em.

Rofet. This is too much, *Fidelia*—And now, to keep you longer in Sufpence wou'd be Cruelty—But the Writer of this Scroll has a Mind darker than Night. You fhall join with me in wondring, that there is fuch a Monfter in the World.

[*Reads.*]

To Mifs ROSETTA BELMONT.

Madam,

AS I write without a Name, I am alike indifferent to your Thanks, or Refentment—Fidelia *is not what fhe feems*—She has deceiv'd You, and may your Brother to his Ruin—Women of the Town know how to wear the Face of Innocence, when it ferves the Purpofes of Guilt—Faddle, *if he pleafes, can inform you far-ther*—But be affur'd, I have my Intelligence from more fufficient Authority.

P. S. *There needs no farther Addrefs in this Matter, than a plain Queftion to* Fidelia—*Is fhe the Sifter of Mr.* Belmont's *Friend?*

Fid. Then I am loft!   [*Afide.*

Rofet. What, in Tears, *Fidelia?*—Nay, I meant to raife your Contempt only—Prithee, look up, and let us laugh at the Malice of this namelefs Libeller.

Fid. No, *Rofetta*—The Mind muft be wrapt in its own Innocence, that can ftand againft the Storms of Malice—I fear, I have not that Mind.

Rofet. What Mind, *Fidelia?*

Fid. And yet that Letter is a falfe one.

Rofet.

Rofet. Upon my Life, it is!—For you are Innocence it felf.

Fid. Oh, *Rofetta!*—No Sifter of Mr. *Belmont*'s Friend kneels to you for Pardon—but a poor wretched Out-caft of Fortune, that with an artful Tale has impos'd upon your Nature, and won you to a Friend-fhip for a helplefs Stranger, that never knew her felf.

Rofet. Rife, *Fidelia*—But take Care!—For if you have deceiv'd me, Honefty is nothing but a Name.

Fid. Think not too hardly of me neither—For tho' I am not what I feem, I wou'd not be what that Letter calls me, to be Miftrefs of the World.

Rofet. I have no Words, *Fidelia*—Speak on—But methinks, you fhou'd not weep fo.

Fid. Nay, now, *Rofetta*, you compel me—For this Gentlenefs is too much for me—I have deceiv'd you, and you are kind—If you wou'd dry up my Tears, call forth your Refentment—Anger might turn me into Stone—but Compaffion melts me.

Rofet. I have no Anger, *Fidelia*—Pray go on.

Fid. When my Tears will let me—I have play'd a foolifh Game, *Rofetta*—and yet my utmoft Fault has been, confenting to deceive you—What I am, I know not—That I am not what I feem, I know—But why I have feem'd otherwife than I am, again I know not—'Tis a Riddle, that your Brother only can explain—He knows the Story of my Life, and will in Honour reveal it—Wou'd he were here!

Rofet. Wou'd he were, *Fidelia!*—for I am upon the Rack—Prithee, go on, and inform me farther.

Fid. There's my Grief, *Rofetta*—For I am bound by fuch Promifes to Silence, that to clear my Inno-cence, wou'd be to wound it—All I have left to fay is, that my Condition of Life only has been affum'd, my Virtue never.

Enter Servant.

Rofet. Well, Sir!

Serv. Mr. *Belmont*, Madam, was juft gone; but

Mr. *Faddle* will wait upon your Ladyſhip immediately.

Roſet. Did they ſay where my Brother went ?

Serv. They did not know—Mr. *Faddle* is here, Madam.   [*Exit.*

SCENE II.

Enter FADDLE *humming a* Tune.

Fad. In Obedience to your extraordinary Commands, Madam—But you ſhou'd have been alone, Child.

Roſet. No trifling, Sir—Do you know this Handwriting?   [*Gives him the Letter.*

Fad. Hum!—Not I, as I hope to be fav'd—Nor you neither, I believe. (*aſide*)—Is it for my Peruſal, Madam ?

Fid. And your anſwering too, Sir.

Fad. Mighty well, Madam. (*reads*) Hum!—*Fidelia*—*Women—of the Town—Innocence—Guilt—Faddle—inform you farther !*—Why, what a Pox, am I brought in for ? —*Intelligence—Queſtion—Fidelia—Siſter of* Mr. Belmont's *Friend.*   [*Stares and Whiſtles.*

Roſet. Well, Sir!   [*takes the Letter.*

Fad. Oh!—I am to guefs at the Writer—Can't, upon my Soul—Upon my Soul, I can't, Child— 'Tis a Woman, I believe tho', by the damn'd Blabbing that's in't.

Fid. The Letter ſays, Sir, that you can inform this Lady farther concerning me—Now, Sir, whatever you happen to know, or to have heard of me, deliver freely, and without Diſguiſe—I entreat it, as an Act of Friendſhip, that will for ever oblige me.

Fad. Let me ſee!—No—It can't be her neither— She is a Woman of too much Honour—and yet, I don't remember to have open'd my Lips about it, to any Soul but her.

Fid.

Fid. You know me then, Sir ?

Rofet. Speak out, Sir !

Fad. Methinks, if thefe Letter-writers were a little more communicative of their own Names, and lefs fo of their Neighbours, there wou'd be more Honefty in 'em—Why am I introduc'd here !—Truly, forfooth, becaufe a certain Perfon in the World is overburden'd with the Secrets of her own Slips, and for a little Vent, chufes to blab thofe of another—*Faddle* inform you farther !—*Faddle* will be damn'd as foon.

Rofet. Hark you, Sir—If you intend to enter thefe Doors again, tell me all you know—for I will have it—You have own'd your telling it elfewhere, Sir.

Fid. What was it you told, Sir ?

Fad. What I fhan't tell here, Madam—Her angry Ladyfhip muft excufe me, Faith.

Rofet. 'Tis very well, Sir !

Fid. Indeed, *Rofetta*, he knows nothing.

Fad. Nothing in the World, Madam, as I hope to be fav'd— Mine is all Hear-fay—And, Curfe upon 'em! the whole Town may be in a Lie, for any Thing I know—So, they faid of Lady *Bridget*—— that fhe went off with her Footman—But 'twas all Slander, for 'twas a Horfe Grenadier, that fhe bought the Commiffion for, laft Week.

Rofet. What has Lady *Bridget*, or the Town, to do with *Fidelia*, Sir ?

Fad. So I faid, Madam—the very Words—Says I, a Woman of the Town ?—Who made her a Woman of the Town ?—Does a Slip or two with Particulars make a Lady a Woman of the Town ?—Or if it did, fays I, many a one has taken up, and liv'd honeftly afterwards—A Woman of the Town indeed !

Fid. Hold your licentious Tongue, Sir !—Upon my Life, *Rofetta*, 'tis all Malice—'Tis his own Contrivance—I dare him to produce another Villain, that's bafe enough to fay this of me.

Fad.

Fad... Right, Madam!—Stick to that, and Egad,
I'll be of your Side.   [*Aloud in her Ear.*

Fid. Infolence! (*strikes him*) Oh, I am hurt beyond all bearing!

Rofet. And I, loft in Perplexity—If thou art link'd
with any Wretch, bafe enough to contrive this Paper,
or art thy felf the Contriver,—may Poverty and a
bad Heart, be thy Companions—But if thou art
privy to any Thing, that concerns the Honour of
this Family, give it Breath—and I'll infure thee both
Protection and Reward.

Fid. I dare him to the Difcovery.

Fad. Ladies—I have had the Honour of a Blow
conferr'd on me by one of you—and am favour'd
with the Offer of Protection and Reward from the
other—Now to convince both, that, in Spite of In-
dignities, or Obligations, I can keep a Secret—if
ever I open my Lips upon this Matter, may Plague,
Famine, and the horn'd Devil confume and feize me.
—And fo, Ladies—I take my Leave. [*Exit finging.*

Rofet. What can this Fellow mean, *Fidelia?*—
Has he not abus'd you?

Fid. Is it a Doubt then? —Wou'd I had leave to
fpeak!

Rofet. And why not, *Fidelia?*—Promifes, unjuft-
ly extorted, have no Right to Obfervance—You have
deceiv'd me, by your own Acknowledgment—and
methinks, at fuch a Time, Matters of Punctilio fhou'd
give Place to Reafon and Neceffity.

Fid. I dare not, *Rofetta*—'Twou'd be a Crime to
your Brother—and I owe Him more than all the
World.

Rofet. And what are thofe Obligations, *Fidelia?*

Fid. Not for me to mention—Indeed, I dare not,
Rofetta.

Rofet. 'Tis well, Madam!—And when you are inclin'd to admit me to your Confidence, I fhall perhaps
know better how to conduct my felf.   [*Going.*

S C E N E.

S C E N E III.

Enter Young BELMONT, *meeting her.*

Rof. Oh, you are come, Brother!—Your Friend's
Sifter, your Ward there, has wanted you, Sir!
Bel. What is it, *Fidelia?*
Fid. I have no Breath to fpeak it—Your Sifter,
Sir, can better inform you.
Rofet. Read that, Sir.
          [*Gives him the Letter, which he reads to himfelf.*
Fid. Now, *Rofetta,* all fhall be fet right—Your
Brother will do me Juftice, and account for his own
Conduct.
Rofet. I expect fo, *Fidelia.*
Bel. Impertinent!—[*Gives back the Letter*]—I met
Faddle, as I came in—and I fuppofe in pure Love of
Mifchief, he has made my believing Sifter here, a
Convert to the Villany of that Letter—But I'll make
the Rafcal unfay every Thing he has faid—or his
Bones fhall ake for't.   [*Going.*
Fid. Stay, Sir, I entreat you!—That I am a
Counterfeit, in Part, I have already confefs'd—
Bel. You have done wrong then.
Fid. But am I a Creature of the Town, Sir?—
Your Sifter muft learn that from you—You have been
once my Deliverer—Be fo now—Tell her, I am
poor and miferable, but not difhoneft—That I have
only confented to deceive her, not defir'd it—Tell
her, I deferve her Pity, not her Anger—'Tis my
only Requeft—Can you deny it me?
Bel. You have faid too much, *Fidelia*—And for
your own Sake, I fhall forbear to mention what I
know of your Story—How far your own Honour
is bound, you are the beft Judge—But a Breach of
the moft folemn Promifes, let me tell you, Madam,
                                              will

will be a wretched Vindication of the Innocence you contend for.

Fid. And is this all, Sir?

Bel. For my own Part, I muſt have better Authority than *Faddle*, or a nameleſs Writer, to believe any Thing to your Diſhonour—And for you, Siſter—I muſt not have this Lady ill-treated—While I am ſatisfy'd of her Innocence, your Suſpicions are impertinent—Nor will I conſent to her Removal, Madam, —mark that—whatever you, in your great Wiſdom, may have privately determin'd.   [*Exit.*

Roſet. You are a Villain, Brother.

Fid. Now I have loſt you, *Roſetta!*

Roſet. When you incline to be a Friend to your ſelf, *Fidelia*—you may find one in me—But while Explanations are avoided, I muſt be allow'd to act from my own Opinion, and agreeable to the Character I am to ſupport.   [*Exit.*

Fid. Then I am wretched!—But that's no Novelty—I have wander'd from my Cradle, the very Child of Misfortune. To retire and weep, muſt now be my only Indulgence.

[*Exit.*

SCENE IV.

Re-enter BELMONT.

Bel. Why, what a Rogue am I!—Here have I thrown a whole Family—and that my own too—into Perplexities, that Innocence can't oppoſe, nor Cunning guard againſt—And all for what?—Why, a Woman—Take away that Excuſe, and the Devil himſelf would be a Saint to me ; for all the reſt is ſinning without Temptation—In my Commerce with the World, I am guarded againſt the mercenary Vices—I think, I have Honour above Lying, Courage above Cruelty—Pride above Meanneſs, and Honeſty nefty above Deceit—and yet, throw but coy Beauty in my Way, and all the Vices, by Turns, take Pofſeſſion of me—Fortune, Fortune, give me Succeſs this once—and I'll build Churches!

SCENE V.

Enter FADDLE.

Fad. What, *Charles!*—Is the Coaſt clear, and the finiſhing Stroke given to my Embaſſy, hah?

Bel. Thou haſt been a moſt excellent Raſcal—and Faith, Matters ſeem to be in a promiſing Condition. —For I have flung That in *Roſetta*'s Way, which if ſhe keeps her Womanhood, will do the Buſineſs.

Fad. Prithee, what's that, *Charles?*

Bel. Why, I have bid her, not to think of parting with *Fidelia.*

Fad. Nay, then, Tip ſhe goes headlong out at Window—But haſt thou no Bowels, *Charles?*—for, methinks, I begin to feel ſome Twitches of Compunction about me.

Bel. I underſtand you, Sir—But I have no more Purſes.

Fad. Why, look you, *Charles?*—We muſt find a Way to lull this Conſcience of mine—Here will be the Devil to do elſe—That's a very pretty Ring, *Charles.*

Bel. Is it ſo, Sir?—Hark you, Mr. Dog—If you demur one Moment to fetching and carrying in this Buſineſs, as I bid you—you ſhall find my Hand a little heavy upon you.

Fad. Pugh, Pox, *Charles!*—Can't a Body ſpeak? —People may be in Good-humour, when they want People to do Things for People, methinks.

Bel. Troop this Moment, with your raſcally Conſcience to the King's-Arms—and wait there till I come, Sir.

Fad

Fad. Why fo I will, *Charles*—A Pox of the fwaggering Son of a—Not fo big neither—if one had but a little Courage.   [*Afide, and going.*

Bel. Hark you, *Faddle!*—Now I think on't, there is a Way yet for thee to make another Purfe out of this Bufinefs.

Fad. Why, one wou'd not be a Rogue for nothing, methinks.

Bel. I faw Sir *Charles* going into *Fidelia*'s Chamber— Thou may'ft fteal upon 'em unobferv'd — They'll have their Plots too, I fuppofe.

Fad. And where am I to come and tell thee, hah?

Bel. At the King's-Arms, Boy.

Fad. But you'll remember the Purfe, *Charles?*

Bel. Softly, Rafcal!   [*Exit Faddle.*

Why, there it is again now!—I am a Fellow of Principle!—And fo I will be, fome Time or other— But thefe Appetites are the Devil—and at prefent I am under their Direction.

                                                [*Exit.*

SCENE VI. *Another Apartment.*

Sir CHARLES *and* FIDELIA *difcover'd fitting.*

Sir *Cha.* He durft not fay, directly, you were that Creature the Letter call'd you?

Fid. Not in Terms, Sir; but his Concealments ftruck deeper than the fharpeft Accufations.

Sir *Cha.* And cou'd Mr. *Belmont* be filent to all this?

Fid. He faid he had his Reafons, Sir—and it was my Part to fubmit—I had no Heart to difoblige him.

Sir *Cha.* You are too nice, Madam—— *Rofetta* loves you, and fhou'd be trufted.

Fid. Alas, Sir!—if it concern'd me only, I fhou'd have no Concealment.

                                                Sir *Cha.*

Sir Cha. It concerns you moſt, Madam—I muſt deal plainly with you — You have deceiv'd your Friend; and, tho' I believe it not, a ſeverer Reproach reſts upon you—And ſhall an idle Promiſe, an extorted one too—and that from a Man, who ſolicits your Undoing, forbid your Vindication? You muſt think better of it.

Fid. 'Tis not an extorted Promiſe, Sir, that ſeals my Lips—But I love him—And tho' he purſues me to my Ruin, I will obey him in this, whatever happens—He may deſert me, but never ſhall have Reaſon to upbraid me.

Sir Cha. 'Tis your own Cauſe, Madam—and you muſt act in it as you think proper—Yet ſtill, if I might adviſe—

Fid. Leave it to Time, Sir *Charles*—And if you believe me innocent, your friendly Thoughts of me, and my own Conſciouſneſs ſhall keep me chearful.

SCENE VII.

Enter FADDLE, *liſt'ning.*

Fad. O, Pox, is it ſo!—Now for a Secret, worth twenty Pieces!   [*Aſide.*

Sir Cha. Has it ever appear'd to you, Madam, that *Faddle* was a Confidant of Mr. *Belmont*'s?

Fid. Never, Sir—On the contrary, a Wretch moſt heartily deſpis'd by him.

Fad. If ſhe ſhou'd be a little miſtaken now! [*Aſide.*

Sir Cha. Can you gueſs at any other Means of his coming to a Knowledge of you?

Fid. None, that I know of, Sir.

Fad. Faith, I believe her.   [*Aſide.*

Sir Cha. One Queſtion more, Madam, and I have done—Did Mr. *Belmont* ever ſolicit your removing from this Houſe?

Fid. Never directly, Sir—He has often, when we

G   have

have been alone, quarrel'd with himself for bringing me into it.

Sir Cha. I thank you, Madam—And if my Enquiries have been at any Time too importunate, allow 'em to the Warmth of an honeft Friendfhip—For I have a Heart, that feels for your Diftreffes, and beats to relieve 'em.

Fid. I have no Words, Sir *Charles*—Let my Tears thank you.

Sir Cha. Be compos'd, my Child—And if *Rofetta's* Sufpicions grow violent, I have Apartments ready to receive you—with fuch Welcome, as Virtue fhou'd find with one who loves it.

Fid. Still, Sir *Charles*, my Tears are all that I can thank you with—For this Goodnefs is too much for me.

Fad. And, fo fhe's a Bit for the old Gentleman, at laft! Rare News for *Charles!* —Or with a little Addition, I fhall make it fo—But I muft decamp, to avoid Danger.   [*Afide, and Exit.*

Sir Cha. Dry up your Tears, *Fidelia*—For, if my Conjectures are well grounded, before Night, perhaps, fomething may be done to ferve you—And fo I leave you to your beft Thoughts.   [*Exit.*

Fid. Then I have one Friend left—How long I am to hold him, Heaven knows—'Tis a fickle World, and nothing in it is lafting, but Misfortune—Yet I'll have Patience ;

> *That fweet Relief, the healing Hand of Heav'n*
> *Alone to fuff'ring Innocence has giv'n ;*
> *Come, Friend of Virtue, Balm of every Care,*
> *Dwell in my Bofom, and forbid Defpair.*

[*Exit.*

A C T

ACT IV.

SCENE I. *An Apartment.*

Enter COLONEL *and* ROSETTA.

R O S E T T A.

I Tell you, I will not be talk'd to.

Col. 'Tis my Unhappinefs, Madam, to raife no Paffion in you, but Anger.

Rofet. You are miftaken, *Colonel*— I am not angry, tho' I anfwer fo—My Gaiety has been difturb'd to-day ; and Gravity always fets upon me like Ill-humour—*Fidelia* has engrofs'd me, and you are talking of yourfelf—What wou'd you have me fay ?

Col. That your Negleft of me has been diffembled, and that I have Leave to love you, and to hope for you.

Rofet. This is very ftrange now !—Why, 'tis not in your Power to avoid loving me, whether you have Leave to hope or not—And as to my diffembling— I know nothing of that—All I know is, that I'm a Woman—and Women I fuppofe diffemble fometimes. —I don't pretend to be a Bit better than a Woman.

Col. Be a kind one, and you're an Angel.

Rofet. Why there now !—When if I wanted to be an Angel, the very Kindnefs that made me one, wou'd leave me in a Month or two, a mere forfaken Woman. No, no, Colonel—Ignorance is the Mother of Love, as well as Devotion—We are Angels before you know us to be Women—and lefs than Women, when you know us to be no Angels—If you wou'd be pleas'd with the Tricks of a Juggler, never enquire how they are done.

Col. Right, Madam, where the Entertainment confifts only in the Deceit.

G 2　　　　　　　　　*Rofet.*

Rofet. And Philofophers will tell you, that the on‑ly Happinefs of Life is to be well deceiv'd.

Col. 'Tis the Philofophy of Fools, Madam—Is the Pleafure that arifes from Virtue a Cheat ?—Or is there no Happinefs in conferring Obligations, where the Receiver wifhes to be oblig'd, and labours to return ?—'Tis the Happinefs of Divinity, to diftri‑bute Good, and be paid with Gratitude.

Rofet. But to give all at once, wou'd be to lofe the Power of obliging.

Col. And to deny all, wou'd be to lofe the Pleafure of obliging.

Rofet. But where the Gift is trifling, you know !

Col. That Trifle, if lent to another's Manage‑ment, might make both rich.

Rofet. This is playing at Crofs-purpofes—But if I were inclin'd to liften, what have you to fay in Fa‑vour of Matrimony ?

Col. To Fools, Madam, 'tis the Jewel of Æfop's Cock—but to the Wife, a Diamond of Price, in a fkilful Hand, to enrich Life—'Tis Happinefs, or Mifery, as Minds are differently difpos'd—The ne‑ceffary Requifites are Love, good Senfe, and good Breeding—The firft to unite, the fecond to advife, and the third to comply—If you add to thefe, Neat‑nefs and a Competency, Beauty will always pleafe, and Family Cares become agreeable Amufements.

Rofet. And yet I have known a very miferable Couple, with all thefe Requifites.

Col. Never, if you'll believe me, *Rofetta*—They have worn 'em in Public, and may have diffembled with Succefs—But Marriage-Intimacies deftroy Diffimula‑tion—And if their private Hours have known no Enjoyment—there muft have been wanting, either the Affection that fhou'd unite, the Underftanding that fhou'd advife, or the Complacency that fhou'd oblige.

Rofet. Do you know now, that you never pleas'd me fo much in all your Life?

Col.

Col. If fo, *Rofetta*—one Queſtion, and then to apply.

Rofet. How if I ſhou'd not anſwer your Queſtion?

Col. 'Tis a fair one, upon my Word—Don't you think, that you and I cou'd muſter up theſe Requiſites between us?

Rofet. Let me conſider a little—Who muſt have Love, pray?

Col. Both of us.

Rofet. No—I have no Mind to have any Thing to do with Love—Do you take that, and give me Underſtanding, to adviſe—So then you chuſe again, and have all the good Breeding, for Compliance——Then I, Neatneſs—and laſt of all, Competency ſhall be divided between us.

Col. A Match, Madam, upon your own Terms! —But if ever you ſhou'd take it into your Head to diſpute Love with me, what other Requiſite are you willing to give up for it?

Rofet. Why—Neatneſs, I think—'Tis of little Uſe to a marry'd Woman, you know.

Col. A Trifle, Madam!—But when are we to come together?

Rofet. As ſoon as we can give Proof, that theſe Ingredients are between us—In a few Years, perhaps.

Col. If our Virtues ſhou'd ſtarve in that Time?

Rofet. Pſh'ah!—You know nothing of the Matter. —Senſe will improve every Day—And Love and good Breeding live an Age—if you don't marry 'em. —But we'll have done with theſe Matters, for I can keep the Ball up no longer—You did not ſay, *Fidelia* upbraided me?

Col. The very Reverſe—'Twas her only Affliction, ſhe ſaid, that you had Reaſon to think hardly of her.

Rofet. Poor Girl!—If you wou'd make Love to me with Succeſs, *Colonel*, clear up theſe Perplexities—Suppoſe I was to diſmiſs my Pride a little, and make her a Viſit with you?

Col.

Col. 'Twou'd be a kind one.

Rofet. Lead on then——For in Spite of my Refentments, I have no Heart to keep from her.

[*Exeunt.*

SCENE II. *Another Apartment.*

Enter *Young* BELMONT, *and* FADDLE.

Bel. If this fhou'd be Invention, *Faddle?*

Fad. I tell thee, I was behind the Screen, and heard every Syllable on't——Why, I'll fay it to his Face, prithee.

Bel. What, that he propos'd to take her into Keeping, and that fhe confented ?

Fad. Not in thofe Words, Man——No, no, Sir *Charles* is a Gentleman of politer Elocution——Pray, Child, fays he, did young *Belmont* ever propofe your removing from this Houfe?——No, Sir, fays fhe, but he has curs'd himfelf to Damnation for bringing me into it. [*Mimicking Sir* Cha. *and* Fid.] Well, Child, fays he, the Thing may be done to Night—Apartments are ready for you——And then, in a lower Voice, he faid fomething about Virtue, that I cou'd not very well hear——But I faw, it fet the Girl a crying——And prefently——in Anfwer to a Whifper of his, I heard her fay, in a very pretty Manner, that fhe thought it was too much for her——But what his Propofals were, the Devil a Syllable cou'd I hear.

Bel. Ha! ha!——Yonder he is, *Faddle*, and coming this Way——We muft not be feen together.

Fad. For a little Sport, *Charles*, fuppofe I fling my felf in his Way, and make Intereft to be Commode to him, hah!

Bel. And get thy Nofe twifted for thy Pains ?

Fad. Why, I can run, if I can't fight, prithee.

Bel. Faith, I never doubted thee that Way——I'll to my Room then, and wait for thee.

Fad.

Fad. But leave the Door open, *Charles.*

Bel. Ha! ha! ha!—You'll not be tedious, Sir?

[*Exit.*

SCENE III.

Enter Sir CHARLES.

Fad. If the old Gentleman fhou'd be in his Airs, tho'—Servant, Servant, Sir *Charles!*

Sir Cha. O, Sir!—You are the Man I was looking for.

Fad. If I can be of any Service, Sir *Charles*—What —and fo hah!—Faith, you're a fly one!—But you old Poachers have fuch a Way with you!—Why here has *Charles* been racking his Brains for Ways and Means, any Time thefe three Months—and juft in the Nick, foufe comes me down the old Kite—and alack-a-day, poor Chick!—The Bufinefs is done.

Sir Cha. Make your felf a little intelligible, Sir.

Fad. And fo, I don't fpeak plain, hah?—Oh the little Rogue!—There's more Beauty in the Veins of her Neck, than in a Landfcape of *Claude* —— and more Mufick in the Smack of her Lips, than in all *Handel!*

Sir Cha. Let me underftand you, Sir.

Fad. Methinks 'twas very laconic tho'—If *Rofetta's* Sufpicions grow violent, I have Apartments ready to receive you. [*Mimicking Sir* Charles]—But a Word in your Ear, old Gentleman — Thofe Apartments won't do.

Sir Cha. O, Sir!—I begin to be a little in the Secret.

Fad. Mighty quick of Apprehenfion, Faith!— And then the little Innocent!—Still, Sir *Charles*, my Tears are all that I can thank you with; for this Goodnefs is too much for me—[*Mimicking* Fidelia]—, Upon my Soul, you have a great deal of Goodnefs,

Sir

Sir *Charles*—a great deal of Goodnefs, upon my Soul.

Sir *Cha.* Why, now I underftand you, Sir—And as thefe Matters may require Time, for the fake of Privacy, we'll fhut this Door.   [*Shuts the Door.*

Fad. Any other Time, Sir *Charles*—But I am really fo hurry'd at prefent—that—Oh Lord. [*Afide.*

Sir *Cha.* Why what does the Wretch tremble at? —Broken Bones are to be fet again, and thou may'ft yet die in thy Bed. [*takes hold of him*] — You have been a Liftener, Sir.

Fad. Lord, Sir!—indeed, Sir!—Not I, Sir!

Sir *Cha.* No Denial, Sir.   [*Shakes him.*

Fad. Oh Sir—I'll confefs—I did liften—I did indeed, Sir.

Sir *Cha.* Does your Memory furnifh you with any other Villany of yours, that may fave me the Trouble of an Explanation?

Fad. I'll think, Sir—What the Devil fhall I fay now!   [*Afide.*

Sir *Cha.* Take Care!—For every Lie thou tell'ft me, fhall be fcor'd ten-fold upon thy Flefh—Anfwer me—How came Mr. *Belmont*'s Sifter by that anonymous Letter?

Fad. Letter, Sir?

Sir *Cha.* Whence came it, I fay?

Fad. Is there no Remiffion, Sir?

Sir *Cha.* None, that thou can'ft deferve—For Honefty is not in thy Nature.

Fad. If I confefs?

Sir *Cha.* Do fo then, and truft me.

Fad. Yes—and fo be beat to Mummy by *Charles*— If you won't tell him, Sir!

Sir *Cha.* I'll think on't.

Fad. Why then, Sir—But he'll certainly be the Death of me—It was by his Contrivance, I wrote the Letter, and fent it from the King's-Arms.

Sir *Cha.* Very well, Sir!—And did you know to what Purpofe it was fent?   *Fad.*

Fad. Yes, Sir—it was to alarm the Family againſt *Fidelia*, that *Charles* might get her into private Lodgings—That was all, as I hope to be fav'd, Sir.

Sir *Cha.* Was it, Sir!—And upon what Principles were you an Accomplice in this Villany ?

Fad. I was out of Money, Sir, and not over valiant—and *Charles* promis'd and threaten'd—'Twas either a ſmall Purſe, or a great Cudgel—And ſo I took one, to avoid t'other, Sir.

Sir *Cha.* And what doſt thou deſerve for this?

Fad. Pray, Sir, conſider my honeſt Confeſſion, and think me paid already, if you pleaſe, Sir.

Sir *Cha.* For that thou art ſafe—If thou woud'ſt continue ſo, avoid me—Be gone, I ſay.

Fad. Yes, Sir—and well off too, Faith.

[*Aſide and going.*

Sir *Cha.* Yet ſtay—If thou art open to any Senſe of Shame, hear me.

Fad. I will, Sir.

Sir *Cha.* Thy Life is a Diſgrace to Humanity— A fooliſh Prodigality makes thee needy—Need makes thee vicious, and both make thee contemptible. Thy Wit is proſtituted to Slander and Buffoonery— and thy Judgment, if thou haſt any, to Meanneſs and Villany. Thy Betters that laugh With thee, laugh At thee—And who are they ?—The Fools of Quality at Court, and thoſe who ape 'em in the City—The Varities of thy Life are pitiful Rewards, and painful Abuſes—For the ſame Trick, that gets thee a Guinea to Day, ſhall get thee beaten out of Doors to Morrow—Thoſe who careſs thee, are Enemies to themſelves—and when they know it, will be ſo to thee— In thy Diſtreſſes they'll deſert thee—and leave thee, at laſt, to ſink in thy Poverty, unregarded and unpity'd—If thou can'ſt be wiſe, think of me, and be honeſt.

[*Exit.*

Fad.

Fad. I'll endeavour it, Sir—A moſt excellent Diſcourſe, Faith—And mighty well there was not a larger Congregation—So, ſo!—I muſt be witty, with a
Vengeance!—What the Devil ſhall I ſay to *Charles*
now?—And here he comes, like Poverty and the
Plague, to deſtroy me at once—Let me ſee!—Ay—As
Truth has ſav'd me with one, I'll try what a little Lying will do witir t'other.

SCENE IV.

Enter Young BELMONT.

Ha! ha! ha! — Oh, the rareſt, Sport, *Charles!*
Bel. What Sport, prithee?
Fad. I ſhall burſt!—Ha! ha! ha!—the old Gentle-
man has let me into all his Secrets.
Bel. And, like a faithful Confidant, you are going
to reveal 'em.
Fad. Not a Breath, *Charles*—Only that I am in
Commiſſion, my Dear—that's all.
Bel. So I ſuppoſe, indeed!
Fad. Nay, *Charles*, if I tell thee a Lie, cut my
Throat—The ſhort of the Matter is—The old Poa-
cher, finding me in the Secret, thought it the wiſeſt
Way to make a Confidant of me—And this very
Moment, my Dear, I am upon the Wing to provide
Lodgings for the Occaſion.
Bel. If this ſhou'd be Apocryphal, as my Fa-
ther ſays!
Fad. Goſpel every Syllable, as I hope to be ſav'd—
Why, What in the Devil's Name, have I to do, to
be inventing Lies for thee?—But here comes the old
Gentleman again, Faith—Oh the Devil! [*Aſide*] Pri-
thee, ſtroke him down a little, *Charles*—if 'tis only
to ſee how awkwardly he takes it—I muſt about the
Lodgings—Ha! ha! ha!—But if ever I ſet Foot in
this Houſe again, may a Horſe-pond be my Portion.
[*Aſide, and Exit.*

SCENE V.

Enter Sir CHARLES, *with a Letter in his Hand,*
speaking to a Servant.

Sir *Cha.* Bid him wait a little, and I'll attend him.
[*Exit Servant.*] What can this mean?—Let me read
it again. [*Reads*

If the Interest of Sir Charles Raymond's *Family be*
dear to him, he will follow the Bearer, with the same
Haste, that he wou'd shun Ruin.

That he wou'd shun Ruin!—This is strange!—
But be it as it will—I have another Concern, that must
take Place first.

Bel. Sir *Charles,* your Servant—Any News Sir?

Sir *Cha.* Not much, Sir—Only that a young Gentleman, of Honour and Condition, had introduc'd a
virtuous Lady to his Family; and when a worthless
Fellow defam'd her Innocence, and robb'd her of her
Quiet, He, who might have dry'd her Tears, and
vindicated her Virtue, forsook her in her Injuries, to
debauch his Mind, with the Assassin of her Reputation.

Bel. If your Tale ends there, Sir, you have learnt
but half on't—For my Advices add, that a certain elderly Gentleman, of Title and Fortune, pitying the
forlorn Circumstances of the Lady, has offer'd her
Terms of Friendship and Accommodation—And, this
Night, she bids Farewel to Maidenhood and a Female
Bedfellow in private Apartments.

Sir *Cha.* You treat me lightly, Mr. *Belmont.*

Bel. You use me roughly, Sir *Charles.*

Sir *Cha.* How, Sir?

Bel. In the Person of *Fidelia.*

Sir *Cha.* Make it appear, and you shall find me a
very Boy in my Submissions.

Bel. 'Twou'd be Time lost—and I can employ it
to Advantage—But remember, Sir, that this House
is another's, not yours—That *Fidelia* is under my

Direction, not yours— and that my Will muſt determine her Removal, not yours.

Sir Cha. Is ſhe your Slave, Sir?—to bear the Bur-
den of your Inſults, without Complaining, or the
Right of chuſing another Maſter?

Bel. And who ſhall be that Maſter?—You, Sir?
The poor Bird, that wou'd eſcape the Kite, is like to
find warm Protection from the Fox.

Sir Cha. Prithee think me a Man, and treat me as
ſuch.

Bel. As the Man I have found you, Sir *Charles*—
Your grave Deportment, and Honeſty of Heart are
Covers only for Wantonneſs and Deſign—You preach
up Temperance and Sobriety to Youth, to monopo-
lize, in Age, the Vices you are unfit for.

Sir Cha. Hark you, young Man!—You muſt curb
this impetuous Spirit of yours—or I ſhall be tempted
to teach you Manners, in a Method diſagreeable to
you.

Bel. Learn 'em firſt your ſelf, Sir—You ſay, *Fidelia* is inſulted by me?—How is it made out?—Why,
truly, I wou'd poſſeſs her without Marriage!—
I wou'd ſo—Marriage is the Thing I wou'd avoid—
'Tis the Trick of Prieſts, to make Men miſerable,
and Women inſolent—I have dealt plainly, and told
her ſo—Have You ſaid as much?—No. You wear
the Face of Honeſty, to quiet her Fears—that when
your Blood boils, and Security has ſtolen away her
Guard, you may ruſh at Midnight upon her Beauties,
and do the Ravage, you are ſworn to protect her
from.

Sir Cha. Hold, Sir!—You have driven me beyond
the Limits of my Patience—And I muſt tell you,
young Man, that the Obligations I owe your Father,
demand no Returns that Manhood muſt bluſh to
make—Therefore hold, I ſay—For I have a Sword
to do me Juſtice, tho' it ſhou'd leave my deareſt
Friend childleſs.

Bel. I fear it not.   Sir

Sir *Cha.* Better tempt it not—for your Fears may come too late—You have dealt openly with *Fidelia*, you fay—Deal fo for once with me ; and tell me, whence came that vile Scroll to *Rofetta* this Afternoon ?

Bel. It feems then, I wrote it!—You dare not think fo.

Sir *Cha.* I dare fpeak, as well as think, where Honour directs me.

Bel. You are my Accufer then?

Sir *Cha.* When I become fo, I fhall take Care, Mr. *Belmont*, that the Proof waits upon the Accufation.

Bel. I difdain the Thought.

Sir *Cha.* Better have difdain'd the Deed.

Bel. I do both—and him that fufpects me.

Sir *Cha.* Away !—You fear him that fufpects you, and have difdain'd neither the Thought, nor the Deed.

Bel. How, Sir ! [*Drawing.*

Sir *Cha.* Put up your Sword, young Man— and ufe it in a better Caufe—This is a vile one—And now you fhall be as ftill thro' Shame, as you have been loud thro' Pride—You fhou'd have known, that Cowards are unfit for Secrets.

Bel. And if I had, Sir ?

Sir *Cha.* Why then, Sir, you had not employ'd fuch a Wretch as *Faddle*, to write that Letter to *Rofetta*.

Bel. The Villain has betray'd me !—But I'll be fure on't. [*Afide*] He durft not fay I did.

Sir *Cha.* You fhou'd rather have built your Innocence upon the Probability of his unfaying it.—For the fame Fear, that made him confefs to me, may make him deny every Syllable to you.

Bel. What has he confefs'd, Sir ?

Sir *Cha.* That to Day, at Dinner, You prompted the Letter that He wrote.—That your Defign was, by vilifying *Fidelia*, to get her difmifs'd, and the Difmiffion, to prepare her Ruin in private Lodgings. —Was this your open Behaviour, Sir ! *Bel.*

Bel. Go on with your Upbraidings, Sir—Speak to me as you will—and think of me as you will—I have deferv'd Shame, and am taught Patience.

Sir *Cha.* Was this well done ?—Did her Innocence, and her undiffembled Love deferve this Treatment ?

Bel. Proceed, Sir.

Sir *Cha.* No, Sir—I have done—If you have Senfe of your paft Conduct, you want not Humanity to heal the Wounds it has given—Something muft be done, and fpeedily.

Bel. What Reparation can I make her ?

Sir *Cha.* Dry up her Tears, by an immediate Acknowledgment of her Wrongs.

Bel. I wou'd do more.

Sir *Cha.* Bid her farewell then, and confent to her Removal.

Bel. I cannot, Sir.

Sir *Cha.* Her Peace demands it—But we'll talk of that hereafter—If you have Honour, go and do her Juftice, and undeceive your abus'd Sifter—Who waits there ?—Indeed, you have been to blame, Mr. *Belmont.*

Enter Servant.

Show me to the Bearer of this Letter.

[*Exit with the Servant.*

Bel. Why, what a Thing am I!—But 'tis the Trick of Vice to pay her Votaries with Shame—And I am rewarded amply!—To be a Fool's Fool too!—To link myfelf in Villany, with a Wretch, below the Notice of a Man !—And to be out-witted by him!—So!—fo!—I may have abus'd Sir *Charles* too—Let me think a little!—I'll to *Fidelia* inftantly, and tell her what a Rogue I have been—But will that be Reparation ?—I know but of one Way—and there my Pride ftops me—And then I lofe her—Worfe and worfe !—I'll think no more on't— but away to her Chamber, and bid Her think for me.   [*Exit.*

A C T

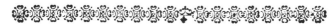

ACT V.

SCENE *continues.*

Enter Sir ROGER *and* Servant. *Sir* ROGER *with a Letter in his Hand.*

Sir *ROGER.*

VERY fine Doings indeed!—But I'll teach the Dog to play his Tricks upon a Father!—A Man had better let a Lion loose in his Family, than a Town-Rake—Where is Sir *Charles,* I say?

Serv. This Moment come in, Sir.

Sir Ro. And why did not you say so, Blockhead?—Tell him, I must speak with him this Moment.

Serv. The Servant says, he waits for an Answer to that Letter, Sir.

Sir Ro. Do as I bid you, Rascal, and let him wait. Fly, I say.   [*Exit. Serv.*

The riotous young Dog!— To bring his Harlots Home with him!—But I'll out with the Baggage.

SCENE II.

Enter Sir CHARLES.

Oh, Sir *Charles!* — 'Tis every Word as we said this Morning—The Boy has stolen her—and I am to be ruin'd by a Law-suit.

Sir Cha. A Law-Suit!—With whom, Sir?

Sir Ro. Read, read, read!   [*Gives the Letter.*

Sir Cha. [*Reads*]

I Am Guardian to that Fidelia, *whom your Son has stolen from me, and you unjustly detain. If you deny*
                                                  her

her to me, the Law shall right me. I wait your An-
swer by the Bearer, to assert my Claim in the Per-
son of

GEORGE VILLIARD.

Why then my Doubts are at an End!—But I must
conceal my Transports—and wear a Face of Coolnefs, while my Heart overflows with Paffion!
                                             [*Afide.*
Sir *Ro.* What, not a Word, Sir *Charles*?—There's
a Piece of Work for you!—And fo I am to be
ruin'd!
Sir *Cha.* Do you know this Villiard, Sir *Roger?*
Sir *Ro.* Whether I do or not, Sir, the Slut fhall
go to him, this Moment.
Sir *Cha.* Hold a little.—This Gentleman muft be
heard, Sir—and, if his Claim be good, the Lady
reftor'd.
Sir *Ro.* Why e'en let her go as it is, Sir *Charles.*
Sir *Cha.* That wou'd be too hafty—Go in with
me, Sir, and we'll confider how to write to him.
Sir *Ro.* Well, well, well!—I wifh fhe was gone
tho'.   [*Exeunt.*

SCENE III. *Another Apartment.*

Enter *Young* BELMONT *and* FIDELIA.

Bel. Afk me not why I did it, but forgive me.
Fid. No, Sir—'tis impoffible—I have a Mind,
Mr. *Belmont*, above the Wretchednefs of my Fortunes—and, helplefs as I am, I can feel in this Breaft
a Senfe of Injuries, and Spirit to refent 'em.
Bel. Nay, but hear me, *Fidelia.*
Fid. Was it not enough to defert me in my Diftreffes?—To deny me the poor Requeft I made
you?—But muft you own your felf the Contriver of
that Letter?—'Tis infupportable!—If I confented to
                                                 affume

aſſume a Rank that belong'd not to me—my Heart
went not with the Deceit— You wou'd have it ſo,
and I comply'd—'Twas Shame enough, that I had
deceiv'd your Siſter—It needed not, that I ſhou'd
bring a Proſtitute to her Friendſhip —This was too
much—too much, Mr. *Belmont!*

Bel. Yet hear me, I ſay!

Fid And then, to leave me to the Malice of that
Wretch!—To have my ſuppos'd Infamy the Tavern
Jeſt of his licentious Companions!—I never flatter'd
myſelf, Mr. *Belmont,* with your Love—But knew
not, till now, that I have been the Object of your
Hatred.

Bel. My Hatred!—But I have deſerv'd your hard-
eſt Thoughts of me—And yet, believe me, *Fidelia,*
when I us'd you worſt, I lov'd you moſt.

Fid. Call it by another Name—for Love delights
in Acts of Kindneſs—Were your's ſuch, Sir?—And
yet muſt I forget all—For I owe you more than Injuries can cancel, or Gratitude repay.

Bel. Generous Creature!—This is to be amiable,
indeed!—But muſt we part, *Fidelia?*

Fid. I have reſolv'd it, Sir, and you muſt yield
to it.

Bel. Never, my ſweet Obſtinate!

Fid. That I have lov'd you, 'tis my Pride to acknowledge—But that muſt be forgot—And the hard
Taſk remains, to drive the Paſſion from my Breaſt,
while I cheriſh the Memory of your humane Offices.
—This Day then ſhall be the laſt of our Meeting—
Painful, tho' it may be—yet your own, mine, and
the Family's Peace requires it—Heaven, in my Diſtreſſes, has not left me deſtitute of a Friend—or if
it had, I can find one in my Innocence, to make even
Poverty ſupportable.

Bel. You have touch'd me, *Fidelia*—and my Heart
yields to your Virtues—Here then let my Follies have

I an

an End—and thus let me receive you, as the everlafting Partner of my Heart and Fortune.

[*Offers to embrace her.*

Fid. No, Sir—The Conduct that has hitherto fecur'd my own Honour, fhall protect yours—I have
been the innocent Difturber of your Family—but
never will confent to load it with Difgrace.

Bel. Nor can it be difgrac'd—I mean to honour it,
Fidelia—You muft comply!

Fid. And repay Generofity with Ruin! —No, Mr.
Belmont—I can forego Happinefs, but never can confent to make another miferable.

Bel. When I repent, *Fidelia!*—But fee where my
Sifter comes, to be an Advocate for my Wifhes!

SCENE IV.

Enter ROSETTA.

Rofet. Oh, Sir, you are found!—You have done
nobly indeed!—But your Thefts are difcover'd, Sir.
—This Lady's Guardian has a Word or two for you.

Bel. Her Guardian! — Upon my Life, *Fidelia,*
Villiard!—He comes as I cou'd wifh him.

Rofet. Say fo when you have anfwer'd him, Brother—Am I to lofe you at laft then, *Fidelia?*—And
yet my Hopes flatter me, that this too, as well as the
Letter, is Deceit—May I think fo, *Fidelia?*

Fid. As truly as of your own Goodnefs, *Rofetta*—
Your Brother will tell you all—Oh, he has made me
miferable by his Generofity!

Bel. This pretended Guardian, Sifter, is a Villain,
and *Fidelia* the moft abus'd of Women—Bounteous
he has been indeed—but to his Vices, not his Virtues,
fhe ftands indebted for the beft of Educations—The
Story will amaze you!—At twelve Years old—

Rofet. He's here, Brother—and with him, my Papa,
Sir *Charles* and the *Colonel*—Now, *Fidelia!*

SCENE

S C E N E V.

Enter Sir ROGER, *Sir* CHARLES, *the* COLONEL
and VILLIARD.

Sir *Cha.* If that be the Lady, Mr. *Villiard,* and
your Claim as you pretend, Sir *Roger* has told you,
fhe fhall be reftor'd, Sir.

Sir *Ro.* Yes, Sir—and your Claim as you pretend.

Vill. 'Tis well, Madam, I have found you—[*going to Fidelia*]—This, Gentlemen, is the Lady—
And this, the Robber who ftole her from me. [*Pointing to Belmont*]—By Violence, and at Midnight he
ftole her.

Bel. Stole her, Sir ?

Vill. By Violence, and at Midnight, I fay—

Bel. You fhall be heard, Sir.

Vill. Ay, Sir, and fatisfy'd—I ftand here, Gentlemen, to demand my Ward.

Sir *Cha.* Give us Proofs, Sir, and you fhall have
Juftice.

Vill. Demand 'em there, Sir. [*Pointing to Belmont and Fidelia*]—I have told you, I am robb'd—If
you deny me Juftice, the Law fhall force it.

Sir *Cha.* A little Patience, Sir. [*to Villiard*] Do
you know this Gentleman, *Fidelia?*

Fid. Too well, Sir!

Sir *Cha.* By what Means, Sir, did you become
her Guardian ?   [*to Villiard.*

Vill. By the Will of her who bore her, Sir.

Sir *Cha.* How will you reply to this, *Fidelia ?*

Fid. With Truth and Honefty, Sir.

Bel. Let him proceed, Madam.

Vill. Ay, Sir—to your Part of the Story—Tho'
both are practic'd in a damn'd Falfhood, to confront
me.

Bel. Falfhood!—But I am cool, Sir—Proceed.

Vill. My Doors were broke open at Midnight by this Gentleman; [*pointing to Belmont.*] my felf wounded, and *Fidelia* ravifh'd from me—He ran off with her in his Arms—Nor, 'till this Morning, in a Coach, which brought her hither, have my Eyes ever beheld her.

Sir Ro. A very fine Bufinefs, truly, young Man! [*To Belmont.*

Fid. He has abus'd you, Sir—Mr. *Belmont* is no- ble— [*To Sir Roger*]

Bel. No Matter, *Fidelia*—Well, Sir!—You have been robb'd you fay? [*To Villiard.*

Vill. And will have Juftice, Sir.

Bel. Take it from this Hand then. [*Drawing.*

Sir Cha. Hold, Sir!—This is adding Infult to In- juries—*Fidelia* muft be reftor'd, Sir.

Sir Ro. Ay, Sir—*Fidelia* muft be reftor'd.

Fid. But not to Him!—Hear but my Story—and if I deceive you, let your Friendfhip forfake me— He bought me, Gentlemen—For the worft of Pur- pofes, he bought me of the worft of Women—A thoufand Times has he confefs'd it, and as often pleaded his Right of Purchafe to undo me—Whole Years have I endur'd his brutal Solicitations—'till tir'd with Entreaties, he had Recourfe to Violence— The Scene was laid—and I had been ruin'd beyond Redrefs—had not my Cries brought the generous Mr. *Belmont* to my Relief—He was accidentally paf- fing by—and alarm'd, at Midnight, with a Woman's Shrieks, he forc'd open the Door, and fav'd me from Deftruction.

Sir Cha. How will you anfwer this, Sir? [*To Villiard.*

Vill. 'Tis falfe, Sir—That Woman was her Nurfe. —Thefe Hands deliver'd her to her Care.

Fid. Alas, Gentlemen!—She found me a helplefs Infant at her Door—So fhe has always told me—and

at

at twelve Years old, betray'd me to that Monster—
Search out the Woman, if she be alive, and let me
be confronted.

Sir Ro. If this be true, Sir *Charles*, I shall bless
myself as long as I live, for getting my Boy. [*Weeps.*

Vill. 'Tis false, I say—A damn'd Contrivance to
escape me—I stand here, Sir, to demand my Ward.
[*to Sir Roger*]—Deny her to me at your Peril.

Bel. He shall have my Life as soon.

Vill. Hark you, Sir. [*To Sir Roger*] There are
Things, call'd Laws, to do Right to the Injur'd—
My Appeal shall be to them.

Sir Cha. That Woman must be produc'd, Sir.
[*To Villiard.*

Vill. And shall, Sir, in a Court of Justice—Our
next Meeting shall be there—'Till then, Madam, you
are secure. [*To Fidelia.*

Bel. Take Care that You are so, Sir, when we have
Occasion to call upon you—You shall have Justice.

Vill. And will, Sir, in Defiance of you. [*Exit.*

Sir Cha. Fear not, *Fidelia*—We believe, and will
protect you.

Roset. My sweet Girl!—But whence came the
Letter this Afternoon?

Bel. 'Twas I that wrote it.

Roset. Oh, monstrous!—And cou'd you be that
Wretch, Brother?

Bel. And will atone for it, by the only Recompence that's left me.

Sir Ro. And what Recompence will you make
her, hah, Rogue?

Bel. I have injur'd her, Sir—and must do her
Justice—If you wou'd retrieve my Honour, or promote my Happiness, give me your Consent, Sir, to
make her your Daughter.

Roset. Why, that's my Brother!—Now I am sure
she's innocent!—And so you will, Papa!

Sir

Sir Ro. But pofitively, I will not, Child—Marry her indeed!—What, without a Shilling!—And be ruin'd by *Villiard* into the Bargain!—If your Story be true, *Fidelia*, you fhall be provided for—But no marrying, d'ye hear, Child?

Fid. You need not doubt me, Sir.

Sir Ro. Why that's well faid, *Fidelia*.

Rofet. And deferves Reward, Sir —Pray, Sir *Charles*, let us have your Thoughts upon this Matter.

Sir Cha. Your Brother's Propofal, Madam, and *Fidelia*'s Denial, are as generous, as your Father's Determination is juft.

Bel. I expected as much, Sir.

Sir Cha. My Opinion was afk'd, Sir.

Bel. And you have given it—I thank you, Sir.

Sir Cha. Think of *Villiard,* Mr. *Belmont*—His Claim may be renew'd, Sir.

Bel. *Fidelia* has deceiv'd you then!—You think otherwife, Sir *Charles*.

Col. My Life upon her Innocence!—And where the Fortune, on one Side, is more than fufficient, how light is all Addition to it, compar'd to the Pof-feffion of Her one loves!—Let me, Sir, be happy in *Rofetta*, [*To Sir Roger*] and give her Fortune to *Fidelia*, to make her an Object worthy of your Son.

Rofet. There's a *Colonel* for you!—What fays my fweet *Fidelia* ?

Fid. I intended to be filent, Madam—But 'tis now my Duty to fpeak—You have been my Deliverer, Sir, from the worft of Evils. [*To Belmont.*] And now wou'd nobly augment the firft Obligation, by a Generofity, too mighty for Acknowledgment—If I had the Wealth of Worlds, it wou'd be too little to beftow—But poor and friendlefs as I am, my Heart may break, but never fhall confent to make my Benefactor a Penitent to his Virtues.

Sir

Sir Cha. 'Tis nobly faid, *Fidelia!*—And now, Mr. *Belmont*, our Difputes will foon be at an End—You have this Day, Sir, reproach'd me often—It remains now, that you fhou'd know me as I am.

Bel. If I have err'd, Sir—

Sir Cha. Interrupt me not, but hear me—I have watch'd your Follies with Concern; and 'tis with equal Pleafure, I congratulate your Return to Honour—If I have oppos'd your generous Inclinations, it was only to give 'em Strength—I am now a Suppliant to your Father, for the Happinefs you defire.

Bel. This is noble, Sir *Charles!*

Sir Char. And to make *Fidelia* worthy of his Son, a Fortune fhall be added, equal to his warmeft Expectations.

Sir Rog. Why ay, Sir *Charles!*—Let that be made out, and I fhall have no Objections.

Fid. What mean you, Sir?   [*To Sir Charles*

Sir Cha. A Minute more, and my fweet Girl fhall be inftructed—You have often told me, Sir, [*To Belmont*] that I had an Intereft in this lovely Creature—I have an Intereft!—An Intereft, that you fhall allow me!—My Heart doats upon her!—Oh, I can hold no longer!—My Daughter!—my Daughter!
   [*Running to Fidelia, and embracing her.*

Fid. Your Daughter, Sir!

Sir Cha. Oh, my fweet Child!—Sir *Roger!*—Mr. *Belmont*, my Son!—Thefe Tears!—thefe Tears!—*Fidelia* is my Daughter!

Col. Is't poffible?

Sir Cha. Let not Excefs of Wonder over-power you, *Fidelia*—For I have a Tale to tell, that will exceed Belief.

Fid Oh, Sir!

Sir Cha. Upbraid me not, that I have kept it a Moment from your Knowledge—'Twas a hard Trial!—and while my Tongue was taught Diffimulation, my Heart bled for a Child's Diftreffes!

   Bel.

Bel. Torture us not, Sir—but explain this Wonder!

Sir Cha. My Tears muſt have their Way firſt—O my Child!—my Child! — [*Turning to Sir Roger and the reſt.*] Know then—That wicked Woman, ſo often mention'd, was my *Fidelia's* Governante—When my miſtaken Zeal drove me into Baniſhment, I left her an Infant to her Care—To ſecure ſome Jewels of Value, I had lodg'd with her, ſhe became the Woman you have heard—My Child was taught to believe ſhe was a Foundling—Her Name of *Harriet* chang'd to *Fidelia*—and to leſſen my Solicitude for the Theft, a Letter was diſpatch'd to Me in *France*, that my Infant Daughter had no longer a Being—Thus was the Father robb'd of his Child, and the Brother taught to believe he had no Siſter!

Fid. And am I that Siſter, and that Daughter?—Oh Heavens! [*Kneels.*

Bel. [*Running to her, and raiſing her*] Be compos'd, my Life! —A Moment's Attention more—and your Tranſports ſhall have a Looſe—Proceed, Sir!

Sir Cha. Where ſhe withdrew her ſelf, I cou'd never learn—At twelve Years old, ſhe ſold her, as you have heard—and never, 'till Yeſterday, made Enquiry about her—'Twas then, that a ſudden Fit of Sickneſs brought her to Repentance—She ſent for *Villiard*—who told her minutely what had happen'd.—The Knowledge of her Deliverance gave her ſome Conſolation—But more was to be done yet—She had Information of My Pardon and Return—and ignorant of my Child's Deliverer, or the Place of her Conveyance, ſhe at laſt determin'd to unburden her ſelf to me—A Letter was brought me this Afternoon, conjuring me to follow the Bearer with the ſame Haſte that I wou'd ſhun Ruin.—I did follow him—and receiv'd from this wretched Woman the Story I have told you.

Fid.

Fid. Oh, my Heart!—My Father! [*Kneels*]—Have I at laft found you!—And were all my Sorrows paft, meant only to endear the prefent Tranfport!—'Tis too much for me!

Sir Cha. Rife, my Child!—To find thee thus virtuous, in the Midft of Temptations, and thus lovely, in the Midft of Poverty and Diftrefs!—After an Abfence of eighteen melancholy Years, when imaginary Death had torn thee from my Hopes!—To find thee thus unexpected, and thus amiable!—is Happinefs, that the uninterrupted Enjoyment of the faireft Life never equal'd!

Fid. What muft be mine then!—Have I a Brother too! [*Turning to the Colonel.*] Oh my kind Fortune!

Col. My Sifter! *embracing her.*]

Fid. Still there is a dearer Claim than all—and now I can acknowledge it—My Deliverer!—

Bel. And Hufband, *Fidelia*!—Let me receive you, as the richeft Gift of Fortune! [*Catching her in his Arms.*]

Rofet. My generous Girl!—The Pride of your Alliance is my utmoft Boaft, as it is my Brother's Happinefs.

Sir Ro. I have a Right in her too—For now you are my Daughter, *Fidelia.* [*Kiffes her.*]

Fid. I had forgot, Sir—If you will receive me as fuch, you fhall find my Gratitude in my Obedience.

Sir Cha. Take her, Mr. *Belmont*, and protect the Virtue you have try'd. [*Joining their Hands.*]

Bel. The Study of my Life, Sir, fhall be to deferve her.

Fid. Oh *Rofetta*!—Yet ftill it remains with you, to make this Day's Happinefs compleat—I have a Brother that loves you.

Rofet. I wou'd be *Fidelia*'s Sifter every Way! — So take me while I am warm, *Colonel*! [*Giving him her Hand.*

K *Col.*

Col. And when we repent, *Rofetta,* let the next
Minute end us.

Rofet. With all my Heart!

Fid. Now, *Rofetta,* we are doubly Sifters!

Sir Cha. And may your Lives, and your Affections
know an End together.

Bel. [*Taking Fidelia by the Hand*] And now, *Fidelia,*
what you have made me, take me—a Convert to
Honour! I have at laft learnt, that Cuftom can be
no Authority for Vice; and however the miftaken
World may judge, He who follicits Pleafure, at the
Expence of Innocence, is the vileft of Betrayers.

Yet Savage Man, the wildeft Beaft of Prey,
Affumes the Face of Kindnefs to betray,
His giant Strength againft the weak employs,
And Woman, whom he fhould protect, deftroys.

F I N I S.

THE
EPILOGUE.

Written by Mr. GARRICK.

Spoke by Mrs. CIBBER.

I Know, You all expect from seeing Me,
    An Epilogue, of strictest Purity;
Some formal Lecture, spoke with prudish Face,
To shew our present joking, giggling Race,
True Joy consists in Gravity and Grace.
But why am I, for ever made the Tool?
Of every squeamish, moralizing Fool,
Condemn'd to Sorrow all my Life, must I
Ne'er make you laugh, because I make you cry?
Madam (say they) your Face denotes your Heart,
'Tis Your's to melt us in the mournful Part.
So from the Looks, our Hearts they prudish deem!
Alas, poor Souls! — we are not what we seem!
Tho' Prudence oft our Inclination smothers,
We grave Ones, love a Joke—as well as others.
From such dull Stuff, what Profit can you reap?
You cry—'Tis very fine,—(Yawns)and fall asleep.
Happy that Bard!—Blest with uncommon Art,
Whose Wit can chear, and not corrupt the Heart!
Happy that Play'r, whose Skill can chase the Spleen,
And leave no worse Inhabitant within.

'Mongst

'Mongſt Friends, our Author is a modeſt Man,
But wicked Wits will cavil at his Plan:
Damn it (ſays one) this Stuff will never paſs,
The Girl wants Nature, and the Rake's an Aſs.
Had I, like BELMONT, heard a Damſel's Cries,
I wou'd have pink'd her Keeper, ſeiz'd the Prize,
Whipt in a Coach, not valu'd Tears a Fardin,
But drove away like Smoke---to Covent Garden;
There to ſome Houſe convenient wou'd have carried
         her,
And then--- dear Soul!---the Devil ſhou'd have
         married her.
But this our Author thought too hard upon her;
Beſides, his Spark, forſooth, muſt have ſome Honour!
The Fool's a Fabuliſt—and deals in Fiction;
Or he had giv'n him Vice—without Reſtriction.
Of Fable, all his Characters partake,
Sir CHARLES is virtuous—and for Virtue's Sake;
Nor vain, nor bluſtering is the Soldier writ,
His Rake has Conſcience, Modeſty, and Wit,
The Ladies too—how oddly they appear!
His Prude is chaſte, and his Coquet ſincere:
In ſhort, ſo ſtrange a Group, ne'er trod the Stage,
At once to pleaſe, and ſatirize the Age.
For You, ye FAIR, his Muſe has chiefly ſung,
'Tis You, have touch'd his Heart, and tun'd his
         Tongue;
The Sex's Champion, let the Sex defend,
A ſoothing Poet is a charming Friend:
Your Favours, here beſtow'd, will meet Reward,
So as You love dear Flattry—ſave your BARD:

GIL
BLAS

GIL BLAS.

A

COMEDY.

As it is Acted at the

Theatre-Royal in Drury-lane.

By Mr. MOORE.

LONDON:

Printed for R. FRANCKLIN, in *Russel-street,*
Covent-Garden, 1751.

[Price One Shilling and Six Pence.]

TO THE

T O W N.

GENTLEMEN,

AFTER the Variety of Fortunes, that poor *Gil Blas* has experienced upon the Stage; the Praife and the Difpraife he has received; the Mirth and the Groans he has occafioned; he throws himfelf into your Clofets, for your cooler and more deliberate Opinions of him. He does not pretend to any extraordinary *Rank*; but flatters himfelf, notwithftanding the Plainnefs of his Drefs, that you will not think him too *low* for your Acquaintance. He can fay, without Vanity, that he could have been *wittier*, had he not preferr'd being *natural*, and thought more of conducting his *Bufinefs*, than of fhewing his *Parts*. He hopes no greater Intricacy will appear in that

A 2 Bufinefs,

Bufinefs, than was neceffary to produce entertaining Situations, and make the Difcovery more
pleafing at laft.　Faults and Defects he has
many; but he humbly prefumes, that a good
Critick will no more expect Perfection upon the
Stage, than a good Man will in Lif*.　He con-
feffes great Obligations to his Friends, and has
no Refentment to his Enemies. His Defire is to
entertain you innocently, and to be at all Times,

GENTLEMEN,

Your moft Obedient Servaut.

February,　13th.

PROLOGUE.

Spoken by Mr. *Woodward,*

In the Character of a *Critic,* with a *Catcall* in his Hand.

ARE *you all ready? Here's your Musick! here!* *
  Author, sneak off, we'll tickle you, my Dear.
The Fellow stop'd me in a hellish Fright——
Pray Sir, says he, must I be damn'd To-night?
Damn'd! surely Friend—Don't hope for our Compliance,
Zounds, Sir!—a second Play's downright Defiance.
Tho' once, poor Rogue, we pity'd your Condition,
Here's the true Recipe—for Repetition.
Well Sir, says he, e'en as you please, so then,
I'll never trouble you with Plays again.
But hark ye, Poet!—— won't you tho', says I?
'Pon Honour—Then we'll damn you, let me die.
Shan't we, my Bucks? Let's take him at his Word—
Damn him—or by my Soul, he'll write a third.
The Man wants Money, I suppose—But mind ye——
Tell him you've left your Charity behind ye.
A pretty Plea, His wants to our Regard!
As if we Bloods had Bowels for a Bard!
Besides, what Men of Spirit, now a-days,
Come to give sober Judgments of new Plays?
It argues some good Nature to be quiet—
Good Nature!—Ay—But then we lose a Riot.
The scribbling Fool may beg and make a Fuss,
'Tis Death to him – What then?—'Tis Sport to us.
Don't mind me tho'—For all my Fun and Jokes,
The Bard may find us Bloods, good natur'd Folks?
No crabbed Criticks—Foes to rising Merit——
Write but with Fire - and we'll applaud with Spirit—
Our Author aims at no dishonest Ends,
He knows no Enemies, and boasts some Friends;
He takes no Methods down your Throats to cram it,
So if you like it, save it, if not —— damn it.

---

* Blowing his Catcall.

EPILOGUE.

Written by Mr. GARRICK.
And spoken by Mrs. *Pritchard*.

As the Succeſs of Authors is uncertain,
   Till all is over, and down drops the Curtain;
Poets are puzzled in our dangerous Times,
How to addreſs You in theſe After-Rhymes.
If they implore and beg, with abject Mind,
Their Meanneſs rather makes you ſick than kind;
And if they bounce and huff it to the Town,
Then You are up—and take the Bullies down.
Of Beaux and Politicks and ſuch like Stuff,
And ev'n of Tawdry too, you've had enough—
On all Degrees, from Courtier to the Cit,
Such ſtale dull Jokes have been ſo often writ,
That nothing can be new—but Decency and Wit.
Thus far our Bard—The reſt is mine to ſay;
I am his Friend, ſo, will attack his Play.
How could his thoughtleſs Head with any Truth
(If Spaniſh Dons are like our Engliſh Youth)
Make his wild Rake ſo ſink from upper Life,
To quit his Miſtreſs, for a lawful Wife!
The Author might have married him—but then
He ſhould have had his Miſtreſs back again.
This is the Scheme our Engliſh Dons purſue,
Tho' One's too much, there's Taſte in having Two.
As for the Lady—I diſlike her Plan,
With You I'm ſure, ſhe had not paſs'd for Man—
Had ſhe with Our young Bloods contriv'd this Freak,
She had been blown and ruin'd in a Week.
And if of Virtue they could not have trick'd her,
They'd damn'd her for a Fool—perhaps have kick'd her.
But Jeſt apart—for all our Bard has wrote,
Our moſt alluring Bait's the Petticoat.
Before that magic Shrine the proudeſt fall,
'Tis that enchanting Circle draws in all.
Let Fools ſay what they will, Experience teaches,
'Tis beſt to marry firſt—then wear the Breeches.

Dramatis Personæ.

M E N.

Don Lewis Pacheco,	*Mr.* Woodward.
Don Felix *de* Mendoza,	*Mr.* Palmer.
Don Gabriel *de* Pedros,	*Mr.* Sowdon.
Gil Blas, *Servant to* Aurora,	*Mr.* Garrick.
Melchior, *Servant to Don* Lewis,	*Mr.* Yates.
Pedro, *Servant to Don* Felix,	*Mr.* Shuter.

W O M E N.

Aurora,	*Mrs.* Pritchard.
Ifabella,	*Mrs.* Bennet.
Laura, *Woman to* Aurora,	*Mifs* Minors.
Beatrice, Ifabella's *Maid,*	*Mrs.* Crofs.
Bernarda, *one who letts Lodgings,*	*Mifs* Pitt.

SCENE. *Salamanca.*

GIL BLAS.

A

COMEDY.

ACT I.

SCENE, *An Apartment at* Bernarda's.

Enter Gil Blas, *with a Portmanteau, and* Bernarda.

Ber. THIS is the Room, Signor—Here, here! You may lay your Portmanteau here. And now, young Man, you are welcome to *Salamanca*.

Gil. Thank you, thank you, Signora. A pleasant Sort of a Situation this! My Master and I are not over nice; if Things are neat, and the People handy about us, we may stay with you some Time.

Ber. I presume, Signor—but I never ask Questions. —What People have a Mind to tell, it would be rude not to hear, you know—But I presume you are come to pursue your Studies.

Gil. Very possibly, Signora. The Sciences are inviting Things; and most likely we shall dabble a little before we go—But my Master, Signora—my Master may want you. He's horridly fatigu'd I'm afraid— As for myself—the Conversation of an agreeable Woman to be sure—*(Bowing)* But I don't know how it is—this College Air has made me a little thoughtful. —I would be alone.

B   *Ber*

Ber. Nay, Signor, Heaven forbid that I fhould difturb you. We fhan't fall out I believe. You look like a fober, difcreet young Man—I'll attend your Mafter, and come back t'you prefently. [*Exit.*

Gil. And come back t'you prefently!—What the Devil do thefe Women fee in Me, that I always get into their good Graces fo!—But now for a little thinking. From *Madrid* to *Salamanca* in eighteen Hours! Why, what a Madcap is this Miftrefs of mine! Here has fhe ftep'd into Breeches; left her Friends in the Lurch; trufted no one with her Secret; and, with only her Woman and myfelf, pofted to *Salamanca*. Can this be a Frolick? No, faith. A hundred and eight Miles, and the worft Road in all *Spain*, is rather too much for a Frolick. Love then!—Ay, ay, Love muft be the Thing. Let a mettled Girl but once get That into her Head, and the Labours of *Hercules* are no more than a Game at Romps to her. Love let it be then. But where's the Man? There I confefs my Sagacity is at Fault. And yet with a little Vanity now, I could be mighty unaccountable in my Guefs. Says my Lady *Aurora* at *Madrid*—and fhe call'd me into her Room too—*Gil Blas*, can you be faithful? Have you a Regard for your Miftrefs? Will you fly with me to *Salamanca*? I have a Secret that will furprize you. From the firft Day too that I enter'd into her Service——

Ber. (Within) Signor *Gil Blas!*

Gil. Who calls there?—— She diftinguifh'd me with Favours; loaded me with Praifes; enquir'd into my Family; lamented my Servitude; admir'd my Addrefs; courted my good Opinion; fmil'd at me; nodded at me; wink'd at me——There muft be fome Meaning in all this——

Ber. (Within) Signor *Gil Blas!* Where are you, Signor *Gil Blas?*

Gil. Here! here! A Pox of your fcreaming! What a delicious Dream has this Hag interrupted!

Re-enter

Ber. O, Signor ! are you here? They told me you were gone down Stairs. Well to be sure! this Master of yours—this Friend I mean——

Gil. There you have hit it, Signora, you have hit it——But has he said any Thing of Me pray?

Ber. Said any Thing! why he talks of nothing else. Signora *Bernarda*, says he, take Care that *Gil Blas* be well treated. I have the greatest Regard for him. He is every Thing in the World to me——

Gil. Gratitude, Signora; only a little Gratitude for good Offices. I serve my Master with Advice, and he pays me with Friendship——that's all.

Ber. Well, how prettily was that said now! But as I was saying—O, to be sure, he's a sweet Gentleman!—And there's Signor *Lopez* too——

Gil. *(Aside)* A Chambermaid in Breeches.

Ber. He may wear what Dress he pleases, but his Looks are too good for a Valet de Chambre. Some Man of Fashion, I suppose.

Gil. Of a very antient Family, Signora—a little reduc'd or so.

Ber. Poor Gentleman! But he's happy in such a Friend. I had a Friend too, but he forsook me; and so I'm reduc'd to lett Lodgings. But let me tell you, young Man—*(The Bell rings, and* Bernarda *is call'd from within)* I never show a Room to any but People of Quality.

(Within) Signora *Bernarda!*

Ber. Nothing but Hurry in this House! *(The Bell rings again)* Presently presently!—Your Master is a Man of Quality, I suppose? But I ask no Questions.

Gil. Nor will give any Answers, I see. *(Angrily)*

Ber. Don't be in a Passion, young Man. *(The Bell rings again)* Coming! coming! [*Exit.*

Gil. *(Musing)* Take Care that *Gil Blas* be well treated—I have the greatest Regard for him—He is every Thing in the World to me——Those were the Words I think——But they meant nothing to

be fure—Friendfhip perhaps—a little of the Platonie
or fo—but no Love—not a Bit of that—And yet now
I could fancy myfelf born to be a great Man. She
call'd me to her yefterday at the Inn, and could not
fpeak for Blufhing—A foft Sign that!—We have another Lodging too in the next Street—Well, and what
then?—Why only that Somebody's to be Mafter there.
——If fhe fhould be really fmitten with my Perfon and
Underftanding!—But a Pox on't, I have been making
Love to the Chambermaid—What's to be done there?
Her Lady muft not be difturb'd.   Jealoufy's an unru-
ly Paffion—The Girl fhall be provided for—Yes—fhe
muft be provided for.

Enter Laura *in Boy's Clothes.*

Lau. (*Slapping him on the Shoulder*) What are you
thinking of, *Gil Blas?*

Gil. Oh, *Laura!*—Is it you?—How d'you do,
Child?—I'm a little bufy.

Lau. Hey-day! Is any Thing the Matter with you?

Gil. Why, look you, Child—When Men of Underftanding withdraw themfelves from Company, they
are not to be broke in upon—People fhould allow 'em
their thoughtful Moments.

Lau. Ha!—A Diforder in your Head, perhaps!—
And fo you don't love me?

Gil. A Citizen of the World muft love every Body.
We are all Links of the fame Chain, *Laura*—But
Times and Circumftances are fubject to change—And
fo--in fhort--the World's a very fickle Sort of a World.

Lau. Very fickle indeed—But I'm forry you don't
love me—I wanted to have made a Fool of you.

Gil. That's a Fib, Huffy.   Gentlemen of my Appearance are not to be play'd Tricks with by Cham-
bermaids.   But a Word in your Ear, Child.   I intend to fhow myfelf a little in *Salamanca*—And if the
Ladies fhould happen to walk with their Eyes open
——why, you muft make yourfelf as eafy as you
can.   Upon my Honour I'll come back, if I can't do
better.

Lau.

Lau. And upon My Honour, I'll forgive you if you can.

Gil. But how does Travelling agree with you, *Laura?*

Lau. Juft as Loving does with You. I am tir'd.

Gil. Like enough, Faith. But how does Donna *Aurora?*

Lau. In as high Spirits as when fhe left *Madrid.* Ah, *Gil Blas*! if You lov'd Me, as well as I fancy She loves Somebody——

Gil. Ha! has fhe faid any Thing?

Lau. A Hint or fo—But You are her Favourite, and to know all prefently.

Gil. Hem! So I fuppofe, Child. No, no, to be fure it is not me,   [*Afide, and ftrutting.*]

Lau. Hey-day! What does the Coxcomb fwell at?

Gil. Hark you, *Laura*—If ever I live to be a great Man, you fhall be provided for.

Lau. The Jackanapes! Why, you don't think my Lady *Aurora* in Love with You?

Gil. With me! in Love with me! Ha, ha, ha! Why fhould fhe be in Love with me? And yet ftranger Things have happen'd, Child.

Lau. Is it poffible the Fellow fhould be in earneft? [*Afide*] 'Tis mighty well, Sir—and fo all your fine Promifes are come to this!

Gil. Why, look you, Child—As to Promifes—— You fhall be provided for—fo don't cry.

Lau. The Gudgeon, what a Swallow he has! [*Afide*]

Gil. What are you thinking of, *Laura?*

Lau. That you are a mercenary Wretch, and that my Eyes are open at laft—Yes, yes, 'tis plain enough now, what we came to *Salamanca* for. [*Angrily.*] But will you really defert me, *Gil Blas?*

Gil. Defert you! What a Thought was there indeed! Don't I tell you, you fhall be provided for? Your Lady fhall be a Friend too. I have fome Intereft

with

with her I believe. [*Strutting about.*] But mum! here she comes. Don't be a Fool and spoil all now.

Lau. I shall certainly die, if I don't laugh. [*Aside.*]

Enter Aurora, *in Boy's Clothes, and* Bernarda.

Aur. Nay, as for that, Signora, I don't dislike the Apartments—Hark you, *Gil Blas*—You must away to the other Lodgings for the small Portmanteau. And be sure you get every Thing in Readiness. But if you would oblige me, return immediately. I have a Secret for you of the last Importance—Remember to make Haste back. [*Apart.*]

Gil. Yes, Sir—If you would oblige me!—Last Importance!—Return immediately! (*Aside.*) I'll be back in a Moment, Sir. [*Exit.*]

Aur. For you, *Lopez*—I shall dress in a quarter of an Hour; so see that every Thing is in Readiness.

Lau. When you please, Sir. [*Exit.*]

Aur. But if Don *Lewis* should disappoint you, Signora!

Ber. He never disappoints me—His Baggage came Yesterday; and I expect him every Moment—Oh! he's the sweetest Gentleman! You'll be so happy together!

Aur. I have heard often of him. But they say he pursues the Ladies at *Salamanca* rather closer than his Studies.

Ber. Nay, as for that Matter—But I say nothing. —People that lett Lodgings must not tell Tales. He's a sweet Nobleman, and may have his Gallantries for any Thing I know.

Aur. A good many I suppose. But you are to be trusted, Signora.

Ber. I thank Heaven, Sir. What one sees, one sees, you know—But Madam *Isabella* would not walk so proudly, if her Secret was not in safe keeping.

Aur. *Isabella*! O! I had forgot—Is not she—?

Ber. The old Advocate's Daughter, Sir. But Don *Lewis* may be mistaken.

Aur.

Aur. D'you think fo?

Ber. Nay, I think nothing, and fay nothing. He may fancy he has her all to himfelf.—But it is not my Way to tell Tales.

Aur. Nor mine to ask Queftions. We are the beft met in the World for that, Signora. You can keep Secrets, and I want to know none—Is fhe handfome?

Ber. Handfome!— She knows how to drefs, Sir. But if a certain Perfon, that fhall be namelefs, did not neglect herfelf a little —— Her Ladyfhip and I are pretty near of an Age I believe—She has a great Spirit tho'.

Aur. Has fhe fuch a Spirit?

Ber. The Devil of a Spirit, Sir —— And then for Intrigue!—But I fay Nothing.

Aur. And yet it vexes you that Don *Lewis* fhould be fo deceiv'd.

Ber. There's the Thing, Sir. Why, he believes her as conftant as a Turtle —— But between you and me, I never lik'd his Friend Don *Gabriel*.

Aur. Has his Friend been falfe too?

Ber. It's no Bufinefs of mine, Sir—But People will talk. There have been ftrange Doings in Don *Lewis's* Abfence.—This *Gabriel*, you muft know, is his Confidant with the Lady—But I have nothing to do with their Intrigues.

Aur. You talk like a difcreet Woman, Signora.

Ber. I thank Heaven Sir, for what I am. I live as you fee; and lett the beft Lodgings in *Salamanca.* You are in a Houfe of Reputation, Sir, and your Secrets will be fafe.

Aur. So I fee indeed. *(Afide.)* *Ifabella* is not handfome then?

Ber. Nothing like it, Sir —— A bad Woman too— a very bad Woman.

Aur. They don't think Don *Lewis* will marry her?

Ber. Out upon her! Marry her! No, no, he knows
better;

better; and befides, he's too wild a Spark to think of marrying any Body.

Aur. So I'm afraid indeed. *(Afide.)* You fhall introduce me to him, Signora.

Ber. By all Means, Sir. You will be the fweeteft Company! But fuch Doings! Thank Heaven, I am not fo young as I was!—For I have had my Temptations as well as others.

Aur. Ay, Signora; and have given 'em too, or I am miftaken.

Ber. Nay, as to that—But I am turn'd of thirty—Would you think it, Sir?—I am turn'd of thirty—But I was always difcreet.

Aur. You may thank Heaven indeed, Signora; for Difcretion is not always a Woman's Virtue.

Re-enter Laura.

What now, *Lopez?*

Lau. Only for the Portmanteau, Sir.

Aur. Stay a Moment—I fhall call for you by-and-by, Signora. *(To Bernarda.)* But be fure you come and tell me when Don *Lewis* arrives.

Ber. Heavens blefs you both! But many an aking Heart will be left behind you in *Salamanca.* *(Exit.*

Lau. And now what News, Madam?

Aur. Only that Don *Lewis* has a Miftrefs here.

Lau. A Score of 'em, I'll warrant you. Did you imagine he came hither only to ftudy?

Aur. 'Tis We are come to ftudy I'm afraid. *(Sighs.)* Ours is a wild Scheme, *Laura.*

Lau. Let it be fuccefsful, and no Matter.

Aur. You have not faid any Thing to *Gil Blas?*

Lau. Not a Syllable, Madam; and for a particular Reafon, I am glad on't.

Aur. What Reafon, prithee?

Lau. Another Time, Madam. Here he comes.

Aur. Do you withdraw then, I am afham'd to let him into the Secret, but there's nothing to be done without him.

Lau.

Lau. Ha! *(looking out)* Let me die if the Fellow has not gone and powder'd himself.

(Aside and Exit.

Enter Gil Blas, *powder'd and dress'd, with a Portmanteau.*

Aur. So soon return'd, and dress'd too, *Gil Blas!* But you are always expeditious.

Gil. To obey a Lady's Commands, Madam—and yours above all others. There's a Willingness in such Obedience, that turns Fatigue to Pleasure.

Aur. Why, you are an absolute Courtier, *Gil Blas!* ——But I told you I had a Secret for you—Heigh! ho!—Come from the Door a little, and tell me if I may trust you.

Gil. If you doubt me, Madam!—

Aur. No, *Gil Blas*, I think you have a Regard for me. I have found in you an Understanding above the Condition of a Servant; and I know too, that by Birth and Education, you have a Right to better Employment. From this Moment you are my Friend. Will you be my Friend, *Gil Blas!*

Gil. Your faithful Servant for ever, Madam—and one that—I don't know—You have made me—But won't you go on, Madam?

Aur. I know not how, *Gil Blas*—I am a Woman, and I find have all the Frailties of a Woman.

Gil. For Heaven's Sake!—

Aur. Yet why should Love be call'd a Frailty?— But then so rash a Love! so forward! so liable to Censure!—I blush to own the Folly I have been guilty of.

Gil. Is it my Condition, Madam?—I am a Servant 'tis true—But then—Why let 'em censure—let 'em censure, Madam——

Aur. I know you are to be trusted; and it may lie in your Care and Secresy to make me happy.

Gil. In mine, Madam!—To make You happy?— Is it possible?

C

Aur.

Aur. Has *Laura* told you nothing?

Gil. Not a Syllable—It was Matter of Diverſion to her—But, ſays I, ſtranger Things have happen'd.—My Lady *Aurora*, ſays I—

Aur. You could not gueſs it ſure?

Gil. She laugh'd at me only for hinting at it.

Aur. And what was your Hint?

Gil. Nay, Madam, I am but a Servant—And till I know it from your own Lips—

Aur. But you'll blame me I'm afraid—Nay all the World will blame me.

Gil. Love, Madam, is a great Leveller we all know—But where the Object is ſo very unworthy—

Aur. Unworthy did you ſay? Why unworthy?

Gil. Not abſolutely unworthy, I muſt needs own—But the Honour is ſo high, Madam.

Aur. So high! What mean you?—He may have a few Faults of Youth perhaps—but his Virtues—

Gil. O, Lord, Madam!——

Aur. Nay, nay, he has a thouſand Virtues——

Gil. All of your own making indeed, Madam—But upon my Knees I conjure you! (*Kneels*) open your whole Heart to me!—We'll fly to the fartheſt Corner of the World to hide your Bluſhes.

Aur. Nay, *Gil Blas*—If Don *Lewis* and I come together, there will be no great Need of bluſhing, or of hiding either.

Gil. Don *Lewis* did you ſay, Madam?——Don *Lewis?*

Aur. You ſeem ſurpriz'd, *Gil Blas!*

Gil. A little, Madam—I did not once think of Don *Lewis*, I muſt own.

Aur. Not think of him! Who was it you did think of?

Gil. I believe I was a little abſent, Madam.

Aur. That's ſtrange methinks! Do you know Don *Lewis?*

Gil. Don *Lewis Pacheco?*

Aur.

Aur. Ay.

Gil. I have feen him, Madam. Yes, yes, the Man's found at laft.   (*Afide.*

Aur. Seen him! You are ftrangely furpriz'd, *Gil Blas!*—But what I am going to tell you will furprize you more.

Gil. Nay, Madam, as to that—I can't be much more furpriz'd.

Aur. I have only feen him neither——I verily believe he does not fo much as know me.

Gil. Indeed, Madam!

Aur. But from the Inftant he caught my Eyes, I felt a Paffion for him fo ftrong, that all my Refolution fince has not been able to conquer it. I told *Laura* of my Love.

Gil. *Laura,* Madam!—O, the Jade!   (*Afide.*

Aur. Why not? What Objection was there to *Laura's* knowing it?

Gil. Objection! None at all, Madam—no Objection—Pray go on.

Aur. I told her of my Love, and bad her enquire into his Temper and Character. She acquitted herfelf fo well, and brought me fuch flattering Accounts of him, that I grew defperate, and hearing he was immediately returning to *Salamanca* to finifh his Studies, I determin'd, in this Difguife, to be here before him, and in the very Houfe where he's to lodge. But now comes my Scheme—Don't be fo amaz'd till you have heard me out.

Gil. A little puzzled or fo——But the Scheme by all Means, Madam.

Aur. My Brother, you know, was with the Army abroad; and has been too long abfent from *Madrid* for Don *Lewis* to have any Knowledge of him—For this Reafon I made bold to borrow his Name; and under the manly Appearance of Don *Felix de Mendoza,* I intend an intimate Acquaintance with Don *Lewis* ——At the other Lodgings——

Gil.

Gil. Ay, Madam, what then?

Aur. There I am to be myfelf——with *Laura* as my Duenna, juſt come from the Country in my Way to *Madrid.* Here I am Don *Felix* in Breeches——and There his Twin-Siſter, Donna *Aurora,* in Petti-coats. Here I ſhall talk to him of myſelf and There he ſhall be introduc'd to myſelf—D'you conceive me?

Gil. Perfectly, Madam. O, Love, Love, what Fools do you make of us! *(Aſide.)* When do you expect him!

Aur. To-day——Every Moment. You look as if the Thing did not pleaſe you.

Gil. O, mightily, Madam! mightily indeed!——Philoſophy I thank thee! I am coming to myfelf a-gain. *(Aſide.)* I like it——There's Spirit in't—and I'll aſſiſt you with my Life.

Aur. Thank you, *Gil Blas*——And whether we ſucceed or not, it ſhall be a Service you ſhan't repent of——But huſh!——we are interrupted.

Enter Bernarda *haſtily, and* Laura.

Ber. News! News, Sir!—I told you how 'twou'd be. The Don's arriv'd, and will kiſs your Hands as ſoon as he is dreſs'd——Oh! ſuch a Couple of you!——But I ſay nothing——only Heaven defend the poor Women in *Salamanca!*

Aur. And did you tell him, Signora—I mean did you pay him my Compliments?

Ber. Did I? To be ſure I did the very Inſtant I had Opportunity. He knows your Family perfectly he ſays.——

Aur. Ha!——

Ber. Tho' he has not the Honour to know Don *Felix.*

Aur. Then all's well again. *(Aſide.)*

Ber. No Matter—You'll be ſoon enough acquain-ted for Miſchief, I'll warrant you.

Aur. Does he dine at Home?

Ber.

Ber. If he can be honour'd with Your Company, he says. *(The Bell rings.)* Coming! Coming!

Aur, I'll certainly attend him. *(Bell rings again.*

Ber. Coming, I say!—Nothing but Hurry in this House! [*Exit.*]

Lau. You look pale, Madam.

Aur. Sick, fick, *Laura,* quite fick!—Would I were at *Madrid* again!

Lau. Courage! Courage, Madam! What defpair of Victory before the Engagement!—Methinks *Gil Blas* looks a little pale too.

Gil. Oh! the Slut! *(Afide)*

Aur. What's the Matter, *Gil Blas?*

Gil. With me, Madam? Nothing in the World, Madam. I was thinking that—only a little concern'd to fee you fo out of Spirits.

Lau. Ha, ha, ha! And fo the Story took a wrong Turn! *(Apart to* Gil Blas)

Gil. Hark you, Huffy—One Word to your Miftrefs, and I defert the Caufe. *(Apart)*

Aur. Nay, nay, no Whifpering. We have not Time. Is every Thing ready in my Room? *(To Laura.)* I muft in, and drefs this Moment. Would this Meeting were well over! for I have but a Woman's Heart after all.

Lau. Never fear, Madam. He does not know Don *Felix.*

Aur. The Certainty of that gives me fome Hopes.

Gil. Every Thing muft depend upon your own Behaviour, Madam.

Aur. For which Reafon, you, *Gil Blas,* are from this Inftant to converfe with Don *Felix* with all the impertinent Freedom of a favourite Servant.

Gil. Very well, Madam——Moft noble Don *Felix,* I'm your Slave.

Lau. Why, there now!—How eafy my Lady has made your Part!——And yet how the Man looks! Ha, ha, ha!

Aur.

Aur. No Laughing, I befeech you —— By which Means, whenever you fee me difconcerted, you can turn the Difcourfe, and give me Time to recover. The fame good Turn, you *Laura*, can do Don *Felix's* Sifter, in the watchful Office of her Duenna.

Gil. Right, Madam —— And fhe'll become the Office admirably.

Lau. I'll affure you, Sir!

Aur. I fee 'twill do —— My Spirits are returning!

Gil. But ftill he muft fee you again and again.

Aur. Perhaps not —— But to guard againft the worft, run immediately to the Inn, and order three poft Horfes to be kept ready faddled, that we may vanifh the very Inftant we fee Occafion.

Gil. The very Thing, Madam! —— I'll go immediately.

Aur. You muft be back to wait at Dinner tho'.

Gil. Without Fail.

Aur. And now to equip myfelf for the Field of Battle! Come, *Laura*. [*Exit.*

Lau. Ha, ha, ha! Pluck up a little Courage, Man, —and don't look fo difconfolate. Things did go a little wrong to be fure —— But I won't tell. [*Exit, and re-enters.*] And yet, upon fecond Thoughts, if Don *Lewis* and my Lady fhould happen to difagree, —who knows but—However, we'll talk of that another Time. [*Exit, laughing.*

Gil. So, fo! I have fool'd myfelf to fome Tune— O, Vanity! Vanity! ——A Canker upon this Tongue of mine for blabbing to *Laura*—— I was to provide for her, with a Pox!—Now will fhe betray me to her Miftrefs, and add a thoufand Lies by Way of Decoration. I can't ftand it—No—I'll e'en fteal off, and leave 'em to fhift for themfelves ——But hold! hold! Will that be honourable? Has not my Lady *Aurora* trufted me with her Secret? —— And won't fhe ftand in Need of my Advice?—— But then to ftay and be the But of a Chambermaid! —— That ftings—No ——it

———it is not in Philofophy to bear that———But hold
again! Does my Lady know what an Afs I have been?
Why, no———Ay, but then this *Laura!* The Secret's
too good to be kept, that's certain—Well! 'Tis but
denying it, and the Matter at leaft remains doubtful.
I muft humour her, and pretend Love to her———Ay,
ay, that will do. *Aurora* muft be ferv'd———I have
promis'd, and will perform———So now I am myfelf
again.

Enter Melchior, *brufhing a Hat, and finging.*

Mel. Not a Petticoat fring'd, or the Heel of a Shoe,
    Ever pafs'd me by Day-light, but at it I flew.

Gil. I fhould know that Voice fure.

Mel. Gil Blas!

Gil. What, *Melchior!* ——— my old Friend and
Companion at *Toledo!*

Mel. And as hearty as ever, Boy———Kifs me.

Gil. But what in the Devil's Name brought You
hither?

Mel. A Partiality for the Sciences. I was always
of a thoughtful Turn, you know—mightily addicted
to be wife——— And fo my Mafter and I are come
hither to finifh our Studies.

Gil. And who may be your Mafter pray?

Mel. The noble Don *Lewis Pacheco*———And we
live as merry as the Morning Lark, Boy—But what
Service are You in, *Gil Blas?* for I fee you wear the
Badge ftill.

Gil. A Whim, *Melchior*—only a Whim. I live
in Friendfhip with Don *Felix de Mendoza.* Your
Mafter and he and I are to be very intimate.

Mel. Gil Blas!

Gil. Ha!

Mel. Why, they have not cur'd you. Do you remember old Stories?

Gil. Ay; and have learnt Philofophy enough to
laugh at 'em———But come, a Hiftory! a Hiftory!
———I muft know your Adventures, *Melchior.*

Mel.

Mel. Would not a Glafs of *Malaga* do better before Dinner?

Gil. Your Adventures firft, if you pleafe, Sir.

Mel. Faith, as for Adventures, a few trifling Services, and as few trifling Intrigues make up the whole Catalogue—— in *Spain* I mean——But I have been in *England*, Poy.

Gil. In *England!* And do they live there as we do?

Mel. Ay, and die there as You may do —— My Mafter and I had like to have dy'd there——A Pox upon the People!——If a Man would live by his Wits among 'em, he muft die by the Law.

Gil. And who was that Mafter, pray?

Mel. His Name d'you mean?—O! a great Count I'll affure you——A moft finifh'd Gentleman. One that could travel the World over, and carry his Fortune in his Fingers—Prefto! begone!—And fnap, a Nobleman's Purfe is in your own Pocket.

Gil. And how were you receiv'd in *England?*

Mel. O! Faith, mighty well. To do 'em Juftice, the *Englifh* are a very good Sort of People. If you don't dive too deep into their Pockets, they are mighty fond of having them pick'd by Strangers.

Gil. Put what Company did you keep?

Mel. The beft you may be fure. We had a Pafport to all the People of Rank.

Gil. And what was that?

Mel. Play, my Poy—the Key to every great Man's Door in *England.* Sometimes indeed, Merit, Title, or Fortune may introduce a Stranger to Notice——but the fureft Recommendation is Play—Do but play deep, and you rank with the beft of 'em.

Gil. But their Women, *Melchior!*—How are their Women?

Mel. Why, that's a Queftion I can hardly anfwer: —We marry'd a Few of 'em—They are mighty fond of Strangers, you muft know—But we did not live long

long enough with our Wives, to make a Trial of their Tempers.

Gil. You are a great Rogue, *Melchior.*

Mel. Ay, *Gil Blas*; if Your Honefty was but equal to My Knavery, I fhould have a pretty good Opinion of you. But, Faith, I am naturally honeft— I do but copy my Mafters.

Gil. You muft mend, Sir, you muft mend—And I don't care if I go in with you, and drink a Glafs to your Reformation.

Mel. And to the Reformation of our Mafters ; for if yours is fuch a Wencher as mine, we fhall have but bad Examples.

Gil. We muft fet 'em then, we muft fet 'em——fo come along——I can ftay but a Moment tho'—You are a great Rogue, a great Rogue, *Melchior.*

Exeunt.

A C T.   II.

S C E N E, *continues.*

Enter Gil Blas, *and* Laura *in Boys Clothes.*

Gil. NOthing but Jollity all Dinner-time—— And then fuch Profeffions of Friendfhip, and fuch Schemes for Raking!—Faith, to my Mind tho', My Lady *Aurora*'s the cleverer Fellow of the two.

Lau. At her Tongue you mean. But what have they talk'd about ?

D

Gil.

Gil. Wenching. What fhould they talk about? The Devil's in thefe Women, when they ftep into Breeches——She has boafted of fuch Exploits! —— I was forc'd to give her a Nod now and then to hold her Hand; for Don *Lewis* will certainly fmoak the Woman by her Want of Confcience.

Lau. I'll affure you, Saucebox! —— But how did you feel yourfelf, *Gil Blas?*—Did not the Sight of Don *Lewis* difcompofe you?

Gil. Nay, prithee now——

Lau. Only a little——Come come, confefs.

Gil, Have you no Mercy, Huffy?

Lau. Ha, ha, ha!—Stay till I have done laughing, and perhaps I may find a little—But hark you, *Gil Blas!* If Matters had turn'd out as you and I fhrewdly fufpected, would you really have provided for me.

Gil. Will the Wench never have done? —Zounds! can't a Man miftake? *Humanum eft errare*—There's Latin for you, you Slut—and the Meaning on't is, that a very wife Man may be an Afs fometimes.

Lau. And fo fine a Scholar too!— That's a Pity— But you love me again now, I fuppofe?

Gil. Moft violently, by this Hand. *(Taking her Hand)* Nay, prithee, don't be coy—'Twas but a little Slip from Virtue. Has Your Virtue never made a Slip, Child?

Lau. Not that you fhall know of, Sir. But how if I fhould fuffer you to kneel to me once more?—— Ah! *Gil Blas!* Thefe Women of Quality will never let you alone, I'm afraid.

Gil. You won't have done then?——One Word more and I vanifh.

Lau. Ha, ha, ha!—Come, I have done, I have done—Here's my Hand upon't.

Gil. And mine —You muft fwear firft tho', never even to think of what an Afs I have been. I have been an Afs *Laura,* and there's an End on't.

Gil.

Lau. Agreed, agreed—And now you fhall gallant me to the other Lodgings.

Gil. But not a Word to my Lady——That's the firft Part of the Condition.

Lau. And the fecond—

Gil. That the Laugh's out, and I hear no more on't—So away, away—For I muft be back in a Moment. [*Exeunt.*

Scene draws and difcovers Don Lewis *and* Aurora *over a Bottle.*

D. L. Ha, ha, ha! And fo the Brother would not fight?

Aur. He did not like me, I believe. I wore a Cockade in my Hat, and had feen fome Service, you know. I was reckon'd pretty good at a home Thruft too—And thefe are Circumftances your modern fine Gentlemen don't relifh fo well.

D. L. But what faid the old Banker, her Father?

Aur. There's a Form, you know, for Fathers upon fuch Occafions——A Form I ought to remember I'm fure; for I have had it repeated to me by thirty or forty of 'em. It runs pretty much in this Manner——— Sir, you have ruin'd my Daughter, and difhonour'd my Family—A Family, Sir!—And fo on—a good deal about the Family—And for a Conclufion, you muft make Amends by Marriage.

D. L. And you anfwer'd in Form too, I fuppofe?

Aur. By a fhort Negative, and a low Bow—And fo the Affair ended.

D. L. But what became of the Girl?

Aur. She ftole to me the next Day, and cry'd a little—But I am a bitter bad Comforter—I can't bear to fee a Woman in Diftrefs—Befides, I was fo engag'd with half a Dozen of her Acquaintance, that I could not afk her to fit down. You may find her in a Nunnery, I fuppofe, counting her Beads, and weeping over the Vanities of the World——Thofe Nunneries are

D 2 vaftly

vaftly oblig'd to fuch Rakes as you and me, Don *Lewis.*

D. L. Faith, I think fo—But you give no Quarter I fee.

Aur. Yes, always—For I never purfue, after the Engagement's over—But what's to be done here? I can't drink—I told you I never drink.

D. L. But I muft, I fuppofe—Unlefs you make me a fecond in Your Engagements.

Aur. Nay, nay, that won't do—I muft fight under Your Generalfhip in *Salamauca.*

D. L. Faith, not under mine. I am a mere Hufband in Love. If I have a Miftrefs that can be faithful, I pitch my Tent there, and cry Peace to all the World.

Aur. Till fhe has cloy'd you, I fuppofe. You have a Miftrefs then?

D. L. Ay——and a kind one.

Aur. And her Name is——*Ifabella.*

D. L. Ha!—Do you deal with the Devil, Don *Felix?*

Aur. A fmall Agent of his——I'll go and tell her you are coming.

D. L. Hold! hold, Sir!—Are you acquainted with her?

Aur No, Faith——not yet.

D. L. Who told you of her?

Aur. Has fhe a Sifter? Or will you introduce me to her Maid? I can cry Hem from the Garret, if the old Advocate comes.

D. L If the old Advocate comes! Did not you tell me, you arriv'd here only this Morning?

Aur. About half an Hour before you.

D. L. And fo knowing already?

Aur. In Amours only—But I'll unriddle—I'll unriddle. You commended My Fellow, that waited upon us at Dinner. That Fellow has more Intelligence than the Inquifition —I'll pit him for a Secret, againft

all

all the Priefts in *Spain.* He knows of your Friend Don *Gabriel* too.

D. L. He knows no Ill of him, I'm fure.

Aur. Only that he's your Confidant with *Ifabella.*

D. L. And the moft faithful in the World. Don *Gabriel* is a Gentleman of Family, tho' without Fortune ; a Man of Probity and Honour. I fent to him this Morning—I wonder he is not come yet. You fhall be acquainted with him.

Aur. I thank you, Sir. And does he vifit *Ifabella,* in Your Abfence ?

D. L. Conftantly. He's my Ambaffador to her.

Aur. 'Tis a nice Truft methinks. I am for no Seconds with a Miftrefs.

D. L. You'll be of another Mind, when you know him.

Aur May be fo—But don't miftake me—I only tell you that *Gil Blas* is in your Secret—Where he got it, I don't know.

D. L. From the Devil I fuppofe, or *Ifabella's* Maid. I know of none elfe that could tell him—But can he keep as well as find ?

Aur. From every body but his Mafter. He's the moft faithful Fellow living. I do nothing without him.

D. L. Mine is fuch Sot, I dare not fend him upon a common Meffage. Will you lend me yours, for a Note to *Ifabella?*

Aur. Ha!—Ay.—Or I'll go myfelf—Won't that be as well ?

D. L. For the Lady perhaps—

Aur. Nay, if you doubt my Honefty—Who waits there ? *Gil Blas !*

Enter Gil Blas.

Gil. Did you call, Sir ?

Aur. Ay. Don *Lewis* has Employment for you— And, d'you hear, Sir ?—The beft Service you can do

your

your Mafter, will be your Faithfulnefs to his Friend.

D. L. You are very obliging, Don *Felix*,

Gil. And what are your Honour's Commands, Sir?

D. L. Only to deliver a Letter. You are a fly Rogue, *Gil Blas.*

Aur. Ask if it is not to *Ifabella*. *(Apart to* Gil Blas.)

Gil. To Madam *Ifabella*, I fuppofe ?—Hem!

D. L. A devilifh fly Rogue—But remember, Sir, that the Secret goes no farther. I fhall find you here, Don *Felix?*—A fhort Note will do.

Aur. As long a one as you pleafe. I am not going out, you know. *(Exit* Don *Lewis*.)

Gil. What Secret's this, Madam? And who is *Ifabella ?*

Aur. A Miftrefs of Don *Lewis*; an Advocate's Daughter in Town. *Bernarda* told me of her; but I have given You the Merit of the Difcovery, to bring you into Employment. If he founds you about it, pretend to know every Thing, and fay nothing.

Gil. I'll warrant you. But am I to deliver the Letter, Madam?

Aur. By all Means; and to act honeftly by Don *Lewis*.

Gil. Honeftly, Madam!

Aur. Ay, honeftly—That's your Cue at prefent.

Gil. Nay, with all my Heart. Any Thing for the Good of the Caufe.

Aur. And bring me an Account of the Lady—of her Perfon and Wit—how old fhe is—with what other Intelligence you can get.

Gil. I'll do't, Madam—But how go Matters here?

Aur. Juft as you faw at Dinner—All Friendfhip and Confidence. I fhall tell him of my Sifter prefently. Is *Laura* at the other Lodgings?

Gil. And drefs'd for the Duenna, Madam.

Aur. Hufh! here comes Don *Lewis*.

Re-enter

Re-enter Don Lewis.

D. L. There, Sir. *(Giving a Letter to* Gil Blas.) You fee the Directions—But remember that *Ifabella's* the Daughter, and not the Father—My Fellow would have needed the Caution, I'm fure?

Gil. And fo, if the Daughter is from Home, I may leave it with the Father, Sir. *(Bowing.)*

Aur. Right, *Gil Blas*—But you need not fear him. *(To* D. Lewis.) Is he to deliver it into her own Hands?

D. L. Or to her Maid's. He'll be call'd up, if the Old Fellow is abroad—You are to be My Servant, Sir.

Gil. Hir'd at *Madrid*, the Day before your Honour fet out—For Women will ask Queftions—I'll fly, Sir. [*Exit.*]

D. L. A lively Fellow this!—But you look grave, Don *Felix*—Nothing has happen'd I hope?

Aur. The Devil and all has happen'd. I am fentenc'd to Sobriety and Pennance for a whole Week—I have a Sifter come to Town.

D. L. A Sifter!—How d'you hear it?

Aur. From *Gil Blas.* He met her Servant it feems, who told him fhe was juft come, and intended ftaying a Week.

D. L. And what brought her hither?

Aur. Sifterly Love and Kindnefs to be fure. She's returning to *Madrid* from a country Vifit, and has taken *Salamanca* in her Way.

D. L. To pafs a Week with her Brother—And does this vex you?—Is fhe handfome?

Aur. Hum!—very like Me.

D. L. Nay, then fhe muft be handfome—Younger than you?

Aur. About a Minute. We are Twins, you muft know.

D. L. And when d'you vifit her?

Aur. This Moment. She'll take it ill elfe. Hang her! the Jade's good Company enough; but fhe thinks

me

me a Rake, and I hate to be tutor'd.

D. L. Shall I attend you?

Aur. No. She'll fall in Love with you; and I defign her for a Nunnery.

D. L. A Nunnery! I muſt ſee her then.

Aur. But *Iſabella* will expect you.

D. L. Not till the Evening. The old Dragon's never ſecure till then.

Aur. And ſo you inſiſt upon ſeeing her? Come along then—And yet, now I think on't, I won't go. Could not you and I ſtart better Game this Afternoon?

D. L. Nay, did not you promiſe me?—I muſt and will ſee her.

Aur. You muſt and will!—Why, then ſo you ſhall. But take Care of yourſelf; for ſhe may play the Devil with you.

D. L. Say you ſo?—But I'll venture.

Aur. To St. *Mark's* then—You muſt be my Guide. But ſhe'll be indiſpos'd, I'm afraid. *(Aſide. Exeunt.)*

SCENE *Changes to* Iſabella's.

Enter Don Gabriel *and* Iſabella.

Iſa. This Morning! Did he arrive this Morning? And why have not I heard from him? But You are his Friend, Don *Gabriel*—He has ſent to You I ſuppoſe?

D. G. Only a Meſſage about an Hour ago, that he deſir'd to ſee me; but I pretended not to be at Home, that I might give You Notice of his Arrival. If I might adviſe you, 'twere beſt not to him.

Iſa. Not ſee him! Why not ſee him? Dreſs up a Tale to him, do—and tell him I have deceiv'd him. The Wretch that can betray his Friend, will be black enough for any Thing.

D. G. Ay, rail at me, and be a Woman. But I have advis'd you for the beſt. Don *Lewis* has ſlighted you. Poſſeſſion has cloy'd him—Or if it has not—a divided Heart will ſatisfy neither of us. I'll ſhare you with no Man.   *Iſa.*

Ifa. Nor ſhall you, Sir. Who told you of a divided Heart? Don *Lewis* has it all. My Perſon indeed has been yours—And what then? I took you for my Convenience—the Proxy of Don *Lewis*—I was form'd for Pleaſure, and will purſue it—Therefore no more of this. I'll ſee Don *Lewis*—Nay if you oppoſe me, I'll tell him of my own Falſehood, that he may puniſh yours.

D. G. You have ſworn to live for Me.

Ifa. Tell it to Don *Lewis* then; and plead your Right in me to Him—Do this, and I am yours.

D. G. I dare do more, Madam.

Ifa. 'Tis falſe. Your Dependance is upon his Bounty. —Nay, and upon mine too--Therefore no more of this.

D. G. You Will ſee him then?

Ifa. I will—and you ſhall be my Meſſenger. Go to him as he deſires-— and tell him with what Eagerneſs I expect him—'Tis your Employment, Sir.

D. G. Can this be *Iſabella?*

Ifa. Ay, Don *Lewis*'s *Iſabella.* Go to him this Moment, and tell him I languiſh for him. But remember, Sir, if I hear a Hint from him to my Diſhonour, I'll ſacrifice You to my Revenge, tho' the Town ſhould ring of me.

Enter Beatrice.

Bea. Not ſo loud, Madam, not ſo loud! Here's a Letter from Don *Lewis*—The Servant will overhear you.

Ifa. I care not if he does. Shew him up Stairs. *(Opens and reads the Letter to herſelf.)*

D. G. Is it the old Servant?

Bea. No, a Stranger.

D. G. I'll not be ſeen then.

Ifa. Your Heart fails you, does it?—But you may have the Pleaſure of liſtening from the next Room.

D. G. I ſcorn the Employment, Madam. My Care is for You. *[Exit.]*

Ifa. Shew up the Servant, I ſay. *(Exit* Beatrice, *and returns with* Gil Blas*)* Do you ſerve Don *Lewis,* Sir?

E   *Gil.*

Gil. I hope fo, Madam. 'Tis my Endeavour to ferve every body.

Ifa. I mean, are you his Servant ?

Gil. Why, as to that, Madam—there's no hiding the Difgrace—I am but a Servant.

Ifa. Is Don *Lewis* your Mafter, I ask ?

Gil. If I like him upon another Week's Trial, Madam.

Bea. O, Sir! he'll give you double Wages for your Wit——

Ifa. And treble for your Manners. You are juft Come to him then ?

Gil. Juft Going to him, Madam—if I can carry an Anfwer to his Letter.

Ifa. Is this your natural Humour, Sir—Or is it put on to fhew your Parts ? But you fhall have an Anfwer prefently. Get me my Writing things, Beatrice—Stay—I'll go into my Clofet. You can wait a Moment I fuppofe ?

Gil. An Age, Madam—if my Mafter would not be impatient. *(Exeunt* Ifabella *and* Beatrice.) A Woman of Spirit, Faith!—I heard a Man's Voice tho', I'll fwear; —and high Words too. If it was not for my Fears now, I fhould be prying into that Room—One Peep however. *(Going to the Door)* No. Philofophy fays, keep your Head out of a Hornet's Neft. A Man there was, and that's enough. I don't mightily love Mifchief—But Don *Lewis* muft know of this—My Lady muft be told too, that *Ifabella's* handfome—If it fhould happen to fret 'em a little—Why, I have been fretted too—'Tis but turning the Tables—I have been the Fool of the Morning—and They may chance to be the Fools of the Afternoon—Every one in his Turn.

Re-enter Ifabella.

Ifa. There, Sir! Deliver that to your Mafter. *(Gives him a Letter.)* You may tell him too how witty you have been.

Gil.

Gil. It is not my Way to boaſt, Madam. Men of real Talents never do that—But I ſhall deliver your Letter, Madam. A fine-made Woman, and a great —Hem!   (*Aſide and Exit.*)

Iſa. Beatrice! Shew the Gentleman down Stairs.

Re-enter Don GabrieL

Well, Sir! what ſay you now?

D. G. That I have thought better of the Affair. May I ſee Don *Lewis*'s Letter, Madam?

Iſa. No. 'Tis in a Style you won't like.

D. G. Your own was to appoint him here, I preſume?

Iſa. At five, Sir. You had beſt ſtay and meet him.

D. G. No, Madam; I'll haſten to his Lodgings.

Iſa. Do ſo—And remember what I told you— One Hint to my Diſadvantage, and your Ruin is inevitable.

D. G. You may depend upon me—and ſo, farewell. Damn'd, deceitful Woman!   (*Aſide and Exit.*)

Iſa. The bluſtering, cringing Hypocrite! I hate him But now to prepare for Don *Lewis*.   [*Exit.*]

SCENE *changes to* Bernarda's.

Enter Don Lewis *and* Aurora.

Aur. Hang her!—'Twas only an Air—Fatigu'd, and indiſpos'd, and a Parcel of Cant!—I was a Fool to ſend your Name in.

D. L. No, Faith—'twould not have been fair elſe. A Brother may be admitted without Ceremony; but there's a Decorum to be obſerv'd with Strangers.

Aur. A Decorum!—Pſhaw!—Her Cap was rumpled perhaps—or ſhe had not nipt her Eye-brows to Day—Decorum!—Theſe Prudes are the Devil. But if *Iſabella* does not engage you for the Evening, ſhall we ſee you at Coffee?

D. L. With all my Heart—Here comes *Gil Blas.*

E 2   *Enter*

Enter Gil Blas.

Well, Sir, did you fee her?

Gil. So the Maid faid, Sir—But whether 'twas really *Ifabella* or not, I can't be certain. She was a devilifh fine Woman tho'.

D. L. And what faid fhe to my Letter?

Gil. Not a Syllable, Sir. She ask'd a few Queftions relating to myfelf, as I was a Stranger. Women, you know, are apt to be inquifitive when they meet with Strangers.

D. L. You are arch, Sir!

Gil. O, Sir! nothing to what I was with Her—I was quite whimfical.

D L. And when am I to fee her?

Gil. That, Sir, is more than I know—She did not open her Lips about that.

D. L. She read my Letter fure?

Gil. Not that I faw Sir.

Aur. Why, this is a ftrange Account, Don *Lewis!*

D. L. He has miftaken the Houfe. *Ifabella* could not behave fo.

Aur. She had Company perhaps.

Gil. Not that I know of, Sir. I heard a Gentleman's Voice indeed—but he was clofetted before I had the Honour of Admittance.

D. L. Are you in Jeft, or Earneft, *Gil Blas?*

Gil. Between both, Sir.

D. L. In Earneft then, what was her Anfwer to my Letter?

Gil. Faith, Sir, I can't tell. She gave it me feal'd up—and I had not the Curiofity to open it. This is her Anfwer, Sir. *(Gives him a Letter.)*

D. L. Mighty well, Sir! Do you ferve your Mafter in this Manner? *(Reads to himfelf.)*

Aur. Ha, ha, ha! You muft bear with him, Don *Lewis*——'Tis always the Rogue's Prologue to a fuccefsful Meffage.

Gil. A Way of fweetening good News, Sir. I hope your Honour will pardon me.

D. L.

D. L. Nay, Sir, if you play your Tricks upon your Matter, I have no Right to complain. But you talk'd of hearing a Man in her Chamber—That was carrying the Jeſt too far, Sir.

Gil. If I had invented it, Sir—But a Man there was, that's certain.

D. L. And cloſetted when You came in?

Gil. I can't ſwear as to the Cloſetting—There may be a Back-ſtairs for any Thing I know.

D. L. But you heard a Man's Voice? That you are ſure of?

Gil. Upon my Honour, Sir.

Aur. And where's the Harm if he did?

D. L. The Harm! The Harm is in her concealing him.

Aur. A Trifle!—Your Friend Don *Gabriel* perhaps.

D. L. No—my Friend would not have hid himſelf. He viſits her at My Deſire.

Aur. Are you to ſee her this Evening?

D. L. She appoints me at five; and then but for an Hour or two—Her Father's expected.

Aur. Will you ſup at my Siſter's then?

D. L. If my Mind's at Eaſe, and you tell me 'twill be proper.

Enter Melchior *with Don* Gabriel.

Mel. Don *Gabriel*, Sir.　　[*Exit. with* Gil Blas.
D. L. My Friend!

D. G. My dear Don *Lewis!* Welcome to *Salamanca* again!

D. L. Don *Felix de Mendoza*——A Gentleman whoſe Acquaintance has done me Honour.
　　　　　　(*Introducing Don* Gabriel *to* Aurora.)
D. G. Once more, my dear *Lewis*, welcome to *Salamanca!* But there are fairer Arms that want to hold you.

D. L. Are you ſure of that, Don *Gabriel?*
　　　　　　　　　　D. G.

D. G. Why that Queſtion?——and with ſo grave a Face too? Have you any Cauſe to doubt it?

D. L. I think not. When ſaw you the Lady?

D. G. You look ſtrangely ſerious methinks—Have you heard of any Thing?

D. L. Nay, Faith, I am no Keeper of Secrets. I ſent to her juſt now by Don *Felix*'s Servant—She deſires to ſee me indeed—There's her Letter. *(Gives him a Letter.)* But the Fellow ſwears to her concealing a Man in the Room.

D. G. Ha, ha, ha! And is this what has vex'd you?

D. L. And with Reaſon too.

D. G. O, to be ſure! But how if I was that Man?

D. L. No—You would not have hid yourſelf.

D. G. Ay, there's the Puzzle now—You are not jealous of me?

D. L. No, Faith. But what need of hiding?

D. G. Becauſe I heard a Knocking at the Door, and thought 'twas the Advocate. I was ſoon undeceiv'd indeed; but as the Servant was a Stranger, and I could not conjure that he was yours, 'twas the wiſeſt Way to keep where I was——At leaſt I thought ſo.

Aur. The Jealouſy of theſe Lovers! How are you now, Don *Lewis?*

D. L. Cur'd——quite cur'd——But my Time's come I believe. *(Looking at his Watch.)* ſhall I ſet you down, Don *Gabriel?*

D. G. Unleſs Don *Felix* pleaſes to command me.

Aur. I thank you, Sir; but I was juſt going out. You know where you are to ſup, Don *Lewis?* We may expect you at Seven I ſuppoſe! Another Night I ſhall deſire the Company of your Friend.

D. L. No Ceremony I beg. You may poſſibly ſee me before Seven——And ſo Adieu!—My Compliments to the Lady.

D. G. Sir, Your moſt humble Servant. [*Exit. with Don* Lewis.]

Aur. Your moſt obedient, Sir——*Gil Blas!*

Enter

Enter Gil Blas.

Did you obferve the Face of Don *Gabriel?* Is not there a good deal of the Rogue in't ?

Gil. There's a good deal of t'other Thing in *Ifabella's* I know.

Aur. There Was a Man in the Room it feems.

Gil. I'll be fworn to it. Was it not Don *Gabriel?*

Aur. Ay. He was forc'd to own it ; but endeavour'd to carry it off with a Laugh. With a little of your Addrefs, *Gil Blas,* we fhall be able to make Difcoveries that he won't like.

Gil. I'll warrant you, Madam. But I wifh I had not gone with that Letter——It has lower'd my Spirits I think.

Aur. Why fo pray ?

Gil. *Ifabella's* fo confounded handfome.

Aur. Handfome!——I have heard a different Account of her.

Gil. And fuch an Underftanding too!——But then for Beauty, I never faw any Thing like it.

Aur. The Creature may be tolerable I fuppofe— How fhould fhe carry on her Trade elfe?

Gil. Here fhe came fmiling into the Room, Madam —twirling a Lock of her Hair——Thefe were her Motions—— fo graceful ! fo majeftick !——I had not Courage to fay a Word to her.

Aur. You can talk enough now methinks.

Gil. Who I, Madam?——Yes, yes, I thought how 'twould be. *(Afide.)* I am forry to offend, Madam——but you defir'd a particular Account of her. Her Shape indeed, if one had a Mind to find Fault——

Aur. Is crooked I fuppofe.

Gil. Rather too delicate, Madam. I am for fomething a little plumper—But then 'tis perfectly eafy— I never faw any Thing fo eafy.

Aur. You are a very fine Judge, Sir!

Gil.

Gil. To be sure I did not expect to see such a Woman——But if we can detect her with Don *Ga-briel*——

Aur. Ay, that's the Thing!—How old is she?

Gil. There's the Comfort, Madam—Quite young. —We shall have the less Cunning to deal with.

Aur. I thought she had been turn'd of Thirty.

Gil. Nineteen next October—So her Maid told me. —Lord, Madam! we shall be too hard for so young a Creature I'll warrant you.

Aur. I wonder what makes me so out of Spirits.

Gil. The Weather perhaps. It has been cloudy all Day.

Aur. I believe it is the Weather.

Gil. No doubt on't, Madam——I wish it had the same Effect upon *Isabella*——I never saw such Spirits since I was born.

Aur. We'll talk no more of her. *(Angrily.)* 'Tis doing her too much Honour. You must away with Me to the other Lodgings. Don *Lewis* will be there at Seven; and I have but just Time to change my Dress.

Gil, And how are we to manage, Madam?

Aur. You shall be instructed there——Heigh-ho! —I wish my Spirits were a little better.

Gil. No Matter, Madam. You are to be fatigu'd with your Journey, you know——A little of *I-sabella's* Spirits tho', would not be amiss.

Aur. I told you we'd talk no more of her——I hate the Creature—— so come along, Sir.   [*Exit.*

Gil. Yes, yes, the Tables are turn'd. But I have been an unmerciful Dog, that's the Truth on't.

                         [*Exit.*

                             A C T

ACT III.

SCENE, Aurora's *other Lodgings.*

Enter Laura, *dress'd as a Duenna, and* Gil Blas.

Lau. KEEP your Diſtance, young Man; and pray learn that Gentlewomen of My Years and Diſcretion are not to be pull'd and haul'd about by the Fellows.

Gil. The Jade's really old, and does not know it. (*Aſide.*) Nay, good Madam Gravity, one Kiſs, if it be but by Way of Bleſſing. (*Kiſſes her.*)

Lau. There then—But theſe are Favours you muſt not expect often. I demean myſelf by admitting Servants to Familiarities.

Gil. Faith, *Laura,* you act it mighty well—and let me tell you too, the Dreſs becomes you better than you think it does.

Lau. You are always flattering me, *Gil Blas.*

Gil. No, Faith, not always. I have not ſaid a Word of your Youth and Beauty theſe two Days.

Lau. That's becauſe you have look'd higher, you know——But mum!——

Gil. I'll ſcamper to *Madrid,* Huſſy.

Lau. Pſhaw! 'Twas only Inadvertency—I did not mean any Thing. You remember your Inſtructions, if Don *Lewis* comes?

Gil. If you would not put them out of my Head, you Slut.

Lau. 'Twas a Miſtake I tell you. Is not it Seven? My Lady has been a Woman this half Hour.

A Knocking at the Door.

Hark! This is certainly Don *Lewis*—To your Poſt! Your Poſt, Sir!

F   *Gil.*

Gil. In a Moment, in a Moment—But be fure you flip round the back Way, and knock at the Door, bang, bang. [*Exit.*

Knocking again, Laura *opens the Door.*

Enter Don *Lewis.*

D. *L.* If I am not miftaken, Madam, thefe are the Lodgings of Donna *Aurora.* Pray is Don *Felix* here?

Lau. He was here a few Minutes ago, Sir; but was call'd out upon Bufinefs. His Servant is within, and if Your Name is Don *Lewis,* I believe he has a Meffage for you.

D. L. My Name is *Lewis,* Madam.

Lau. I'll call the Servant, Sir, (*Exit.*

D. *L.* Call'd out upon Bufinefs! This is a little odd methinks: But here comes *Gil Blas.*

Enter Gil Blas.

Where's your Mafter, Sir?

Gil. This Moment gone out, Sir. An Exprefs from *Madrid* has brought him a whole Bundle of Difpatches. I believe Matters are going a little wrong at Court; for he look'd devilifhly political upon reading his Papers.

D. *L.* Did he leave no Commands for me?

Gil. Yes, Sir; that he'd be back in a few Minutes; and that he had defir'd my Lady *Aurora* to entertain you. Her *Duenna* is juft gone to tell her, Sir, I believe fhe's hardly drefs'd yet—— I'll go and enquire.

D. *L.* You need not hurry yourfelf. Your Mafter will return in a few Minutes, you fay——and Donna *Aurora* knows already that I am here.

A Knocking at the Door.

Gil. I knew he would not ftay, Sir. (*opens the Door, and looks out,*) Ha! —well, and what fay You?— You knock with Authority methinks!—It is not my Mafter, Sir; but a Meffenger from him. I'll attend you in a Moment. (*Exit, fhutting the Door after him*

D. *L.*

D. L. Hark!—By all this Ruſtling of Silk now, this ſhould be the Lady—and here ſhe comes—A delicate Creature by my Soul!—and her Duenna with her!——A little prudiſh, or ſo——But no Matter—I can be as prudiſh as ſhe ——.

Enter Aurora, *in Women's Clothes, and* Laura.

This is ſo obliging, Madam—But I'm afraid my abrupt Appearance, in the Abſence of Don *Felix*, will carry more of Curioſity than Reſpect with it— If ſo, Madam——

Aur. No Apology, I beg, Sir. My Brother has deſir'd me to detain you. I expect him every Moment.

D. L. I hope no ill News, Madam.

Aur. I hope not, Sir —only ſome family Matters, I believe, which require Diſpatch. They concern a Gentleman in *Salamanca* too. I doubt my Brother has not found him at home.

D. L. An Angel, by all that's heavenly! (*Aſide.*) You'll pardon me, Madam—but I never ſaw Features ſo like as Your's and my Friend's—You are his very Picture.

Aur. Every Body ſays ſo, Sir—when we are aſunder. We are Twins indeed—but when we are together, the Likeneſs is not ſo great.

Lau. Well put that. (*Aſide.*

D. L. His Voice too!

Lau. I don't know, Sir, whether their Voices mayn't be more alike than their Faces.

Enter Gil Blas.

Gilb. My Maſter has ſent a Meſſage, Madam, that he's ſurrounded with Papers, and can't be back till Supper-time. But if Don *Lewis* is here, he inſiſts upon finding him at his Return.

Aur. You know where he is, I ſuppoſe?

Gil. At the *Phœnix*, Madam.

Aur. He may want you perhaps. Go to him and and haſten him. Tell him he muſt leave Buſineſs till To-morrow; his Friend will think him rude elſe.

Gil. Yes, Madam. (*Exit.*

D. L.

D. L. An abfolute Angel! (*Afide.*

Gil. Won't you be feated, Sir?

D. L. If really I ought to ftay. ———

Aur. Sincerely then, I fhall be glad of your Company. I fecure my Brother by engaging his Friend.

D. L. Now, Madam, you oblige me to ftay.

(*They fit.*

Aur. If You have Sifters, Sir, you know how to excufe the Indifference of Brothers. They think us mighty impertinent Sort of Company.

D. L. Why fo, Madam?

Aur. There are Things call'd Pleafures, Sir. I believe My Brother has a good many—and a Sifter is apt to remark a little too gravely upon 'em.

D. L. The fweet Prude!——(*Afide.*) Not where they are innocent, Madam.

Aur. As my Brother's are—You are wanting to your Friend, Don *Lewis*, if you don't fay That—But come, confefs now—Is not he a little too wild?

Lau. Ay, in my Confcience, a meer Rake!

D. L. He's young, and fpirited, and a Man of Rank, Madam; the World will make Allowances for him.

Aur. You are much in his Heart, I affure you.

Lau. And may help to reform him, Sir——God knows he wants to be reform'd.

D. L. Why, to confefs the Truth, Madam, I have been giving him fome little Advice——He is not naturally bad—rather too volatile, that's all ——

Aur. I fhall laugh out prefently. (*Afide.*

D. L. And I am of a contrary Turn ———over-thoughtful perhaps — too apt to be ferious upon Trifles——

Aur. Nay, I would not have you too ferious neither — Virtue may be drefs'd up with too much Formality——But I beg your Pardon, Sir.

D. L. I lov'd him, at firft, for his own Sake, Madam; but now I have the Honour of knowing his Sifter, my Care for him will be doubled.

Aur.

Aur. You are very obliging, Sir——But your Acquaintance has been fo fhort —— he muft have been ftrangely open with you.

D. L. You are his Sifter—and yet I am guilty of a Breach of Truft—But he really was open with me to a Degree of Imprudence —— Nothing but the Franknefs of his Temper could account for't.

Aur. 'Twas always his Way, Sir—He told you of the Banker's Daughter I fuppofe?

D. L. I wifh he had not, Madam——I loft all Patience with him——To boaft, fays I, of bringing an innocent Creature to Ruin !——Fie, fie, Don *Felix!*— But your young Men of Quality think they have a Right to do any Thing.

Aur. Very true, Sir——What a noble Hypocrite have I fet my Heart upon! *(Afide.)* But pray, Sir— I'm afraid I am going to be impertinent —— You know moft of the Families in this Town?

D. L. I know 'em all, Madam—— But my Intimacies are few—I converfe chiefly with my Books — But why d'you afk, Madam?

Aur. Only, Sir, that a Lady here has very politely made an Offer of vifiting me——How fhe came to know me I can't find out——But 'till I have a little Hint of Characters—For Appearances are deceitful.

D. L. They are indeed, Madam——But if you tell me her Name, 'tis moft likely I fhall know her.

Aur. My Brother faid fo, Sir——He laugh'd a little indeed——but he is fo wild you know——

D. L. Too wild, Madam——But what was her Name?

Aur. And that's mighty odd now——I have really forgot her Name—— What was it, *Laura?*

Lau. I think it was *Ifabella,* Madam.

Aur. Ifabella was the Name——D'you know her, Sir?

D. L. Know her, Madam ! ——I — really don't recollect——

Aur. Nay, no great Matter, Sir—— I thought you might have known her.   *D. L.*

D. L. I'll enquire, Madam——I think I have heard of such a Name——So! so!—— (*Aside.*)

Aur. An Advocate's Daughter, I think, *Laura.*

Laur. So the Meſſenger ſaid, Madam; and that ſhe wou'd wait on you this Evening.

D. L. I hope not, Faith — (*Aside.*) There are ſeveral Advocates in Town, Madam — but I have no Acquaintance with their Daughters.

Aur. I did not know but you might, Sir—But 'tis too late to be deny'd to her—You'll know her when you ſee her perhaps.   [*Knocking at the Door.*]

Lau. I believe this may be the Lady, Madam.[*Exit.*

D. L. The Devil it is, (*Aside.*) —— I am afraid I treſpaſs upon your Time, Madam — To morrow I ſhall hope — (*Going to the Door.*)

Aur. Nay, Sir, I muſt inſiſt upon detaining you— My Brother won't forgive me elſe.

D. L. The Lady's a Stranger, Madam —— And I am no Company for Strangers.

Aur. She may be an Acquaintance, you know.

D. L. If you pleaſe, Madam, I'll wait in the next Room.

Aur. By no Means, Sir; we muſt not loſe you.

D. L. What will become of me? (*Aside.*)

Re-enter *Laura with* Gil Blas.

Aur. O 'tis *Gil Blas!*——What a Fright have I put him in! (*Aside*) Well, Sir! Is he coming?

Gil. Not in haſte, Madam, I'll venture to ſay—— There's a Lawyer with him.

Aur. A Lawyer with him!——He might have left his Law-Affairs till Morning.

Gil. I believe not, Madam. They have a Roll or two of Parchment to read—and then Writings muſt be ſign'd——Pray, Madam, had not you a Relation in the *Indies?*——Don——Don——

Aur. *Iſmael*—my Father's firſt Wife's Brother—— What of Him?

Gil. Nay, not much; only that the poor Gentleman's dead, and theſe Diſpatches bring the News.

Aur.

Aur. But did your Mafter fend no Meffage ?—— If the Lady fhou'd come, *Laura*, I'll be deny'd to her.

D. L. Thank Heaven for that. (*Afide.*)

Gil. The Meffage was, Madam—that you would not wait Supper for him——As for Don *Lewis*, he fays, if he's heartily tir'd, he may leave you ; but he'll take no other Excufe.

Aur. I believe, Sir, I muft not ask you to ftay then.

D. L. Only till I can Make the Excufe.

Aur. What think you of a Party at Piquet then ? I fhall prate too much elfe.

D. L. With all my Heart, Madam —But not for that Reafon.

Aur. Get Cards in the next Room. (*To* Laura) My Friend will fhew you the Way, Sir.——You are fo averfe to new Acquaintance, that I'll be deny'd to all but my Brother.

D. L. You'll oblige me, Madam. —— Never fo out of Countenance in my Life ! (*Afide.*)

Aur. I have a fhort Meffage for *Gil Blas*, and will attend you prefently. [*Exit D. L.*]

Gil. And fo Matters go on fwimmingly, Madam ?

Aur. To my Wifh, *Gil Blas* —— But he has fo abus'd me !

Gil. As Don *Felix*, I fuppofe ?

Aur. And I have fo tormented Him with *Ifabella*— The Scheme took ; he really believ'd fhe was coming to vifit me.—If he does not like me ! —— Nay, I am fure he does like me——He could not have been fo alarm'd elfe.

Gil. Proof pofitive, Madam—But I had like to have forgot—— I found a Letter for you at *Bernarda's.*

Aur. For Me ! You frighten me ! My Brother has not found me out fure ! He certainly knows of my Efcape by this Time.

Gil. Never fear, Madam——It is not a Poft-Letter ; an old Woman brought it. (*Gives a Letter.*)

Aur.

Aur. (Opening and reading it) A Billet-doux, by my Manhood!—You ſhall hear it.   *(Reads)*

' If your Journey has not fatigued you, and
' you have Courage to face a Woman To night, I
' know of one that will engage you.   You will find
' her exactly at Eight, in the cloſe Walk behind *St.*
' *Anne*'s. If ſhe coughs twice, you may ask her
' how her cold does ?

To Don *Felix de Mendoza. (Looking at the Superſcription)* Is this a Trick ?—Or have I really made a Conqueſt ?

Gil. O, a Conqueſt no doubt!

Aur. But where can ſhe have ſeen me ?—No Matter where.——If the Aſſignation be real, the Creature's Diſappointment may ſhame her into Modeſty——How abandon'd are ſome Women !—— *(Throws the Letter upon the Ground)* But Don *Lewis* will think me long.
                                                    [*Exit.*]

Gil. Her Diſappointment may ſhame her into Modeſty !—Very likely truly !—Now, in my poor Opinion, her being diſappointed by one Lover may make her the more eager to ſnap at another.——At leaſt, as I've an Hour upon my Hands, I'll try— *(Takes up the Letter)* Exactly at Eight !——I have no Time to loſe, Faith.   [*Runs out*]

Scene changes to Bernarda's.

Enter Melchior.

Mel. A Pox o' theſe Univerſities, ſay I !—Theſe young Collegians follow their Studies ſo cloſely—there's not a Wench to be had for 'em—No, not ſo much as a Tradeſman's Wife, that will look civil upon a Livery. —And what would vex a good Chriſtian's Heart, the Maids at Home here are above Fifty.—I have been all round the Town—but 'twont do—'twill not do.—

Enter Gil Blas.

Gil. Come, come, the Things ! the Things !—— I muſt dreſs this Moment— the Lady will be impatient elſe. *(Strutting about.)*   *Mel.*

Mel. Ha !—Are you mad, *Gil Blas ?*

Gil. Only a little in Hafte—Women of Condition are not to be trifled with—Is every Thing ready in the Dreffing-room ?—Here, here, Boy ! (*Takes the Letter out of the Cover, and gives it to* Melchior.)— To the adorable Signor *Gil Blas*—So the dear Creature writes. (*Puts the Cover in his Pocket.*) You can read, I think, *Melchior* ——A Volume of Love in four Lines !—And no Ceremony you fee !

Mel. (*Reading.*) If fhe coughs twice you may afk her how her Cold does—An old *Abigail,* troubled with the Phthifick !——And is this to you !

Gil. To me—to me——flipt into my Hands by her Duenna this Moment——So come along, I fay—— But hold ! hold ! —I am thinking that a lac'd Coat would fit mighty eafy upon me. You fhall lend me one of your Mafter's, *Melchior.*

Mel. Indeed but I won't——I'll tell you what tho'——I can lend you a Regimental Coat of my own.

Gil. Of your own ?

Mel. A little old or fo—but perfectly genteel——I bought it for my own Intrigues.

Gil. Your own Intrigues !——O ! you gallant Devil you,——But we'll try it however——You fhall go too, *Melchior.*

Mel. As Your Servant, I fuppofe.

Gil. Why, one would not be unattended upon thefe Occafions. This Amour will make a devilifh Noife in Town.

Mel. Yes ; for you'll tell it every Body—and the poor Devil may lofe a good Service by it.

Gil. A Woman of Quality, upon my Honour—— ——So come along—come along—You fhall fee what a Gentleman I make.

Mel. And what a Gentlewoman the Lady makes ——for She'll borrow a Drefs too, to be Company for your Honour. Ha, ha, ha !　　　[*Exeunt.*

Scene changes to a Grove.

Enter Isabella *and* Beatrice.

Isab. (*Looking at her Watch*) We are before our Time, *Beatrice*; it wants a Quarter of Eight—D'you think he'll come?

Beat. 'Tis the same Thing, I believe, whether he does or not.——I have a mighty indifferent Opinion of these handsome Boys. Don *Lewis* is a Man, Madam.

Isab. And the Man of my Heart, *Beatrice*—But this dear Variety! —That's the Bait to catch Women with.

Beat. But to be struck so at first Sight! and That only from your Window, as he passed by!—'Twas swallowing the Bait somewhat greedily.

Isab. Is not he a Man of Quality, prithee?—young, handsome, and a Stranger?—You know too how my Heart loves travelling.

Beat. Why, those are Reasons I grant you. But to hasten Don *Lewis* away, after an Absence of three Months!—Nay, and when you could have kept him the whole Evening!—There's the Wonder.—Besides, how do you know that Don *Felix* has receiv'd your Note?

Isab. Or that he'll come if he has? Or that I shall like him if he does? Or that He'll like Me?—Or twenty Things besides?—And yet here I am, and as well pleased as ever I was in my Life——So no preaching When the Disappointment comes, we shall have Time to moralize upon't.

Beat. How if Don *Gabriel* should be upon the Watch?

Isab. Let him if he dares——Or if he should——I can silence him with Don *Lewis*. I could curse myself for yielding to that Fellow——There was Variety for you!——I hate him, because he wants me to hate every Body but himself.

Beat. And yet you lov'd him once, Madam.

Isab.

Isab. I lov'd Pleasure——and that did as well. But let me hear no more of him. I shall look as ugly as Death at the very Thoughts of him.

Beat. I beg your Pardon, Madam——I should not have mention'd him, only that I fear'd he was upon the Watch. It was certainly Don *Gabriel* that we saw in the Street just now.

Isab. There let him stay then——We have better Things to talk of——Hark!——I hear Voices——We'll walk this Way a little. [*Exeunt.*

Enter Gil Blas, *dress'd as an Officer, and* Melchior.

Gil. Don't stare so, *Melchior*——You have waited upon several Gentlemen in your Time.

Mel. Never upon so fine a Gentleman.

Gil. A Soldier, *Melchior*——a little of the Soldier——with an honourable Scar or so——But don't flatter me——I hate to be flatter'd—And yet will any one tell me, that this is not the exact Air of a Man of Quality? (*struts about.*)

Mel. Or if it should not be quite so exact, what think you of a Man of Quality's Taylor?

Gil. To be sure now this is not Envy——and yet it smells damnably on't too. Narrow-minded People are always sneering at their Superiors——But don't mind me, *Melchior*, I'm not angry——A Pox on't! Why does not the Lady appear?

Mel. Ay, poor Soul! But you must excuse her, *Gil Blas*——she may have twenty Things to wash up this Afternoon——and then there's herself, you know, after all.

Gil. You'll be brought to Shame presently, Sir— Ha!——Who are those yonder? (*looking out*) What think you now, *Melchior?*

Mel. That we shall have our Bones broke, if you offer to speak to 'em. I'll have no Hand in affronting Gentlewomen.

Gil. Keep your Distance then, and hide behind the Trees—— You are a damn'd mean-spirited Fellow, *Melchior.*

Mel.

Mel. I am for no broken Bones —— that's all.
(*Exeunt.*

S C E N E *changes to another Part of the Grove.*

Enter Ifabella *and* Beatrice.

Ifab. Are they following us?
Beat. Only one of 'em — and he's juft here.
Ifab. My Veil! My Veil then! (*Veils herfelf*) And now for the Signal.

Enter Gil Blas. Ifabella *coughs.*

Gil. Yes, yes, we are all right. (*Afide*) Hem! — The Dampnefs of the Evening, Madam, has encreas'd your Cold, I'm afraid.

Ifab. And made my Cough troublefome — If fo, Sir—Ha!—I don't know you.

Gil. You diflike the Cut of my Coat, perhaps — But 'tis my King's Livery, tho' Service may have worn it bare—I am no Fop, Madam.

Ifab. Your Addrefs was fo familiar, I took you for an Acquaintance.

Gil. Rather for one that Was to be an Acquaintance. But don't be frighten'd, Madam —I am a Man of Honour, and a Soldier.

Ifab. Is that any Thing to me, Sir?

Gil. It may, if you will but hear — Do you know any Thing of this Letter? (*Shewing the Letter*) To Don *Felix de Mendoza*—That's the Direction.

Ifab. And what then, Sir?

Gil. Why then, Madam, you have trufted a Boy with a Secret, which he could not keep — and you ought to be glad 'tis in the Hands of a Man, Madam.

Ifab. How if it is not mine, Sir?

Gil. Only that it goes fnug into my Pocket again. (*Puts the Letter in his Pocket*) And fo, if you'll let me gallant you Home, if I don't know whofe Letter it is, I fhall at leaft know whofe it is not, Madam.

Ifab. Is there any Need of that?

Gil.

Gil. Yes, Faith, Madam, and great Need——For the Soul of me I can't ftir now, till I know who did Not write this Letter.

Ifab. You muft tell firft how you came by it.

Gil. With all my Heart, Madam. Don *Felix* gave it me. There, fays he, Don *Antonio.* —— My Name is *Antonio*, Madam —— You are a Man of Wit and Pleafure, and always at a Lady's Service —— If fhe's a fine Woman, tell her I'll be ready at the next Summons——'Twould have been the fame Thing, if your Name had been to the Letter —— I'mean the Lady's Name who wrote it.

Ifab. I don't doubt it—And for your Honefty, I'll confefs that the Letter Was mine —So now you may give it me, and leave me.

Gil. If it was not for a little dear Curiofity—Will you let me fee your Face, Madam? Upon my Soul, if I don't like it, I'll run and fend Don *Felix* t'you.

Ifab. But fuppofe you fhould like it?

Gil. I'll cut his Throat if he comes near you —— One Peep, Madam, for Love's Sake!

Ifab. I have a great Mind, *Beatrice* —— For, in Spite of his odd Figure, I begin to like him devilifh ly: Nay, and he has oblig'd me too. (*Apart.*)

Gil. Have you confider'd it, Madam?

Ifab. There, Sir. (*Flings afide her Veil*)

Gil. *Ifabella*, by St. *Jago!* ——That I fhould not know her Voice! (*Afide.*)

Ifab. And now you may run to Don *Felix.*

Gil. To Your Arms, my Angel! — I can run no-where elfe.

Ifab. Hold! hold!—not fo faft!—Your Bufinefs is with Don *Felix*——You may tell him how ugly the Lady was, he had the Gallantry to difappoint.

Gil. Faith, and fo I will —— and no great Lie neither (*Afide.*) But I'll be as filent as Death, Madam. ——What do you intend to do with me?

Ifab. I intend to bid you Good-night——That's all, Sir.

Gil.

Gil. Have you no Mercy with fo much Beauty ?—
By Heavens, I won't ftir without you.

Ifab. I fhall find a Way to make you. Come,
Child, we muft be going. (*To* Beatrice.)

Gil. Yes, Child, we muft be going.

Ifab. You don't intend to follow us?

Gil. No——I intend to go along with you.

Ifab. Was there ever fuch Affurance ? —— I'll cry
out.

Gil. I'll ftop your Mouth. (*Offering to kifs her.*

Ifab. Not for the World!——We fhall be difcover'd.
—If you Will follow, let it be at a Diftance——Any
Thing to get Home.

Gil. But will you promife to let me in, when you
Are at Home?——Upon my Soul, I'll break your
Windows elfe.

Ifab. Keep your Diftance then—The Man's bewitch'd I think—— I hope he won't lofe me tho'
(*Afide, and exit with* Beatrice.

Enter Melchior *at the other Door.*

Mel. Hip! hip!—*Gil Blas !*

Gil. I'm in Hafte, I'm in Hafte, *Melchior* —— So
come along——come along——There fhe goes !

Mel. Take care that fomebody does not Come——
You have been watch'd I can tell you.

Gil. Ha !—— But fo it is when a Man intrigues
with Women of Quality—Zounds ! I fhall lofe Sight
of her——Before you keep clofe to me. (*Exit.*

Mel. Which, if I do, hang me. No, Faith——If
I ftand the Brunt of a Battle, there muft be Plunder.
——The Impudence of this Rafcal!——But fince the
Devil's let loofe among the Women, I'll e'en make
another Trial for myfelf——So Fortune or a Blanket
attend you, my Dear. (*Exit.*

Enter Don Gabriel.

D. G. Yes, yes, 'twas an Appointment ! I faw
her unveil. I faw how her Eyes gloated upon him—
A Stranger too!——How came fhe acquainted with
him ?——No Matter——I fhall know prefently. By
the

The Help of this Key (*Pulling out a Key*) I can steal upon 'em thro' the Garden. She hates me, and I'll be reveng'd. Don *Lewis* shall know of all. She threatens me with Ruin; but no Matter. My Letters to her are burnt —— I saw 'em burnt —— My Friend shall be prepar'd —Her Gallant shall feel me too— A Curse light upon the Sex——and a double Curse upon the Fools that trust 'em.   (*Exit.*

S C E N E *changes to* Isabella's.

Enter Isabella *and* Gil Blas.

Isab. Follow me to my very Dressing-Room!—Of all the impudent Fellows I ever saw in my Life ——

Gil. You like Me the best. —Why, Faith, as you say, there's nothing like Impudence upon these Occasions.——You look devilishly tempting.

Isab. You talk devilishly saucy.

Gil. Is that your Chamber?

Isab. And what then?

Gil. Nay, nothing at all.

Isab. The Door's lock'd.

Gil. We'll see that presently —— No struggling now——Nay, then! (*Catches her in his Arms.*)

Isab. I won't be pull'd so—I'll call out.

Gil. It shall be from the next Room then.

Isab. Is the Devil in you?

Gil. Ten thousand of 'em, my Angel! —Don't you find how strong I am? (*Carrying her to the Door.*

Isab. I do——I do—Mercy! Mercy!

Enter Beatrice.

Beat. Undone, undone! Madam! —— There's Don *Gabriel* come in the Backway, and running up Stairs.

Gil. Don *Gabriel!*—The Devil he is! If he should know me now!—Lock'd sure enough! (*Aside, and trying to open the Chamber Door*) What's to be done now, Madam?

Isab. Oh! never mind him—I'll treat him as he deserves.   *Gil.*

Gil. That's more than I shall, I am sure—Yes, yes, 'tis Don *Gabriel!*——How will this end? [*Aside.*]

Enter Don *Gabriel.*

D. G. So, Madam, you are found at last!

Isab. You shall repent this, Sir.

D. G. Perhaps not——

Isab. Leave me this Moment.

D. G. Not till I have Satisfaction here, Madam.
(*Looking at* Gil Blas.)

Gil. O Lord! O Lord! (*Aside*) Have I done you any Injury, Sir?

D. G. You have, Sir, —— who Are you?

Isab. A Gentleman and My Friend. You are answer'd, I hope.

Gil. Ay, Sir; a Gentleman, and this Lady's Friend—You are answer'd, I hope.

D. G. The Gentleman shall be try'd Sir, —Follow me this Moment.

Gil. She won't let us fight sure! (*Aside.*)

Isab. How, if I desire him to stay?

Gil. Ay, Sir—how if the Lady desires me to stay?—I'll meet him in the Morning, Madam. [*Apart.*]

Isab. I am Mistress of myself, and accountable to no Man; therefore leave me this Moment.

Gil. I wish he would. [*Aside.*]

Isab. Hark you, Sir——(*To D. Gabriel.*)

Gil. He does not know me—that's my Comfort—I should certainly have been kick'd else. [*Aside.*]

Isab. You have found me with a Stranger—I appointed him——Tell it Don *Lewis*——But remember You and I fall together. (*Apart.*) Leave me, I say—I am Mistress of my own House, and Will be so of my Conduct.

D. G. You shall find, Madam, you are accountable to Me—For You, Sir—

Gil Now it comes. [*Aside.*]

D. G. I must be acquainted with you.

Gil. O, Sir——As to that ——You shall know me Time enough—My Name, Sir——My Name is Don
Antonio

Antonio Callabavaro de Paſſiado—And hark you, Sir
—*(Whiſpers.)* No Words before the Lady — You
have heard of the *Callabavaro*'s?

D. G. No Matter, Sir—I'll be punctual—And now,
Madam, I ſhan't ſtay to diſturb you. Your mean
deſcending to ſuch a Wretch as this, has taught me
to deſpiſe you. When we meet next, my Friend ſhall
be of the Party. Think on't and tremble. [*Exit.*]

Iſab. I laugh at you.

Gil. So do I—now he's gone. *(Aſide.)* Who is he,
Madam?

Iſab. A Villain. *(Walking in Confuſion.)*

Gil. Would I were gone too—For the Devil of any
Paſſion has he left me but Fear. *(Aſide.)*

Iſab. Was it a Challenge you gave him?

Gil. A Challenge, Madam!—Was it for a Man of
Rank, and a Soldier too, to be ſaluted with a—who
are you—and I muſt be acquainted with you?——I'll
be damn'd angry, and ſo ſteal off. [*Aſide.*]

Iſab. Has this Man Courage or not? *(Aſide.)* You
are thoughtful, Sir.

Gil. His Name is Don *Gabriel*, you ſay——

Iſab. And lodges in the Square—Every body knows
him.

Gil. And lodges in the Square!——Every body
knows him!

Iſab. I don' blame your Reſentment.——

Gil. O ho! *(Aſide.)* I'll not ſleep till I have found
him.

Iſab. A Villain and a Coward, Sir.

Gil. Yes, yes, I muſt murder him I ſee. *(Aſide.)*
Shall I bring you an Account of him To-morrow?

Iſab. To-morrow!

Gil. Ay, Madam, To-morrow——I am unworthy
of you till then—Reputation, Madam!—Reputation!
—A Soldier's Reputation!

Iſab. To-morrow then at four——You'll remember
the Hour?

H   *Gil.*

Gil. Or die for my Revenge—I am no Boaster, Madam —— But Tomorrow *Don Antonio Callabayaro de Paſſiado* ſhall bring you Proofs of his Birth and Courage —— Angels guard you — Well off, Faith! (*Aſide and exit.*)

Iſab. 'Tis well, Don *Gabriel!*——You have broken in upon my Pleaſures, and may anſwer for it with your Life.

Enter Beatrice.

Beat. Is not this Gentleman a Sort of a Bluſterer, Madam?

Iſab. He is not a Don *Gabriel*, and therefore no Favourite of Your's. But he's a pretty Fellow, and I like him—Nay, and I'll Have him too—You had beſt tell Don *Gabriel* of my Appointment with him Tomorrow.

Beat. Have you any Cauſe to ſuſpect me, Madam?

Iſab. I am in doubt about it—When I have Certainty, I ſhall know how to behave. This *Gabriel* is a Villain; but let him betray me if he dares—A Fig for Reputation! I'll have done with it—My Life ſhall be a Life of Pleaſure, let the World ſay what it will, Follow me. (*Exeunt.*)

A C T IV.

SCENE *Bernarda's.*

Enter Aurora *in Boy's Clothes and* Gil Blas.

Aur. O! I have kill'd myſelf with laughing! That *Iſabella* ſhould be the Writer of that Aſſignation!——

Gil. Or that I ſhould be her Gallant!—Faith, Madam, I was only upon a Frolick—Little did I think of meeting *Iſabella*.

Aur. You have not faid a Word to Don *Lewis?*

Gil. I have not feen him, Madam.

Aur. What's o'Clock?

Gil. Almoft Time for Me to be a Soldier again —— Paft Three, Madam —— But I have not kill'd Don *Gabriel* — I've been worfe than my Word there.

Aur. O! he's beneath your Notice ——You are too fine a Gentleman.

Gil. The fine Gentleman may get his Bones broketho

Aur. Never fear, never fear ——Every Thing we do has Fortune in't.——But, upon my Word, Don *Lewis*'s Eyes were fo fix'd upon me laft Night, that I could hardly keep my Countenance.

Gil. For Heaven's Sake, no Blufhing now, Madam. ——Don *Felix* muft be impudent——You may blufh the more for't when you are *Aurora.*

Aur. You muft affift me then. Watch both our Looks; and when you fee Occafion, break into our Difcourfe with any Thing you can invent —— No Matter how abfurd.

Gil. Never fear, Madam.

Aur. To bind him fafter to me, I'll be as whim-fical as I can make myfelf.

Gil. In the Perfon of Don *Felix.*

Aur. I mean fo. *Ifabella*'s the Theme. If he talks to me of *Aurora*, as I have a thoufand little Whifpers he will, *Ifabella* muft be the Bar to his being ferious with me.—Run and tell him I am drefs'd.

Gil. In a Moment, Madam. [*Exit.*

Aur. (*Mufing.*) Right! right!——I have it!—— Difgrace my Rival firft——be cool to my Friend—— give my Lover one fhort Sight of me in Petticoats; by Stealth too, to make it fweeter——and then to Horfe——And if he does not follow me to *Madrid* ——I have not the Charms I think I have.

Enter Don Lewis *and* Gil Blas.

D. L. What, but juft drefs'd!——Faith you ftaid it out laft Night. I began to fufpect you were play-ing the Devil.

Aur. Bufinefs, upon my Honour——We mix'd a little Wine with it indeed.

D. *L*. But was there no Wench in the Cafe?

Aur. Pfhaw! You don't think me fo ill bred—— 'Twas You had the Wench. How long did you ftay with her?

D. *L*. About Half an Hour————But 'twas the fhorteft Half Hour I ever knew in my Life.

Aur. Tho' it lafted——let me fee——from Seven in the Evening to One in the Morning——unlefs you went any where elfe.

D. *L*. No, faith——And what's worfe, I fhall never wifh to go any where elfe. (*Sighs*)——But my dear Don *Felix*, not a Word of *Ifabella*——How could you laugh fo Yefterday, when your Sifter enquir'd about her? It was not kind in you.

Aur. Faith, I could not help laughing——A fine Acquaintance for my Sifter, upon my Word!—— But are you and I to be afham'd of what we do? I think we are of Quality enough to be afham'd of nothing.

D. *L*. Well, well——But no laughing——no *Ifabella*, I beg of you.

Aur. I won't——I won't——

D. *L*. Let me look at you a little.

Aur. Ha!——What the Devil ails you?

D. *L*. Upon my Soul, I'll give you Half my Eftate, if you'll fend for *Aurora*'s Gown and Cap, and wear 'em for an Hour.

Gil. Sir, Sir!——I'll wear 'em for the leaft Farm upon your Eftate.

Aur. *Aurora*'s Gown and Cap!——And what then?

D. *L*. Only that I may kneel t'you, and kifs the Back of your Hand——Zounds! you'd be her very felf! her fweet, fweet felf!

Aur. The Man's mad, I believe. (*Turning away.*)

D. *L*. Stark ftaring mad! Incurably mad!—— 'Tis all Your Doing, Don *Felix*——and You muft take Care of me.

Aur.

Aur. I don't underſtand you.

D. *L.* Nor I myſelf——only that my Buſineſs is done. ——

> *O! that the Gods, in Pity to Mankind*——

Gil. *Had made Her ugly——or Don* Lewis *blind!*——
Go on, Sir——We ſhall make it out between us.

D. *L.* I ſhall never come down to Proſe again.

Gil. Proſe, Sir!——My Lady *Aurora* was never thought of in Proſe——Try your Hand once more.

D. *L.* Hold your prating, Raſcal——Hark you, Don *Felix,* ——I have ſeen your Siſter.

Aur. I know it. And you're enclin'd to be mighty merry about her——But let me tell you, I have known Men that have lik'd her.

D. *L.* Is there any particular one She likes?

Aur. Every Soul that likes Her, I ſuppoſe.

Gil. A grateful Diſpoſition that! (*Aſide.*)

D. *L.* Shall I ſpeak plainly of her?

Aur. Ay, if you don't abuſe her.

D. *L.* You won't be in Earneſt, I ſee.

Aur. Yes, Faith, if I thought You were ſo.

D. *L.* In Earneſt then, I love your Siſter——And in Earneſt too, I muſt have Your Leave to tell her ſo.

Aur. You Have told her ſo, perhaps.

D. *L.* No, upon my Honour. If ſhe has gueſs'd at my Heart, 'twas only from the Looks I could not hide from her.

Aur. My Siſter had her Looks too, I ſuppoſe.

D. *L.* None, but what Civility and Good-humour gave her.

Aur. I am glad of that tho'——for I was ſadly afraid of myſelf. (*Aſide.*) This is a very odd Affair, Don *Lewis.* My Leave to tell her ſo!——Impoſſible!——You can't be in Earneſt.

D. *L.* I am, by all my Hopes——Moſt abſolutely in Earneſt.

Aur. What!——When I am privy to your Intrigue with another?

D.

D. L. Iſabella!——You ſhall ſoon ſee an End of That Affair.

Aur. Why, what d'you intend?

D. L. To ſee her once more, and have done with her for ever.

Aur. Has ſhe us'd you ill?

D. L. Not that I know of——

Gil. No Matter for that, Sir——Don *Lewis* may uſe Her ſo I hope.

Aur. Hold your Peace, Sir — And learn to know the Times when your Impertinence may be borne. (*Angrily.*) Look you, Don *Lewis*——I can be neither Friend nor Enemy in this Buſineſs till I ſee my Siſter —and That ſhall be preſently.

D. L. And at your Return, *Iſabella* ſhall be no longer an Objection. (*Going.*)

Aur. Stay, Don *Lewis.* I own I am perplex'd, and know not how to act. I wiſh you had kept this Declaration a Secret from me. I had News for you, that Friendſhip requir'd me to tell —— and now it will look like an officious Concern for my Siſter.

D. L. What is it?——Speak!

Aur. *Iſabella*'s a ——I won't name the Word nei-ther——But *Gil Blas* knows it, and can prove it.

D. L. With all my Heart, Faith——What is it, *Gil Blas?*

Gil. Nay, Sir, no great Matter—— Only that I happen'd to ſee a Gentleman let out at her Back-door laſt Night.

D. L. Don *Gabriel,* I ſuppoſe?

Gil. No, upon my Soul, Sir — Quite another Sort of a Gentleman——A rampant young Fellow of about My Size——I never ſaw a finer Figure of a Man ſince I was born.

D. L. At what Time of the Evening was this?

Gil. About Nine—when You were with my Lady *Aurora.*

D. L. And did you dog him?

Gil.

Gil. His Sword was a little of the longeft — Lord,
Sir! he'd have fpitted me like a Lark——He was not
above My Size neither——But the fineft put together!
——I don't believe you'll match him in all *Spain.*

D. *L.* You are fure 'twas *Ifabella's* Back-door?

Gil. I'll fwear to that, Sir — and to her Maid's
letting him out. You have bewitch'd my Miftrefs,
fays fhe, in a Whifper. ——And he took the Way to
bewitch the Maid too—for I faw him put a fwinging
Purfe into her Hand—And then he was turning upon
his Heel, Sir——But you'll remember To-morrow at
Four, fays fhe — My Miftrefs will die if you don't
come——O! damn your Miftrefs, thought I to myfelf—Ay, ay, fays he—And the Dog was fo carelefs!
——Ay, ay; tell her I'll come and die With her——
Hey! *Sancho! Diego! Lopez!*—And away he flid, Sir,
in a Minuet-Step, with three Footmen at his Heels.

D. *L.* If this Story be true, I fhall be neither
angry nor forry. For to deal plainly with you, Don
Felix, fince I have feen your Sifter, all Women elfe
are indifferent to me.

Enter Melchior.

Mel. Don *Gabriel* is below, Sir.

D. *L.* Shall I afk him up?

Aur. By all Means—Defire the Gentleman to walk
up. (*To* Melchior, *who goes out.*) Will you tell him
of this Difcovery?

D. *L.* To be fure I will——and you fhall fee him
ftare as if a Fit had feiz'd him. Don *Gabriel* has too
much Honefty in himfelf to find out the Want of it
in another.

Gil. To be fure, Sir, a mighty worthy Man——
But liable to be impos'd upon.

Re-enter Melchior *with Don* Gabriel, *and Exit.*

D. *G.* Servant, Servant, Gentlemen——I have
News for you, Don *Lewis.*

D. *L.* I have News for You too——*Ifabella's* the
Devil.

D. *G.* That's My News—How did you hear it?

D. *L.* From

D. L. From. *Gil Blas* here.

Gil. Yes, Sir, from Me.

D. G. From you!——What Intelligence have You?

D. L. The Intelligence of his Eyes and Ears. He faw a Gentleman let out at her Back-door laft Night, and over-heard an Appointment for To-day.

D. G. That's well——But he could not tell you that I broke in upon 'em——Such a pitiful, contemptible, rafcally, fneaking, cowardly Wretch!——I could have torn her Piece-meal for even looking at him.

Gil. Sir!—Pitiful, contemptible, rafcally, cowardly!——Faith, to my Mind now, the Gentleman was a mighty good-looking Sort of a Gentleman.

D. G. A Gentleman!——A Monkey has more Manhood in him.

Gil. Paffion, Sir! Paffion!——You faw him thro' the falfe Medium of Paffion.

D. G. Paffion!——What, with a Worm!——The Wretch was beneath trampling upon.

Gil. O Lord! O Lord!——But there's certainly fome Miftake in this—We don't mean the fame Perfon, Sir.

D. G. Was not he drefs'd in Red?

Gil. Yes, he was. But 'twas not the Colour of his Coat that ftruck me——'Twas his Air—his—his Dignity——Come, he had fome Dignity—You muft allow him a little—Dignity.

D. G. O!—Abundance of Dignity!

Gil. Some People's Eyes!——That's all I fay—Some People's Eyes!

Aur. Gil. Blas!——Why, I think Accounts differ a little. (*Apart.*)

D. L. But what did you do with him?

D. G. Would you think it?——The Fellow challeng'd me.

Gil. I told you he had Courage, Sir. (*To Don Lewis.*)

D. G. Ay

D. G. Ay——But he forgot the Appointment.
I waited for him two Hours after the Time this
Morning, with a Horfewhip for my Weapon.

Gil. And did you think he'd come, Sir?——As if
a Gentleman would come to be horfe-whipt!—O fad!
O fad!

D. L. How do you know of the Affignation To-
day?

D. G. Her Ladyfhip's Maid was with me. The
Fellow meets her at Four, fhe fays; and fhe'll open
the Door to us——fo come away with Me.

D. L. To your Lodgings?

D. G. Ay. I have fomething elfe to tell you. She
has a Plot to make Me as black as herfelf. We
have only Half an Hour to confult in.

D. L. I'll follow you then——I have a Word for
Don *Felix* firft.

D. G. You won't be long?——I'll wait for you in
your own Apartments—Don *Felix*, your Servant.[*Ex.*

Aur. And d'you intend going to her Houfe?

D. L. Yes—and taking Leave of her in Form.

Aur. You'll punifh the Gentleman tho'?

D. L. Yes, Faith, will I——

Gil. So! So! (*Afide.*)

D. L. Moft heartily——

Gil. I'll not go, that's flat. (*Afide.*)

D. L. By giving him the Lady.

Gil. O ho!——then all's fafe. (*Afide.*)

D. L. But Don *Gabriel* expects me. Shall I meet
you at *Aurora*'s?

Aur. No—I fhall ftay but an Hour there; and
fhould take it as a Favour if you left her to herfelf, till we meet To-morrow.

D. L. Nay, that's too much——I have Leave to
vifit her this Evening.

Aur. You'll oblige by deferring this Vifit.

D. L. You hurt me, Don *Felix*——I did not expect
fuch Coolnefs.

I *Aur.*

Aur. I am forry for that.   You may find me warmer To-morrow perhaps.

D. L. Well, Sir——it muſt be as You pleaſe. If *Iſabella*'s the Objection, I am going to her for the laſt Time. Adieu.   [*Exit.*

Aur. Yours, Sir. Poor Fellow, how I have teaz'd him!——But Oppoſition is your only Quickener. You muſt away to the Appointment, *Gil Blas.*

Gil. I ſhall certainly be kick'd.

Aur. No, no, 'tis but diſcovering yourſelf, and the Matter ends in a Laugh——But a Word before you go——When the Buſineſs is over at *Iſabella*'s——

Gil. I wiſh it Was over.

Aur. You muſt hurry Don *Lewis* to *Aurora.*

Gil. Hey-day !——I thought you inſiſted upon his keeping away.

Aur. Ay, that, by Your Inſtructions, I may be ſure of ſeeing him. I'll be deny'd to him, when he comes tho'——*Laura* ſhall tell him that my Brother's with me——who ſhall reſent this Viſit——He has made a Point, you know, of his not ſeeing me.

Gil. You'll appear to him in Breeches then ?

Aur. Not till To-morrow.——But to haſten him to *Aurora*, you muſt hint to him that you have Suſpicions of your Maſter——That he has no Sincerity in him——That he has private Deſigns, and intends oppoſing him with his Siſter. You may fling in a Hint too, that the Lady likes him——that her Brother's out of the Way——In ſhort, any Thing——ſo you get him to viſit me, and to break his Promiſe with Don *Felix.*

Gil. Which if I don't——

Aur. Away, away then !——But don't forget, and go to the Appointment in thoſe Cloaths.

Gil. What forget the very Eſſence of a Gentleman !——I'll ſend *Melchior* for a Chair for you—— Hey ! *Melchior* ! Call a Chair for my Maſter——and then, d'you hear? —Call another for Me. [*Exit.*

Aur. And now I ſhall know, in a few Hours, the Succeſs of this wild Scheme.——But how if my Brother
ther

ther fhould be at *Madrid!*——Nay, if he fhould have trac'd me hither!——The Comfort is, that he knows nothing of *Gil Blas*, or *Gil Blas* of Him——fo they may meet and pafs without Difcovery——As for myfelf, he fhall find it hard to catch me—unlefs upon the Road to *Madrid*—and then it fhall be the Fault of my Horfe——Well! If ever Woman took fuch Pains for a Man! Why—I hope fhe got him, that's all. [*Exit.*

SCENE *another Apartment.*

Enter Don Lewis *and Don* Gabriel.

D. *L.* Why did not you tell me of this?——You have fufpected her a good while then?

D. *G.* Of an immoderate Love of Pleafure. But I had no downright Proofs of her Infamy, and therefore faid nothing.

D. *L.* And whenever you upbraided her, fhe threaten'd you with Deftruction?

D. *G.* Ay. I fhould not wonder if fhe told you I had ravifh'd her. Give Don *Lewis* but a Hint of my Difhonefty, fays fhe, and your Ruin is inevitable—I'll fwear to him that you have whor'd me——That his Friend, his Bofom Friend, the Man whom he fupports, has whor'd me. 'Tis not your Innocence that fhall guard you from my Revenge.

D. *L.* Was this Yefterday?

D. *G.* Yefterday, when I broke in upon her. And my Life upon't fhe keeps her Word.

D. *L.* I hope fo, Faith. My honeft *Ifabella!* Why, this is exactly as I could wifh it. How heard you of the Appointment To-day?

D. *G.* Her Ladyfhip's Maid was with me—She'll open the Door to us.

D. *L.* I fhall be quite the Gentleman with her.

D. *G.* And fhe the Devil with You——But come; we muft haften to our Place of Rendezvous——*Beatrice* will appear at the Window, if the Fellow comes.

D. *L.* Away then——You are hurt, Don *Gabriel,* but I am pleas'd with her Infamy. [*Exeunt.*

I 2 SCENE

S C E N E *changes to* Ifabella's.

Enter Ifabella *and* Beatrice.

Ifab. You have fecur'd the Garden-Door?

Beat. Safe enough, I'll warrant you.

Ifab. And you have heard nothing of the Stranger and Don *Gabriel* To-day?

Beat. Not a Syllable.

Ifab. I wonder if they met—— But Don *Gabriel* thought better on't perhaps.

Beat. Or the Stranger, Madam.

Ifab. I have a better Opinion of him. Is it Four yet?

Beat. The Clock has juft ftruck.

Ifab. Leave me then—— And fee you admit no one but Him.

Beat. Yes, Madam. And yet you may have other Vifitors, or I am fee'd to no Purpofe. (*Afide, and exit.*

Ifab. I have Reafon to fufpect this Wench——She's a Creature of Don *Gabriel*'s——But let the worft happen, I am prepar'd for't. (*A Knocking at the Door.*) Hark!—— here's fomebody coming——I grow old and ugly by thinking of this *Gabriel* — But here comes one to make me young again.

Enter Beatrice *with* Gil Blas, *drefs'd.*

Gil. Servant, Madam——Handfomer than ten thoufand Angels —— I believe we fhan't want You, Child. (*To* Beatrice.) And befides, I don't mightily like that Face of yours.

Beat. Sir!—— I fhan't ftay to frighten you. But you may chance to fee Faces prefently, that you'll like lefs. (*Afide and exit.*)

Ifab. What have you done with Don *Gabriel?*

Gil. What a Gentleman of My Rank ought to do with the Vulgar——Nothing at all, Madam.

Ifab. Haven't you feen him then?

Gil. Upon my Honour, not I——Poverty is apt to make Men defperate——And we Gentlemen of affluent

Fortunes,

Fortunes, who know how to enjoy Life, know how to prize it too!

Iſab. Your Servant, Sir. My Woman will open the Door for you. (*Turning away.*)

Gil. Ha! —What! — Is any Thing the Matter, Madam?

Iſab. Nothing at all, Sir, —— Good-bye t'you.
(*Going.*

Gil. You are not in Earneſt ſure? — Juſt as I expected.   (*Aſide.*)

Iſab. Your Way lies there, Sir. (*Pointing to the Door.*) I have Buſineſs.

Gil. And ſo have I, Faith. (*Getting between her and the Door.*) Look you, Madam——This won't do. ——You and I muſt not part ſo.

Iſab. Is this the Man of Honour and Courage! — That could not ſleep for his Revenge!—Is this——

Gil. Why, really, Madam, I did intend to have cut his Throat—— But I don't know how it was, I chang'd my Mind.

Iſab. As I have mine, Sir—Begone this Moment. (*A Noiſe without.*)—What Noiſe is that?

D. G. (*Without.*) Don't tell Me—Did not we ſee him go in?

Beat. (*Without.*) You are miſtaken, Sir— 'Twas a Gentleman to Me—My Miſtreſs is not at Home.

D. L. (*Without.*) We'll try that preſently.

Iſab. Don *Lewis* too! —— Nay, then! —— But let 'em come.   (*Aſide.*)

Gil. Is the Devil in the Houſe?——But if you love Blood, Madam, you ſhall ſee whether I have Courage or not.

      Enter Don Lewis *and Don* Gabriel.

D. L. Don't be alarm'd, Madam——The Viſit is a little abrupt indeed—but you know how to excuſe it— I have ſeen that Face before. (*Looking at* Gil Blas.

Gil. And may poſſibly ſee it again, Sir.

Iſab. Well, Sir!——You have found me!

      D. L.

D. L. Reports are often falfe, Madam — I thank you for the Satisfaction of my Eyes.

Ifab. 'Twas a Satisfaction I intended you——So I have a Right to your Thanks —— I fhall deferve Don *Gabriel's* too.

D. G. You have 'em with all my Heart, Madam. —But we muft thank the Gentleman, Don *Lewis.*

Gil. Nay, Sir, as to that —— I fhan't infift upon Ceremony.

D. L. (*Walking up to* Gil Blas.) I have certainly feen this Face——May I beg to know where, Sir?

Gil. You fhall know it at a proper Time, Sir:

D. L. Where did you fteal thefe Cloaths?—They don't fit you.

Gil. Steal 'em, Sir?

D. G. Ay, Sir, fteal 'em—But you have forgot, I fuppofe —— as you did your Appointment with Me, Rafcal! (*Takes him by the Collar.*)

Gil. Hands off, Sir!——You are two to one upon me——But I expect to be treated like a Soldier.

D. G. Like a Soldier, Sirrah! (*Shakes him.*)

Ifab. Is this Behaviour for My Houfe, Sir? (*To D.* Gabriel, *who lets him go.*)

Gil. 'Tis mighty odd Behaviour, Madam.

D. G. Say you fo, Sir? (*Offers to take hold of him.*)

D. L. (*Interpofing.*) Hold, Don *Gabriel!* — You'll frighten him into Fits.

Gil. No, Sir——nor both of you.

D. G. Prithee let me come at him.—I'll only fhake him a little.

Ifab. You fhall repent this Outrage.

Gil. Why, that's very kind now——(*Afide.*) Pray, be compos'd Madam——You fhall find me a Match for 'em prefently —— For You, Don *Lewis*, I know you.

D. L. Ha! —— You know my Name indeed —— Where was it you knew me?

Gil. Your Memory fails you, Sir——But I can re-frefh it.

D. L.

D. _L._ Do it this Moment then.

D. _G._ I'll quicken him a little. (*Offers to take hold of him again.*

D. _L._ Hold, I fay!——Who are you, Sir?

Gil. A Gentleman, Sir——and one that has oblig'd you——You have infulted a Man, Sir, that has done you Services ——Services, Sir, that I fhan't upbraid you with——tho' it is Ingratitude in you to forget 'em——I have never clean'd your Shoes indeed—— No, Sir, I am above it — But I have run of your Errands——I have really run of your Errands —— The Name of Don _Antonio Callabavaro de Paffiado_ may found ftrange t'you perhaps——But I have another at your Service—— Look in my Face, Sir —— What think you of your Friend Don _Gil Blas de Santilane?_

D. _L._
and _Gil Blas!_
D. _G._

Gil. The very fame, Sir—— Don _Felix_'s humble Servant, and your Honour's—A Pox upon this Patch! ——I fhall tear away my Skin with it——(*Pulls off his Patch.*) There, Sir!—And now I believe you'll beg my Pardon.

Ifab. Am I impos'd upon?——Who are you?

Gil. Only Don _Felix_'s Servant, Madam—The fame that brought you a Letter yefterday from Don _Lewis._ ——You remember how you admir'd my Wit, Madam!

D. _L._
and _Ha, ha, ha!_
D. _G._

Ifab. Am I detected with a Servant then? (*Snatches Don Lewis's Sword, and runs at* Gil Blas.) Die, Villain!

D. _L._ Hold, Madam! — This Sword is mine —— (*Wrefts it from her Hands.*)

Gil. Pray take Care of her, Gentlemen.

Ifab. Well, Sir! you have difarm'd me. Give me the Sword again, and I'll direct it properly. (*Looking*
at

at Don Gabriel, *who laughs*) Ay, laugh at me, do——
You have caught me——But your triumph fhall be
fhort. I am difgrac'd by a Contrivance——and your
Glory is, that three Men have been too hard for a
Woman.

Gil. No, Madam——They knew no more of me
than your Ladyfhip.

Ifab. No Matter. They have hurt my Pride only.
I am innocent with You, Sir—I found you to be a
Wretch.

Gil. Very true, Madam.

Ifab. But with that Villain there, I have been guilty.
(Pointing to D. Gabriel.)

D. L. That we expected, Madam.

D. G. Ha, ha, ha!—No Interruptions, I beg, Sir.

Ifab. Yes, Sir, for a Moment——that you may
laugh once more. But remember 'tis the laft Time.

D. G. Pray proceed, Madam.

Ifab. To Your everlafting Ruin. Read thefe Letters,
Sir, *(giving Letters to Don* Lewis) and fee to whom
they are directed. What, thunder-ftruck! *(To D.*
Gabriel) You faw 'em burnt, did you ?—But not all,
Sir——You fhould have been fecure of that. I knew
you to be a Villain, and referv'd thefe for your De-
ftruction.

D. L. The Letters are in Your Hand, Don *Gabriel.*
(Reading.)

D. G. Forg'd——Every Word of 'em forg'd.

D. L. I'll read, Sir.

Gil. How like a Rogue he looks! I fhall afk him
about my Dignity prefently. *(Afide.)*

Ifab. I can tell you the Contents, Sir. *(To Don* Gabriel) A few Pieces of private Hiftory to blacken your
Friend. 'Twas a Point you labour'd at, to fecure me
to yourfelf. Don *Lewis* will tell you, whether they
are forg'd or not.

D. L. Thefe Letters muft be mine, Madam. *(Putting them in his Pocket.)* For You, Sir! *(Walking up
to Don* Gabriel.) Never fee my Face again. You are
fallen

fallen even below my Refentment——The Hand-writing is Yours, Sir—tho' I had doubted my own Eyes, but for Circumftances in the Letters, that only You were privy to. Farewel both. I leave you fit Company for one another. Come, *Gil Blas.* (*Going*)

Gil. Sir! Sir!—Only for a Moment, Sir—I came In like a Gentleman, and methinks would fain go Out like one——And fo, Madam, as our Intrigue is at an End——

Ifab. Begone, Sir.

Gil. I fay, Madam, as our Intrigue is at an End, I wifh you all the Happinefs with that good-looking Gentleman, that a reafonable Woman can expect—He's a little heavy or fo—but a Man of excellent Morals——And fo I take my Leave——

D. L. Come, Sir——I have a Word for you too.

Gil. I'll attend you, Sir.

Ye Loves and Graces hover round this Pair,
And make their Virtues your peculiar Care.

(*Exit with* Don *Lewis.*)

D. Gabriel *and* Ifabella *ftand for fome Time looking at each other.*

Ifab. Leave me.

D. G. You have undone me.

Ifab. And therefore I am happy——fuperlatively happy!

D. G. I have undone You too.

Ifab. No Matter—Leave me, I fay.

D. G. I dare not leave you!—I doat upon you.

Ifab. I hate you.

D. G. 'Twas my Love for you that did this——Is there no Way to make Amends?

Ifab. Yes——by leaving me.

D. G. Don *Lewis* is happy!——He loves another, and laughs at both of us.

Ifab. Ha!——Love another!——Does he love another? Name her to me this Moment.

D. G. Aurora, the Sifter of Don *Felix*——To-morrow perhaps will fee 'em marry'd——She's here at *Sa-*

K   *lamqnca.*

lamanca. He told me of her himself——He told me too that he was weary of you——That he wanted an Excuse to break with you—And now, at this Moment, in the Arms of his *Aurora,* he's rejoicing at your Difgrace.

Ifab. 'Tis well!——I wanted only this to make me mad. You love me, you fay—How fhall I be fure on't?

D. G. Put me to the Trial.

Ifab. What Trial?—You would make Amends too. ——What Amends?——Come, be Villain enough to prompt me. Don *Lewis* is your Enemy.

D. G. I hate him.

Ifab. Is that all?

D. G. What mean you?

Ifab. Nothing.

D. G. I hate him, and would be reveng'd.

Ifab. I——love him, and would be reveng'd.

D. G. How?

Ifab. Guefs.

D. G. Ha!——

Ifab. You hefitate!——I thought you Villain enough for any Thing.

D. G. What's the Reward?

Ifab. The Poffeffion of me for ever. I'll plunder my Father, and fly with you the next Moment.

D. G. How am I fecure of that?

Ifab. Come with me to my Clofet.

D. G. Agreed, Madam. (*Exeunt.*)

SCENE *changes to* Aurora's.

Enter Aurora *in* Boy's Clothes, *and* Laura.

Aur. What are they doing at *Ifabella's* all this Time?

Laur. Toffing *Gil Blas* in a Blanket perhaps.

Aur. No, no, Don *Lewis* will be pleas'd. I don't like his ftaying fo long tho'.

Laur. Don't be impatient, Madam.

Aur. No, not impatient—But why does not he come?——*Gil Blas* was to hurry him to me.

Laur.

Laur. All in good Time—But you are ſo violent, you won't give him an Hour to get rid of a Miſtreſs.

Aur. Yes —— if 'twould lead him to a Wife —— You don't conſider the Conſequence of this Viſit.

Laur. The Conſequence !—Nay, Madam, if you conceal'd any Thing ————

Aur. A thouſand Things——I have a little World in this Heart, and but one Tongue to tell what paſſes in't.

Lau. 'Tis a Woman's Tongue tho'.

Aur. And yet it won't do My Buſineſs —— But if Don *Lewis* makes no Attempt to ſee me this Evening, I have a great Mind he ſhall never ſee me again. ——The Fellow can have no Spirit in him.

Lau. And beſides, Madam, how are we to quarrel with him To morrow ? Or why is the Siſter to be ſent away, if Don *Lewis* does not break his Promiſe with the Brother ?

Aur. Or how ſhall I be ſure he loves me ?—The Caſe ſtands thus —— Says the impertinent Don *Felix*, I muſt have no Viſiting at my Siſter's To-night —— Says the gallant Don *Lewis*, it muſt þe as You pleaſe——Ay, but ſays *Gil Blas* ——For I am ſure he has not forgot his Inſtructions —— how if *Aurora* loves you ? And how if her Brother ſhould intend you a Trick ? If This does not bring him, I'll poſitively never ſee him again.

Lau. No more I would, Madam.

Aur. I have ventur'd boldly for Him —— and if he fails me, but in a ſingle Grain of equal Love and Spirit—I'll to Horſe for *Madrid* this very Night— What has He to riſk ?——Why, the Diſpleaſure of a Boy——Let him ſtay but an Hour from me, and if ever he ſees me again, it ſhall be thro' the Grate of a Nunnery—— I'll lower theſe mad Flights ; ſay my Prayers all Day—and never think of Man again. (*A Knocking at the Door.*)

Lau. Oho! Are you there, Sir!——You'll be no Nun, Madam.

Aur. I hope not——You know how to deny me to him——But remember To-morrow at Nine——I muſt be ſure of him at Nine——Don't let him come farther than the Door tho'——My Brother's in the next Room with me—and if he ſees him—O Lord! O Lord!—

Lau. I'll warrant you, Madam.   [*Exit.*

Aur. Yes, yes, the Man's my own again—I began to be frighten'd tho'—Now muſt poor *Aurora* be pack'd to *Madrid* upon this Viſit——If People make Promiſes, they ſhould keep 'em——I am not a Man to be trifled with——Ha!——The Door opens! She won't let him in ſure !——What's the Matter, *Laura?*

Re-enter Laura, *and after her*, Gil Blas, *dreſs'd.*

Lau. You are very impertinent, methinks. (*To* Gil Blas.)   The Gentleman would take no Denial, Sir. (*To* Aurora.) He Muſt ſpeak with you, he ſays.

Aur. Have you any Buſineſs with Me, Sir ?

Gil. If you are Don *Felix de Mendoza,* Sir.

Lau. Ha, ha, ha! Don't you know him, Madam ?

Aur. Gil Blas ! —— A very Soldier-like Appearance, upon my Word! Ha, ha, ha !

Gil. No Laughing, Madam.   The *Callabavaro's* are grave Men, mighty grave Men.

Aur. Well, and what? And how?—

Gil. And When, Madam?—That's the Queſtion— He'll be here preſently—We have done the Buſineſs— detected Don *Gabriel* too——Such a Pair of 'em ! But we left 'em together.

Aur. And where's Don *Lewis ?*

Gil. At the Tavern—chucking down a ſecond Bottle of Champaign to your Ladyſhip's Health.

Aur. Alone ?

Gil. With an old Prieſt. Madam—I pretended Buſineſs at *Bernarda's,* to give you Notice of his Coming.   But we have had the Devil to do.

Aur. At *Iſabella's?*——Tell me how it went.

Gil.

Gil. Only one Thing wanting, Madam ——The Lady was not difgrac'd enough.

Aur. Is not it over then? And was not fhe detected?

Gil. Yes, yes, Madam, fhe was detected ——But then it was with Me ——There was fomething in My Appearance that ———

Aur. No Trifling now, *Gil Blas.*

Gil. Why then, Madam, every Thing happen'd as you could wifh——But the Buftle has been fince.

Aur. What Buftle?

Gil. With Don *Lewis*, Madam——He muft needs know who fet me upon this Intrigue ——Was it your Mafter, fays he?——If *Ifabella* has been My Miftrefs, fhe ranks too high for His Footman.

Aur. But you fatisfy'd him, I hope?

Gil. By telling the whole Truth, Madam —Lord! Sir, fays I, my Mafter does not think of you——— unlefs 'tis to fpite you ——————You may fancy him your Friend perhaps ———But he's No-body's Friend——He loves Mifchief——Go to my Lady, Sir. ——Your Bufinefs is with Her.——All this was in the Street, Madam——He was fadly out of Spirits, he faid——hurt to the Heart by Don *Gabriel* — So with much ado, I inveigled him to the Tavern ———

Aur. And ply'd him with the Whimfies of your Mafter?

Gil. And with Bumpers too—or I had not work'd him up to vifit you ———What, fays I, and fo my Mafter has infifted upon your keeping from his Sifter To-night!———And why was it, d'you think? Only to fend her to *Madrid*, that you may never fee her again——I'll tell you a Secret——She loves you, and He knows it ——Love me, fays he! (*In a drunken Tone*) For the Champaign began to mount, Madam. ——Does the dear Creature love me?——No, no —— it's impoffible, it's impoffible—Does her Duenna love Me, fays I?——For I told him all about it, *Laura*—

Lau. Coxcomb!

Gil.

Gil. If *Aurora* loves me, fays he, a Fig for her Brother——There's my Purfe, you Dog ——Here it is, Madam ——T'other Bumper, Prieft, and I'll fly to her in a Moment ———(*A Knocking at the Door.*) This is he, Madam ——I muft not be feen by him.

Aur. This Way, this Way then!——*Laura* undertakes him now——Slip thro' the Back-door, and attend his Coming at *Bernarda's.* (*Knocking again.*)

Lau. He grows impatient, Madam.

Aur. I have Schemes that I want Time to tell you of——But wait for him at *Bernarda's*——You muft ply him with a few more of your Mafter's Whimfies —— Now, now, *Laura!*   (*Exit.*

Gil. But don't depend upon your Face, Child—— He's a little tipfy, you know, and may be outrageoufly loving.   (*Exeunt different Ways.*)

SCENE *changes to the Street.*

Enter Don Felix *in a Riding-Drefs, and* Pedro.

D. F. Have done, Sir! The Honour of my Family's at Stake, and I'll have no Reft till I'm reveng'd.

Ped. Only confider, Sir——All laft Night we were Whip and Spur upon the Road——And now at Night again, when we fhould be taking a comfortable Supper——here we are, groping about the Streets in a ftrange Place. I don't like it, Sir——I muft needs tell you, I don't like it.

D. F. Will you have done, Sir?

Ped. There's another Thing too——You are not fure 'tis my Lady *Aurora* that we have hunted hither. You can't fwear fhe went off in Boy's Cloaths—— All we know of the Matter is from Scoundrel Poftboys and lying Inn-keepers——And then, Sir, you were forc'd to put Words into their Mouths.

D. F. Have we heard nothing here, Sirrah?

Ped. A mighty Matter indeed! That here's one Don *Felix,* who lives with one Don *Lewis,* who lodges with

with one *Bernarda*—Lord, Sir! here may be twenty Don *Felix*'s, for any Thing We know.

D. F. I tell you, 'tis my Sifter. I have a thoufand Circumftances to convince me. She has affum'd My Name, and lives in Infamy with Don *Lewis*—I'll fee 'em before I fleep——So away, Sir.

Ped. Hark! Don't you hear a Noife?——This is the Devil of a Place, Sir.

Enter at a Diftance Don Gabriel, *and three or four Affaffins.*

D. G. Stand at the Corner there. Thefe are Strangers. I have trac'd him to the Tavern yonder, and this is his Way Home. I'll give the Word as foon as he appears. [*Exit, with Affaffins.*

Ped. Did you hear 'em, Sir?——We fhall certainly be murder'd.

D. F. No, no——They are in Purfuit of another ——and here he comes perhaps. Stand by a little—— If they attack him, I'll defend him.

Ped. Defend him, Sir!——What defend a Stranger! ——O, Lord! O, Lord——I wifh there was another Stranger to defend Me! (*They retire within the Scenes.*)

Enter Don Lewis *drunk.*

D. L. Here again, Faith! This is the third or fourth Time that I have turn'd this damn'd Corner in my Way Home. The Devil's upon a Frolick To-night, and the Rafcal has kick'd the Streets out of their Places.

D. F. A Gentleman! and in Liquor!——Nay then he demands my Affiftance. (*Apart.*)

Ped. You forget my Lady *Aurora*, Sir——And befides, a Man in Liquor never comes to any Harm.

D. L. 'Twas damn'd hard tho' in the dear Angel not to fee me——I was forc'd to take up with my old fnuffling Prieft again——And egad, we drank Bumpers to *Aurora*, till the Room turn'd round. Thank Heaven, I can find my Way Home tho'. (*Going.*

D. *F.*

D. F. (Coming forward) Sir! Sir! If you go That Way, there's Danger.

D. L. Danger!——Well, and what then? Who the Devil are You?

D. F. A Gentleman——and one that may be of Service t'you. There are Villains at the next Corner, laying in wait for Murder—You are in Liquor, Sir, and their Bufinefs may be with You.

D. L. With Me, ha!——And why not with You? Muft a Man be murder'd beeaufe he's a little tipfy ?— But come along, Sir!—Here's old Trufty— (*Drawing his Sword.*) If they are for Murder, I'll murder 'em——So come along, I fay.

D. F. Not That Way, Sir—The Rifk is too great.

D. L. Why, go your Own Way then —— and fo Good-night. I am a regular Man, Sir — and always go the fhorteft Way Home. Hey!—where Are you, Murderers? *(Going.)*

D. F. Stay, Sir——Let me prevail upon you.

D. L. Not if you were the fineft Whore in *Salamanca.*

Ped. O, Lord! O, Lord!—All this for a drunken Stranger too. *(Afide.*

Re-enter Don Gabriel *and Affaffins.*

D. G. That's he. If the Stranger affifts him, he muft die too—Fall on!

D. F. (Drawing his Sword.) Villains!

D. L. Come on!—A hundred of you! (*They engage: Don* Gabriel *and the Affaffins are driven off the Stage.)*

Ped. (Coming forward) Watch! Watch! Murder! Watch!

D. L. Hold your Bawling, Sirrah!——And don't make a Difturbance——We'll enjoy the Victory in Peace. Well pufh'd, Faith!

D. F. How Are you, Sir?

D. L. Sound as a Roach, old Boy. You're a brave Fellow upon my Soul. What fay you to a Bottle at the next Tavern now, that we may grow a little acquainted ? **D. F.**

D. F. No, Sir, I'm engag'd —— And yonder's the Watch to take Care of you.

Ped. We'll all go together, Sir—Watch! Watch!

D. L. Hold your Bawling, I fay!——I am a little drunk, Sir, as you fee —— But my Name is Don *Lewis Pacheco.* I lodge hard by here, at *Bernarda*'s ——and if you'll call upon me in the Morning, I'll thank you as one fober Gentleman ought to thank another.

D. F. Don *Lewis Pacheco!* I have heard of you, Sir.

D. L. Heard of me, Sir! That is not the Thing—Come and fee me.

D. F. You may depend upon me. Do you know a young Gentleman, lately arriv'd here, who calls himfelf Don *Felix de Mendoza?*

D. L. Know him!—He's fuch a Sort of a Fellow, Sir, that the Devil does not know him—— He does not know himfelf I believe——

D. F. You are acquainted with him then?

D. L. Acquainted with him!

D. F. And may tell me where to find him.

D. L. Find him, Sir!—You may find him with a Whore I fuppofe——Not a Wench in *Salamanca* efcapes him.— But he has us'd me ill, Sir, and fo I know nothing of him——I know a Lady, call'd Donna *Aurora* tho'—and that's better — I could tell you a Story now, if I had a Mind——But no Matter —— I'm a very happy Man, Sir —— and that's enough. You'll fee me to To-morrow? Here, Watch! Watch! (*Exit.*)

D. F (*Paufing, and looking out*) They have got him I fee. What think you now, *Pedro?*

Ped. That we had better have gone with the Watch, Sir.

D. F. Fortune has made me his Deliverer, to fave him for my Revenge. To-morrow he'll be fober.

Ped. And fo you'll go back to the Inn, Sir?

D. F. My Sifter is his Strumpet—— To-morrow he'll be fober.

L

Ped.

Ped. Pray come along, Sir. — My Lady *Aurora* to be fure.—Hark !—Pray come along, Sir.

D. *F.* To-morrow he'll be fober. [*Exeunt.*

A C T V.

SCENE *draws and difcovers Don* Felix *at an Inn, fealing a Letter.*

D. *F.* WHO waits there?—*Pedro!*—'Tis Morning now ; and my Gentleman has had the Night to fleep in——*Pedro,* I fay !—— (*Enter Pedro.*)—What's o'Clock ?

Ped. Paft Eight, Sir.

D. *F.* Go with this Letter to *Bernarda*'s ; and fee that you deliver it fafe.

Ped. I hope it is not to Don *Lewis,* Sir. (*Looking at the Superfcription*) I don't know the Street.

D. *F.* But you can afk, Sir. 'Tis Time he fhould be ftirring.

Ped. Would not it be better, Sir, to find out my Lady *Aurora?*

D. *F.* Do as I bid you, Sir—And let me know that you have deliver'd it into his own Hands. I fhall be walking in the Grove behind *St. Luke*'s.—— You'll find the Place, Sir.

Ped. Yes, Sir, I fhall find the Place — But I don't mightily like this Bufinefs. Women will be Women, Sir. And if Don *Lewis* and my Lady fhould be playing the Fool at *Salamanca* here — I believe, Sir, it would be our wifeft Way to go back to *Madrid.*

D. *F.* Will you go where I fend you?

Ped. You know I don't like Fighting, Sir — And perhaps, if you'd confider a little——I am in a ftrange Place, Sir—and if Matters fhould mifcarry — You have been a very good Mafter, Sir ; and 'twould
break

break my Heart if——Pray, Sir, may I fell the
Horfes?

D. F. Another Word, Rafcal! and I'll——

Ped. I'm gone, I'm gone, Sir —— I did but mention it—— A Pox of this Fighting! If a Gentleman
can but get himfelf run thro' the Lungs, he never
confiders what becomes of a poor Servant. (*Afide.
and exit.*

D. F. Another Time this Fellow's Fears could divert me. But my Thoughts are upon Revenge—So
now for *St. Luke*'s and Don *Lewis.* [*Exit.*

SCENE *changes to* Bernarda's.

Enter Don Lewis *and* Melchior.

D. L. In Bed, Sir! Why in Bed before I came Home?
Mel. I was taken very ill, Sir.

D. L You were drunk, Sir—But have you heard
nothing? Do you know of no Difturbance in the
Streets laft Night?

Mel. Difturbance, Sir! I heard none.

D. L. How came I Home, Rafcal?

Mel. The old Way, Sir—by the Watch—fo *Gil
Blas* fays—and that your Honour was a little——

D. L. Drunk I fuppofe — and what then?—D'you
quote Precedent, Sirrah? If I am drunk, 'tis Reafon
enough that You fhould be fober.

Mel. I was taken violently ill, Sir——I could not
fleep all Night.

D. L. And did you hear no Noife?
Mel. Not a Breath, Sir.

D. L. Nor any Talk of an Attack in the Street?
Mel. None, Sir.

D. L. Has no one call'd upon me this Morning?
Mel. Not a Soul, Sir.

D. L. I have a confus'd Heap of Things in my Head,
but remember hardly any Thing diftinctly. That I
was attack'd laft Night I remember. That I was deliver'd

liver'd by a Stranger too I remember——But who he was, or how I got Home, there my Memory fails me.

Enter Bernarda.

Ber. A Letter, Sir.   (*Gives a Letter.*)

D. L. From whom?

Ber. The very Queftion I ask'd, Sir—But I am not over-curious, you know. A Servant brought it, and faid you'd know how to anfwer it.

D. L. You may go in, Signora.

Ber. I fhan't ftay to difturb you, Sir.   (*Exit.*)

D. L. This Letter perhaps may explain Matters. (*Opens and reads the Letter to himfelf.*)

Mel. The different Effects of Liquor upon different Conftitutions!——Why, here am I now as good hu-mour'd a Fellow as any in the Univerfe—and my Mafter there, all Fire and Gun-powder. He muft live fober, or I fhall take him to Tafk I believe.
[*Afide.*]

D. L. So, fo, fo! Where's *Gil Blas?*

Mel. I believe he's within, Sir.

D. L. Tell him I want him. (*Exit* Melchior.) A Challenge! Is it poffible?——Does the Boy play with me? Or is he really in earneft?——To fend it in a Letter too!—Do we live at a Diftance then? Does not one Roof lodge us? One Table board us?——I have dealt openly by him.——

Enter Gil Blas.

Where's your Mafter, Sir?

Gil. Upon his Pleafures I fuppofe. I have feen no-thing of him fince Yefterday.

D. L. Since Yefterday!—Was not he at Home laft Night?

Gil. No, Faith, Sir——'Tis well if he comes Home to Night.——His Frolicks don't commonly end fo foon—But I wifh Gentlemen would confider a little—Servants muft fleep, Sir—We muft have our natural Reft, as well as——

D. L. I am ferious, Sir. D'yeu know nothing of him?

Gil.

Gil. Not a Syllable, Sir.

D. *L.* Read That then. (*Gives him the Letter*) Aloud, Sir.

Gil. I hope no Accident has happen'd.

D. *G.* Read, I fay.

Gil. (*Reads*) ' Don *Lewis* has abus'd my Sifter,
' and difhonour'd a noble Family ; but if Bra-
' very can exift with Bafenefs, he will be ready
' to vindicate with his Sword the Wrongs he has
' done to   *Felix de Mendoza.*
    ' P. S. I wait fingly in the Grove behind
' *St. Luke*'s.'

D. *L.* You know the Hand, Sir ?

Gil. To be fure, Sir, it is my Mafter's Hand—
Not that I ever faw it before tho'.   (*Afide.*)

D. *L.* Can you guefs at the Meaning ?

Gil. The Meaning, Sir !—Why, are you furpriz'd
at it, after what I told you Yefterday ?——The Meaning is, Sir, that he's a pretty Swordfman, and wants to
be Doing a little.

D. *L.* Upon what Foundation ?

Gil. Is not it mention'd in the Letter, Sir ?

D. *L.* I fpeak to be underftood, Sir. He fays I
have abus'd his Sifter——Upon what Foundation does
he fay it ?

Gil. I am thinking, Sir. Yes, yes, 'tis a Trick of
my Lady's that's plain.—One of her Schemes that fhe
talk'd of Yefterday—But why not confult Me ?—No
Matter—There can be no fighting in the Cafe——So
I'll e'en carry on the Humour.   (*Afide.*)

D. *L.* What are you puzzling about?

Gil. Puzzling, Sir ?——No, Faith, the Matter's
pretty plain, I think. My Mafter has fent you a
Challenge——And as every Thing muft be done in
Form, you know, he firft of all cooks you up the Af-
front, and then very decently demands the Satisfaction.
—That's the whole on't, Sir.

D. *L.* You trifle with me.

Gil.

Gil. I wifh I did, Sir——I knew 'twould come out ¡ and therefore I gave you a few Hints.—Why, Sir— There's hardly a Morning that I carry up his Choco- late, but it's an even Bett, that he fends me down with a Challenge.

D. L. But why am I fingled out?

Gil. You vifited his Sifter laft Night—'Tis all as I told you Sir—And befides, you're a new Face—He loves dearly to engage with new Faces, Men or Women. He was in a Humour for fighting too——I have him before my Eyes this Moment—winding himfelf up, Sir—Yes, fays he, I Muft fight this Morning—— Let me fee——A new Face now——Ay, it fhall be Don *Lewis*—A pretty Fellow——a very pretty Fel- low——underftands the Sword too—And then he loves my Sifter—Loves her!— How's that!—Have a Care! Is not fhe a Woman?——Is not he a Man? —— Hey! Pen and Ink there! — So down he fits, and away comes that Challenge—Modern Honour, Sir!

D. L. Is this poffible?

Gil. Not fo probable, perhaps ; but all true, Sir. Why, there was Don *Antonio* at *Madrid* — and no longer ago than laft Week —— They were the beft Friends in the World, Sir—But I don't know how it was, my Mafter happen'd to find out that he fquinted with one Eye. And fo he did fquint —— He look'd fomewhat in this Manner. *(fquints.)* Upon which my Mafter fent him a Challenge——Sir, you have fquinted at me—I am a Gentleman—And fo on, in the com- mon Form——Left-Eye, Affront, Sword and Satif- faction——With a Poftfcript fuch as yours —— I wait fingly in the *Orange Grove*—And there they fought, Sir, —— Modern Honour again! — They were fine Swordfmen indeed ; fo neither of 'em were kill'd— But Things might have been otherwife, you know.

D. L. And is he fober at thefe Times?

Gil. Mad, Sir—only mad. Very little given to Drink. Good-natur'd too —— mighty good-natur'd at Intervals— But a fpoilt Child, Sir——a little un-
                                                                fortunate

fortunate in a fond Mother——Very unlike his Sister *Aurora.*——There's a Temper for you!—The Tears that this Brother of her's has cost us!

D. L. He must be cur'd, *Gil Blas.* You see the Place he appoints in his Letter — I'll encounter with no such Madman——Besides, he's the Brother of my *Aurora*——The Friend too, to whom I owe my Acquaintance with her—Go to him yourself; and tell him, I'll meet him no where but at his Sister's. If he thinks himself wrong'd, let him tell me so there. Away, Sir.

Gil. 'Tis a little dangerous, methinks, in this Humour of his—But I'll do't. What the Devil can this Challenge mean? She had better have consulted Me a little—Only that I have no Head—no Head in the World—Ha, ha, ha! ——Poor Don *Lewis.* (*Aside, and exit*)

D. L. But now, how to manage it with *Aurora!* Should I tell her of this Challenge, it may hurt her too sensibly. The hot-brain'd Madman? How have I injur'd him?——'Tis well tho' that I know him. *Aurora*, perhaps, may let me into the Secret — I'll away to her presently. *Melchior!*

Enter Melchior.

If Don *Felix* should happen to ask for me, I am at Donna *Aurora's* —— And d'you hear, Sir? Let me find you sober when I come Home—Call me a Chair.

[*Exeunt.*

SCENE *changes to a Grove.*

Enter Don Felix *and* Pedro.

D. F. To the Woman of the House! Why the Woman of the House? I bad you see Don *Lewis*, and give the Letter into his own Hands.

Ped. She said he was not up, Sir.

D. F. You should have call'd him up then.

Ped. You need not fear, Sir ——The Letter will rouse him, I'll warrant you.

D. F.

D. F. Do You be gone then——And hark you, Sir! As you know my Secret, you had beſt keep it. Upon Pain of Death, return ſilently to your Inn—— If I ſee but your Shadow, your Life ſhall anſwer for't.

Ped. I am gone, Sir——So! ſo! Here will be fine Doings preſently!—— But I ſhall have the Horſes—— That's my Comfort.   [*Aſide, and Exit.*

D. F. Why does not he come?——But Cowardice is inſeparable from a bad Mind. My Siſter was modeſt, prudent, and amiable—— What Arts have been us'd to corrupt her, I know not. Her Diſhonour ſits heavy upon me—I muſt have Blood for't.

Enter Gil Blas.

Gil. Every Step of the Way have I been thinking of this Challenge—What, in the Name of Wonder, can it mean? I have met No-body —— and this is the Place I think ——

D. F. Who are You, Sir?

Gil. Ha!——I preſume, Sir, by that Queſtion, you don't live at *Salamanca.*

D. F. Who Are you, I ſay?

Gil. Who am I, Sir!—I was only looking for my Maſter——Did you ſee him?

D. F. Your Maſter!——Who's your Maſter?

Gil. Don *Felix,* Sir——No Offence I hope —They told me he was here. A damn'd hot Fellow this. (*Aſide.*)

D. F. I am Don *Felix.*

Gil. That's mighty ſtrange now, that I ſhould not know my own Maſter —— But 'tis Don *Felix de Mendoza* that I want.

D. F. Mendoza !——I am Don *Felix de Mendoza.*

Gil. The Devil you are! But not our *Mendoza* I hope ——O Lord! O Lord! (*Aſide.*)

D. F. I begin to ſuſpect. This muſt be my Siſter's Servant ſent hither by Don *Lewis* and her to inſult me. (*Aſide.*) Anſwer me, Sir —— Who ſent you hither?

Gil.

Gil. Who fent me hither!——Lord! Sir, you frighten me fo!——My Mafter, Sir——I hope you are not angry.

D. F. Who fent you, I fay?

Gil. If you would not frighten me, Sir ——

D. F. Don *Lewis* and *Aurora* fent you.

Gil. Aurora, Sir?

D. F. Ay, Sir, *Aurora*——No Concealments, as you value your Bones. (*Shaking his Cane at him.*)

Gil. Concealments, Sir!——I don't know what you mean——I don't indeed, Sir. Yes, yes, Don *Felix* fure enough!——But I'll confefs nothing.. (*Afide.*)

D. F. Where are they?

Gil. Who did you fay, Sir?

D. F. Don *Lewis* and *Aurora*——Where are they?

Gil. As for Don *Lewis,* Sir—— he lodges at *Bernarda's,* the great Lodging-houfe there——He went out juft now, Sir——But the other Gentleman——— Who did you call him, Sir??—Signor *Aurorio?*= I believe I don't fpeak his Name right.

D. F. You fhall be taught it then. (*Offering to ftrike him.*)

Gil. Hold! hold! Sir!—*Aurora* I think you faid. —Is it a Man or a Woman, Sir?

D. F. My Sifter *Aurora*——And now you know me, tell me of her, or I'll have your Life, Dog. (*Offering to draw*)

Gil. For Heaven's Sake, Sir! —— I can bring you to Don *Lewis* and my Mafter—They may tell you of her perhaps.

D. F. Do it this Moment then——Away, Sir!—— And for Security I'll hold you faft. (*Takes hold of him.*)

Gil. That's the Way, Sir ——I'll go firft, if you pleafe.

D. F. Will you fo!—But we'll go together, Sir.

Gil. So! fo!—Here's a fine Piece of Bufinefs! — This is my Head now! (*Afide.*) [*Exeunt.*

SCENE *changes to* Aurora's *Lodgings.*

Enter Aurora *in Boy's Clothes, and* Laura.

Aur. Why does not *Gil Blas* come?

Lau. They say he went out; but no Body knows whither.

Aur. I wish we don't want him——For if Don *Lewis* does not beat me as a Man, I shall imagine he does not love me as a Woman.

Lau. Never fear, Madam——He'll be angry enough, I'll warrant him——What, send away his Mistress, and he not resent it!——'Tis well I am to be by, let me tell you.

Aur. I think he loves me; and this shall be the last Trial——Let him follow me to *Madrid*, and he shall make a Wife of me as soon as he pleases——(*A Knocking at the Door.*) Here he comes!——

Lau. Hide! hide then!

Aur. I'm in a sad Trembling, I'm sure——Would to Heaven all was over! [*Exit.*

Lau. And now for a grave Face, and a long Story. (*Opens the Door.*)

Enter Don Lewis.

Softly! Softly! Sir——I thought 'twas you—— But you are come to a sad House.

D. L. A sad House!——Why, what's the Matter?

Lau. Speak lower, Sir——Have you seen *Gil Blas* this Morning?

D. L. Ay, what of Him?

Lau. Has he told you nothing?——But how should he?——He did not know it himself.

D. L. No. But I have told Him.——He'll be here presently. Does *Aurora* know it?

Lau. Know what, Sir?——But pray speak softly.

D. L. The Challenge.

Lau. The Challenge! What Challenge?

D. L. Does not she know it then?——A Challenge from Don *Felix.*

Lau.

Lau. Impoffible !—This can't be a Trick of *Gil Blas*', fure! (*Afide.*) A Challenge did you fay ?

D. L. Ay, a Challenge—I fpeak plain I think —— Does fhe know nothing of it ?

Lau. My Miftrefs, Sir?—How fhould fhe ?—But You are not in the Secret I fee.

D. L. What Secret ?——Prithee don't diftract me.

Lau. Lower, lower, Sir ! — Don *Felix* is in the next Room, and will hear every Word.

D. L. Don *Felix!* How long has he been here ?

Lau. Ever fince laft Night.

D. L. Has not he been out this Morning ?

Lau. No. Why d'you ask fo impatiently ?

D. L. You amaze me !——He appointed me juft now to meet him behind St *Luke*'s ; and faid he waited for me thete—— But *Gil Blas* has undertaken him !—Is he come back ?

Lau. Not that I know of ——*Gil Blas* has under-taken him !——This muft be a Trick of his then. (*Afide.*)

D. L. Where's *Aurora* ?

Lau. Would I could anfwer that Queftion, Sir !—— But I fee you know nothing of what has happen'd.

D. L. Of what has happen'd !—— You fet me upon the Rack.

Lau. My Lady's gone, Sir.

D. L. Gone ! gone !——Where's fhe gone ?

Lau. You muft ask That of your Friend Don*Felix.*

D. L. I fhall run mad — But prithee tell me —— How went fhe ?—When went fhe ?—By whofe Au-thority ?

Lau. At Midnight—In a Coach——By Don *Felix*'s Authority.

Lau. Don *Felix !* —— Bring me to him this Mo-ment.—But I'll be patient till I know all. — Prithee tell me.

Lau. That unlucky Vifit laft Night, Sir —— He was fitting at the Window, and faw you—But to tell you how he look'd !—No, Sir, I can never tell you how

he

he look'd. 'Tis well, fays he — mighty well—And away he ftrided to my Lady's Dreffing-room.

D. L. Go on——Prithee go on.

Lau. You have receiv'd, fays he, the laft Vifit from Don *Lewis.*

D. L. Did he Say fo?

Lau. The very Words, Sir —— I hope Not, fays my Miftrefs—The laft Vifit from Don *Lewis!* —— Echoing his Words, you know—Pray, Sir, how came, I by the firft?—Was it of My feeking?—But I love Don *Lewis* —

D. L. Could fhe confefs fo much?

Lau. More, more, Sir——She grew as loud as he. —— I wifh you had heard her —— And if Don *Lewis* loves Me, fays fhe, as I think he does, the World fhan't divide us —— My Heart at leaft fhall be his; and if there's any Cunning in Woman, my Perfon fhall go with it.

D. L. The generous Creature! —— And what follow'd?

Lau. Storming, Sir—— A World of Storming. He lov'd you once, he faid —— but had charg'd his Mind——You muft know he's very apt to change his Mind——You were a Man of loofe Principles; a debauch'd Rake——and a thoufand Things befides—— And then he went out, and then he came in again——. But we foon found what he went out for——

D. L. What? what?

Lau. In lefs than an Hour, Sir, a Coach and fix ftop'd at the Door—and up came three ill-looking Fellows.——In fhort, with the Affiftance of Don *Felix,* they hurry'd my poor Lady down Stairs—forc'd her into the Coach—tumbled a few of her Things in— crack went the Whip—and away they drove, God knows whither.

D. L. At what Hour was this?

Lau. At ten laft Night—I begg'd hard to attend her; but the Doors were fhut upon me.

D. L. Enough, enough, *Laura*—Where is this Madman?　　(*Going in.*)　　　　　　*Enter*

Enter Aurora.

Aur. If you mean Me, Sir, I am here.

D. L. 'Twere better you had been elsewhere, Sir. But I receiv'd your Note, and now am ready to anfwer it.

Aur. What Note, Sir ?——Did I fend you any ?

D. L. You have forgot it then !—But your Mind, I fee, can change upon more Occafions than one.

Lau. Own it, Madam——A Challenge—*Gil Blas*'s Doing.   (*Apart.*)

Aur. Well, Sir——I fent you a Note.

D. L. And this is my Anfwer. (*Drawing.*) Draw.

Aur. What, draw before a Woman !—Hark you, *Laura*, ftep into the next Room a little, that we may kill one another without your fcreaming.

D. L. You are merry, Sir—— But I have Reafon to be otherwife.   Where's *Aurora ?*

Aur. Gone, Sir,—*Salamanca* did not agree with her.

D. L. You have us'd me bafely.

Aur. I have fent away my Sifter.

D. L. You fay too, that I have abus'd your Sifter.

Aur. No, Faith, not that I remember.

D. L. How, Sir !

Lau. In the Challenge, Madam—Own it all. (*Apart.*

Aur. What I wrote, Sir, I believ'd—But I can't pretend to recollect every Thing I write.

D. L. Your Note was written not an Hour ago.

Aur. May be fo——I can't fay as to the Time—— There's no carrying every Thing in one's Head, you know.

D. L. Can this be Don *Felix ?* the Brother of *Aurora ?*—This Shuffler ? This Wretch ?

Aur. What you pleafe, Sir——And yet, after all, I am the very Man.

D. L. This Coolnefs is Infult.

Aur. My Sifter's gone, Sir, and fo is my Anger.

D. L. Draw this Moment!——Or follow me to *Luke*'s.

Aur. Nor one, nor the other.

D. L. Will nothing provoke you ?   *Aur.*

Aur. My Sifter's coming back again.

D. L. What think you of a Blow, Sir ? (*Strikes off her Hat.*)

Aur. A Blow !—I don't think there's much in that, from a Friend. (*Stooping for her Hat*) And yet you may live to repent it.

D. L. I do already, that I have ftruck a Coward— Are not you a Coward ?

Aur. Sometimes fo—fometimes not—Thofe Things are merely accidental——But let me tell you, Sir, (*Walking up to him*) if I affume the Coward now, it is that I may lower myfelf to a Level with You.

D. L. With me !—Have a Care, Sir——What means this ftrange Behaviour ?

Aur. The Man, who has betray'd his Friend, is Company for Cowards.

D. L. Ha !

Aur. Why was My Character to be expos'd ? Sifter or no Sifter, 'tis the fame to Me. I open'd my Heart t'you with a Franknefs you were not worthy of ; told all my Follies ; laugh'd over the wanton Sallies of my Blood—and thought the Secret as fafe in Your Breaft as in my own——There's an Infolence in Her Virtue, that makes me wifh the World had known me, rather than my Sifter.

D. L. You can't be in Earneft fure !—She infolent !— With all the Sweetnefs natural to her Innocence, fhe only laugh'd and wifh'd you wifer.

Aur. There again——You were to reform me !—— You, good Man ! pity'd my Youth——had often told me the Confequence of this wild Behaviour——

D. L. So !—fo !

Aur. And made no doubt but Time and your ghoftly Admonitions would bring me to the Paths of Virtue— There's a Meannefs, Don *Lewis,* in Hypocrify, not to be brook'd by a Woman of Her Temper.

D. L. Ha !——You alarm me now indeed !

Aur. I fear you have loft her for ever by it.

D. L.

D. L. D'you fear it?——Then you are my Friend ſtill.

Aur. Her Departure laſt Night ſo ſuddenly, and all My Behaviour this Morning, which you have thought ſo ſtrange, were at her own Deſire.

D. L. At her own Deſire!——Why *Laura, Laura* ſaw her forc'd away——would have follow'd her, but You ſhut the Doors upon her.

Aur. Laura had her Inſtructions too.

Laur. I was bid to ſay ſo, Sir.

D. L. All my own Folly!—I ſee it!—I ſee it!

Aur. Aurora muſt be won by Openneſs—No Maſk. —No Secret to come out hereafter—And if ever you ſee her more——

D. L. Ever ſee her more!——

Aur. Speak to her with the Freedom you have done to Me. Hide not a Folly from her, that you would bluſh for, if a Wife ſhould know it.—Do this, and I am ſtill enough your Friend, to think and tell her, you deſerve her.

D. L. Generous Don *Felix!* (*Offering to embrace her.*)

Aur. Hold, Sir!—Now for the Blow you gave me. (*Draws.*) Draw!

D. L. Not for the World!——I'll beg Pardon in Public—Do any Thing!—

Aur. I love you, Don *Lewis*——But I am a Sol- dier, and muſt live with Honour——Draw this Mo- ment.

D. L. I dare not——I have injur'd you——

Aur. Draw, I ſay. (*She purſues him, and he re- treats.*)

Lau. For God's Sake, Sir! (*To* Aurora) — Here's ſomebody coming—Hark!

Gil. (*Without*) Stay but one Minute, Sir!— Only till I go in.

D. F. (*Without.*) Not an Inſtant, Raſcal—I muſt ꞇut your Throat at laſt, I find.

Aur.

Aur. Ha !——Who are thefe ? (*Afide.*) This Af‑
fair will keep, Sir. (*Putting up her Sword.*)

D. *L.* What new Turn now ? (*Afide.*)

       Enter Don Felix, *collaring* Gil Blas.

Gil. Mercy ! Mercy !——Good dear Sir, Mercy !

Aur. My Brother ! (*Runs and leans upon the Scene.*)

Lau. Don *Felix*, as I'm a Chriftian !

Gil. The Gentleman in White, Sir——That's my
Mafter.

D. *F.* I fee it is (*Letting* Gil Blas *go.*)

Gil. Never fo frighten'd in all my Life ! (*Afide.*)

D. *F.* Ay, blufh for Shame ; (*To* Aurora) for you
have ftamp'd Difhonour on a Family, that till now
was without Stain.

D. *L.* I don't like this——I'm afraid, Don *Felix*,
you have too many Tricks.

D. *F.* (*Turning quick*) Tricks, Sir!—If You are
Don *Lewis*, your Manners are as foul as your Morals.
—But I am not to be play'd with.

D. *L.* Nor I, Sir—as you fhall All find (*Putting
his Hand to his Sword*)

D. *F.* You fhall have Occafion for your Sword
prefently——But firft, I muft have a Word or two
here. (*Looking at* Aurora.)

Aur. You look fo, Sir——you frighten me.

D. *F.* Which Shame and Difhonour could not do.
——Are not you a Wretch ?

Aur. No, indeed.

D. *L.* What am I to think ?——Where am I got ?
——With whom ?

D. *F.* Could *Aurora* do this ?——The modeft, in‑
nocent *Aurora ?* She has broke a Heart that lov'd
her with that Tendernefs——

D. *L.* You love *Aurora!*——

D. *F.* Again ! ——'Tis well——To You then,
Don *Lewis*——You receiv'd a Note this Mornmg.

Aur. Ha !——Courage affift me now, and we fhall
do ! (*Afide.*)

                           D. *L.*

D. L. I did——a Challenge——And there ſtands
the Writer.

Aur. I writ no Challenge.

D. L. You dare not deny it, ſure!

Aur. I writ none, I ſay.

D. L. This is too much ——

D. F. Hold, Sir!———'Tis Me you are to deal
with——Where my Honour's at Stake, I am not to
be banter'd with.

D. L. Nor I——*Laura* knows he writ it.

Lau. I, Sir! not I——You told me ſo, indeed.

D. L. Is that all?——*Gil Blas* too——Come hither, Raſcal, and ſpeak the Truth.

Gil. What am I to ſay now? (*Aſide.*)

D. L. Speak!

Gil. I thought ſo, Sir.

D. L. You knew the Hand, Villain!——Here's
the Note——(*Shews it* Gil Blas) Deny it if you
dare.

Gil. Kill me, Sir——kill me——I am in your
Power——I really thought it was his——and ſo I
ſaid it——But I beg your Pardon, Sir——I never ſaw
a Line of his Writing in my Life.

D. L. I am diſtracted——You ſee, Sir, the Confuſion I am in. (*To Don* Felix) If this Note is yours,
I am ready to anſwer it.

D. F. The Whole of your Behaviour aſtoniſhes
me——That you have Courage I know.

D. L. How know it, Sir?

D. F. Your Defence laſt Night againſt the Ruffians was a brave one.

D. L. The Ruffians!—more and more ſtrange!

D. F. This Sword was of Service t'you.

D. L. Was it?——I thank you, Sir.

D. F. You were then in a Condition unfit for my
Revenge.

D. L. Revenge!—For what?

D. F. For violating the Honour of my Siſter. I
am Don *Felix de Mendoza,* the Brother of *Aurora*—

N   The

The fame Don *Felix* that call'd You to an Account this Morning for the Wrongs you have done him.

D. L. The Brother of *Aurora!*——Who then is this? (*Pointing to* Aurora.)

D. F. Is not fhe *Aurora?*——If there was a Poffibility of your Ignorance I could be calm——But we have talk'd too long——Follow me this Moment.

D. L. No. I am rivetted here——*Aurora!* Can the wild, the tormenting Don *Felix* be *Aurora?*

Aur. Even fo, Sir——The very individual She.

D. F. And is it true?——Can it be true, that he knew it not, till this Inftant?

Aur. Upon my Honour, Sir.

D. L. And mine——Nay, I hardly can believe it now.

Aur. I told you, you'd repent ftriking me —— How do you intend to give me Satisfaction?

D. L. By loving you for ever!—Laft Night, Don *Felix*, you gave me my Life ——If you would make that Life happy to me, give me your Sifter.

D. F. And would you marry this wild Thing?

D. L. With her own Confent, 'tis my only Wifh.

D. F. What fays *Aurora?*

Aur. Only that I love him, Sir—and fhould break my Heart, if he would not have me.

D. L. My frank *Aurora!*

Aur. I am a very honeft Madcap, Sir, as you fee. I lov'd you, and therefore I purfu'd you. If I have ftep'd a little out of my Sex to make fure of you, let Love be my Excufe.

D. L. My generous Girl!

D. F. Then, Sir, we are Brothers ——And *Aurora* once again my Sifter—Take her, Don *Lewis*—But I muft know of all her Pranks.

D. L. And I too, how the Scheme has been conducted.

Aur. And I, Brother, what good Genius brought You hither, in the very Inftant I could have wifh'd for you.

Gil.

Gil. Here he ſtands, Madam, at your Elbow ——
A little in Diſgrace indeed — Not wanted now, and
therefore not regarded.

D. L. Poor *Gil Blas!*

Gil. What Sort of a Genius, I wonder, had the
Management of My Affairs?

Aur. A lucky one, as you ſhall find.

D. F. Here's to begin. *(Gives* Gil Blas *a Purſe.)*
Let this be an Excuſe for what happen'd in the
Grove.

Gil. Your Honour did frighten me a little.

Enter Bernarda.

Ber. 'Tis well I have found you, Don *Lewis!* ——
I have great News for you!

D. L. For Me?

Ber. You were attack'd laſt Night——But little do
you gueſs by whom —— *Iſabella*'s contriving, every
Bit on't.

D. L. *Iſabella*'s!

Ber. I never lik'd that Don *Gabriel*——He was the
Man, Sir—But he's finely handled.

D. L. Not dead, I hope?

Ber. Wounded, that's all ————

Gil. He'll be hang'd, that's my Comfort. *(Aſide.)*

Ber. Wounded in Half a Dozen Places—He won't
die tho'—But He was of another Mind, or he would
not have ſent for Me——*Iſabella* ſet him at Work—
And this Morning ſhe has robb'd her Father, and
left Don *Gabriel* to his Fate.

D. L. Why, that's as it Should be ——But we
have happier Things to think of——You are in the
Dark, Don *Felix*, but ſhall know all preſently

Aur. This was an Eſcape, indeed!—— My noble
Brother, let me thank you for his Life —And now if
you will follow *Bernarda* to my Lodgings, I'll but
ſtay to be a Woman again, and attend you for the
Laugh. There I was the Friend of Don *Lewis* —
Here the Siſter of his Friend——And you ſhall know
how

how merrily we pafs'd our Time. Lead on, Sir,
(To Don Lewis*)* I'll follow you in a few Minutes.

    D. L. To give me that Happinefs, which a falfe
Friend and falfer Miftrefs promis'd me in vain.

    To all my Follies, here I bid adieu,
Reclaim'd and fix'd by Virtue, and by You.

F I N I S.

Lately Publifh'd, by R. **Franckin,**

Written by the Author of this C O M E D Y,

  1. **F**ABLES for the Female Sex. Adorn'd with **17**
    Copper Plates. Price 5 *s.*
  2. The Foundling; a Comedy. As it is acted at the
Theatre-Royal in *Drury-Lane.* Price 1 *s.* 6 *d.*
  3. The Trial of *Selim* the *Perfian,* for divers high Crimes
and Mifdemeanors. Price 1 *s.*

THE
GAMESTER

NOTE

The third speech from the bottom of p. 64 ("Look at it . . .") is mistakenly attributed to Beverley; it should be spoken by Stukely.

THE
GAMESTER.

A
TRAGEDY.

As it is Acted at the

Theatre-Royal in *Drury-Lane.*

LONDON:

Printed for R. FRANCKLIN, in *Ruffel-Street,*
Covent-Garden; and Sold by R. DODSLEY,
in *Pall-Mall,* M.DCC.LIII.

[Price One Shilling and Six Pence.]

TO THE

RIGHT HONOURABLE

HENRY PELHAM.

S I R,

IT was a very fine Piece of Oratory of a young Lawyer at the Bar, who as Council againſt a Highwayman, obſerved that the Proſecutor had been robbed of a certain Quantity of Ore, which being purified by Fire, cut into circular Pieces, and impreſſed with the Image of a King and the Arms of a State, brought with it the Neceſſaries, the Conveniencies and the Luxuries of Life. I'll be hanged, ſays an honeſt Country Gentleman who was ſtand-

ing

ing by, if this flourishing Fool does not mean Money. But if he had said it in one Word, would not all the rest have been implied?

Just such a Censure as this should I deserve, if in an Address to Mr. *Pelham* I endeavoured to enumerate the Qualities he possesses. The Characters of great Men are generally connected with their Names; and it is impossible for any one to read the Name of Mr. *Pelham*, without connecting with it, in his own Mind, the Virtues of Humanity.

It is therefore sufficient that I desire his Acceptance of this Play; that I acknowledge the Obligations I owe him, and that I subscribe myself

His most grateful,

and

most obedient Servant,

E DW. M OORE.

PROLOGUE.

Written and Spoken by Mr. GARRICK.

L I K E fam'd La Mancha's *Knight, who* Launce *in hand,*
Mounted his Steed to free th' enchanted Land,
Our Quixote *Bard sets forth a Monster-taming,*
Arm'd at all Points, to fight that Hydra——GAMING.
Aloft on Pegasus *he waves his Pen,*
And hurls Defiance at the Caitiff's Den.
The First on fancy'd Giants spent his Rage,
But This has more than Windmills to engage.
He combats Passion, rooted in the Soul,
Whose Powers at once delight ye and controul ;
Whose Magic Bondage each lost Slave enjoys,
Nor wishes Freedom, tho' the Spell destroys.
To save our Land from this MAGICIAN's *Charms,*
And rescue Maids and Matrons from his Arms,
Our Knight Poetic comes ——And Oh! ye Fair!
This black ENCHANTER's *wicked Arts beware!*
His subtle Poison dims the brightest Eyes,
And at his Touch, each Grace and Beauty dies.
Love, Gentleness and Joy to Rage give Way,
And the soft Dove becomes a Bird of Prey.
May this our bold Advent'rer break the Spell,
And drive the Dæmon to his native Hell.
Ye Slaves of Passion, and ye Dupes of Chance,
Wake all your Pow'rs from this destructive Trance!
Shake off the Shackles of this Tyrant Vice:
Hear other Calls than those of Cards and Dice:
Be learn'd in nobler Arts, than Arts of Play,
And other Debts than those of Honour pay.
No longer live insensible to Shame,
Lost to your Country, Families and Fame.
Cou'd our romantic Muse this Work atchieve,
Wou'd there one honest Heart in Britain *grieve?*
Th' Attempt, tho' wild, wou'd not in vain be made,
If ev'ry honest Hand wou'd lend its Aid.

E P I-

EPILOGUE.

Written by a FRIEND,

And Spoken by Mrs. PRITCHARD.

ON ev'ry Gamester in th' Arabian *Nation*,
'Tis *said*, that Mahomet *denounc'd Damnation*;
But in Return for *wicked Cards and Dice*,
He *gave them black-ey'd Girls in Paradise*.
Should *he thus preach, good Countrymen, to You*,
His *Converts would, I fear, be mighty few*.
So *much your Hearts are set on sordid Gain*,
The *brightest Eyes around you shine in vain*.
Shou'd *the most heav'nly Beauty bid you take her*,
You'd *rather hold* —— two Aces and a Maker,
By your *Example, our poor Sex drawn in*,
Is *guilty of the same unnat'ral Sin*;
The *Study now of every Girl of Parts*
Is *how to win your Money, not your Hearts*.
O! in *what sweet, what ravishing Delights*,
Our *Beaux and Belles together pass their Nights*!
By *ardent Perturbations kept awake*,
Each *views with longing Eyes the other's*——Stake.
The *Smiles and Graces are from* Britain *flown*, $\}$
Our *Cupid is an errant Sharper grown*,
And *Fortune sits on Cytherea's Throne*.
In all *these Things tho' Women may be blam'd*,
Sure *Men, the wiser Men shou'd be asham'd*!
And 'tis a *horrid Scandal I declare*
That *four strange Queens shou'd rival all the Fair*,
Four *Jilts with neither Beauty, Wit nor Parts*,
O Shame! *have got Possession of their Hearts*;
And *those bold Sluts, for all their Queenly Pride*,
Have *play'd loose Tricks, or else they're much bely'd*.
Cards *were at first for Benefits design'd*,
Sent *to amuse, and not enslave the Mind*.
From *Good to Bad how easy the Transition*!
For *what was Pleasure once, is now Perdition*.
Fair *Ladies then these wicked Gamesters shun*,
Whoever *weds one, is, you see, undone*.

Dramatis Personæ.

M E N.

Beverley,	*Mr.* Garrick.
Lewfon,	*Mr.* Moffop.
Stukely,	*Mr.* Davies.
Jarvis,	*Mr.* Berry.
Bates,	*Mr.* Burton.
Dawfon,	*Mr.* Blakes.
Waiter,	*Mr.* Ackman.

W O M E N.

Mrs. Beverley,	*Mrs.* Pritchard.
Charlotte,	*Mifs* Haughton.
Lucy,	*Mrs.* Price.

The GAMESTER.

A

TRAGEDY.

ACT I.   SCENE I.

Enter Mrs. Beverley *and* Charlotte.

Mrs. *Beverley.* BE comforted, my Dear; all may be well yet. And now, methinks, the Lodgings begin to look with another Face. O Sifter! Sifter! if thefe were all my Hardfhips; if all I had to complain of were no more than quitting my Houfe, Servants, Equipage and Shew, your Pity wou'd be Weaknefs.

Char. Is Poverty nothing then?

Mrs. *Bev.* Nothing in the World, if it affected only Me. While we had a Fortune, I was the happieft of the Rich: And now 'tis gone, give me but a bare Subfiftance and my Hufband's Smiles, and I'll be the happieft of the Poor. To me now thefe Lodgings want nothing but their Mafter. Why do you look fo at me?

Char. That I may hate my Brother.

B   Mrs. *Bev.*

Mrs. *Bev.* Don't talk fo, *Charlotte.*

Char. Has he not undone you?—Oh! this pernicious Vice of Gaming! But methinks his ufual Hours of four or five in the Morning might have contented him; 'twas Mifery enough to wake for him till then. Need he have ftaid out all Night? I fhall learn to deteft him.

M*rs. Bev.* Not for the firft Fault. He never flept from me before.

Char. Slept from you! no, no, his Nights have nothing to do with Sleep. How has this one Vice driven him from every Virtue! Nay, from his Affections too!—The Time was, Sifter——

Mrs. *Bev.* And is. I have no fear of his Affections. Would I knew that he were fafe!

Char. From Ruin and his Companions—— But that's impoffible. His poor little Boy too! What muft become of him?

Mrs. *Bev.* Why, Want fhall teach him Induftry. From his Father's Miftakes he fhall learn Prudence, and from his Mother's Refignation, Patience. Poverty has no fuch Terrors in it as you imagine. There's no Condition of Life, Sicknefs and Pain excepted, where Happinefs is excluded. The Hufbandman, who rifes early to his Labour, enjoys more welcome Reft at Night for't. His Bread is fweeter to him; his Home happier; his Family dearer; his Enjoyments furer. The Sun that roufes him in the Morning, fets in the Evening to releafe him. All Situations have their Comforts, if fweet Contentment dwell in the Heart. But my poor *Beverley* has none. The Thought of having ruin'd thofe he loves, is

Mifery

Mifery for ever to him. Would I could eafe his Mind of that!

Char. If he alone were ruin'd, 'twere juft he fhou'd be punifh'd. He is my Brother, 'tis true; but when I think of what he has done; of the Fortune you brought him; of his own large Eftate too, fquander'd away upon this vileft of Paffions, and among the vileft of Wretches! O! I have no Patience! My own little Fortune is untouch'd, he fays. Wou'd I were fure on't.

Mrs. *Bev.* And fo you may — 'twould be a Sin to doubt it.

Char. I will be fure on't——'Twas Madnefs in me to give it to his Management. But I'll demand it from him this Morning. I have a melancholy Occafion for't.

Mrs. *Bev.* What Occafion?

Char. To fupport a Sifter.

Mrs. *Bev.* No, I have no Need on't. Take it, and reward a Lover with it. The generous *Lewfon* deferves much more. Why won't you make him happy?

Char. Becaufe my Sifter's miferable.

Mrs. *Bev.* You muft not think fo. I have my Jewels left yet. I'll fell 'em to fupply our Wants; and when all's gone thefe Hands fhall toil for our Support. The Poor fhould be induftrious—— Why thofe Tears, *Charlotte?*

Char. They flow in Pity for you.

Mrs. *Bev.* All may be well yet. When he has nothing to lofe I fhall fetter him in thefe Arms again; and then what is it to be poor?

Char. Cure him but of this deftructive Paffion, and my Uncle's Death may retrieve all yet.

Mrs. *Bev.*

Mrs. *Bev.* Ay, *Charlotte,* could we cure him.
But the Difeafe of Play admits no Cure but Poverty ; and the Lofs of another Fortune wou'd
but encreafe his Shame and his Affliction. Will
Mr. *Lewfon* call this Morning ?

Char. He faid fo laft Night. He gave me
Hints too, that he had Sufpicions of our Friend
Stukely.

Mrs. *Bev.* Not of Treachery to my Hufband ?
That he loves Play I know; but furely he's
honeft.

Char. He wou'd fain be thought fo ; therefore
I doubt him. Honefty needs no Pains to fet itfelf off.

Mrs. *Bev.* What now, *Lucy?*

Enter Lucy.

Lucy. Your old Steward, Madam. I had not
the Heart to deny him Admittance, the good old
Man begg'd fo hard for't.   (*Exit* Lucy.

Enter Jarvis.

Mrs. *Bev.* Is this well, *Jarvis?* I defir'd you
to avoid me.

Jar. Did you, Madam? I am an old Man,
and had forgot. Perhaps too you forbad my
Tears ; but I am old, Madam, and Age will be
forgetful.

Mrs. *Bev.* The faithful Creature! how he moves
me.   (*To* Char.

Char. Not to have feen him had been Cruelty.

Jar. I have forgot thefe Apartments too. I
remember none fuch in my young Mafter's Houfe;
and yet I have liv'd in't thefe five and twenty
Years. His good Father would not have difmifs'd me.   Mrs. *Bev.*

Mrs. *Bev.* He had no Reason, *Jarvis.*

Jar. I was faithful to him while he liv'd, and when he dy'd, he bequeath'd me to his Son. I have been faithful to Him too.

Mrs. *Bev.* I know it, I know it, *Jarvis.*

Char. We both know it.

Jar. I am an old Man, Madam, and have not a long Time to live. I afk'd but to have dy'd with him, and he difmifs'd me.

Mrs. *Bev.* Prithee no more of this! 'Twas his Poverty that difmifs'd you.

Jar. Is he indeed fo poor then?——Oh! he was the Joy of my old Heart——But muft his Creditors have all?——And have they fold his Houfe too? His Father built it when He was but a prating Boy. The Times I have carry'd him in thefe Arms! And, *Jarvis*, fays he, when a Beggar has afk'd Charity of me, why fhould People be poor? You fhan't be poor, *Jarvis*; if I was a King, no-body fhould be poor. Yet He is poor. And then he was fo brave!——O he was a brave little Boy! And yet fo merciful he'd not have kill'd the Gnat that ftung him.

Mrs. *Bev.* Speak to him *Charlotte*; for I cannot.

Char. When I have wip'd my Eyes.

Jar. I have a little Money, Madam; it might have been more, but I have lov'd the Poor. All that I have is yours.

Mrs. *Bev.* No, *Jarvis*; we have enough yet. I thank you tho', and will deferve your Goodnefs.

Jar. But fhall I fee my Mafter? And will he let me attend him in his Diftreffes! I'll be no Expence to him: and 'twill kill me to be refufed. Where is he, Madam?

Mrs. *Bev.*

Mrs. *Bev.* Not at home, *Jarvis.* You ſhall ſee him another Time.

Char. To-morrow, or the next Day — O, *Jarvis!* what a Change is here!

Jar. A Change indeed, Madam! My old Heart akes at it. And yet methinks—But here's ſomebody coming.

Enter Lucy *with* Stukely.

Lucy. Mr. *Stukely*, Madam. (*Exit* Lucy.

Stu. Good Morning to you, Ladies. Mr. *Jarvis*, your Servant. Where's my Friend, Madam?
(*To Mrs.* Bev.

Mrs. *Bev.* I ſhou'd have aſk'd that Queſtion of You. Have not you ſeen him to-day?

Stu. No, Madam.

Char. Nor laſt Night?

Stu. Laſt Night! Did not he come home then?

Mrs. *Bev.* No. Were not you together?

Stu. At the Beginning of the Evening; but not ſince. Where can he have ſtaid?

Char. You call yourſe'f his Friend, Sir; why do you encourage him in this Madneſs of Gaming?

Stu. You have aſk'd me that Queſtion before, Madam; and I told you my Concern was that I could not ſave him; Mr. *Beverley* is a Man, Madam; and if the moſt friendly Entreaties have no Effect upon him, I have no other Means. My Purſe has been his, even to the Injury of my Fortune. If That has been Encouragement, I deſerve Cenſure; but I meant it to retrieve him.

Mrs. *Bev.* I don't doubt it, Sir; and I thank you—But where did you leave him laſt Night?

Stu. At *Wilſon*'s, Madam, if I ought to tell; in Company I did not like. Poſſibly he may be
there

there ftill. Mr. *Jarvis* knows the Houfe, I believe.

Jar. Shall I go, Madam?

Mrs. *Bev.* No, he may take it ill.

Char. He may go as from himfelf.

Stu. And, if he pleafes, Madam, without
naming Me. I am faulty myfelf, and fhould conceal the Errors of a Friend. But I can refufe
nothing here.   (*Bowing to the Ladies.*

Jar. I would fain fee him methinks.

Mrs. *Bev.* Do fo then. But take care how you
upbraid him. I have never upbraided him.

Jar. Would I could bring him Comfort!
                              (*Exit* Jarvis.

Stu. Don't be too much alarm'd, Madam.
All Men have their Errors, and their Times of
feeing 'em. Perhaps my Friend's Time is not
come yet. But he has an Uncle; and old Men
don't live for ever. You fhou'd look forward,
Madam; we are taught how to value a fecond
Fortune by the Lofs of a firft.
                              (*Knocking at the Door.*

Mrs. *Bev.* Hark!— No—that Knocking was
too rude for Mr. *Beverley.* Pray Heaven he be
well!

Stu. Never doubt it, Madam. You fhall be
well too——Every Thing fhall be well.
                              (*Knocking again.*

Mrs. *Bev.* The knocking is a little loud tho'—
Who waits there? Will none of you anfwer?——
None of you, did I fay?——Alas! what was I
thinking of!——I had forgot myfelf.

Char. I'll go, Sifter——But don't be alarm'd
fo.   (*Exit* Charlotte.

                                          Stu.

Stu. What extraordinary Accident have you to fear, Madam?

Mrs. *Bev.* I beg your Pardon; but 'tis ever thus with me in Mr. *Beverley*'s Abfence. No one knocks at the Door, but I fancy it is a Meffenger of ill News.

Stu. You are too fearful, Madam; 'twas but one Night of Abfence; and if ill Thoughts intrude (as Love is always doubtful) think of your Worth and Beauty, and drive 'em from your Breaft.

Mrs. *Bev.* What Thoughts? I have no Thoughts that wrong my Husband.

Stu. Such Thoughts indeed would wrong him. The World is full of Slander; and every Wretch that knows himfelf unjuft, charges his Neighbour with like Paffions; and by the general Frailty hides his own——If you are wife, and would be happy, turn a deaf Ear to fuch Reports. 'Tis Ruin to believe 'em.

Mrs. *Bev.* Ay, worfe than Ruin. 'Twou'd be to fin againft Conviction. Why was it mention'd?

Stu. To guard you againft Rumour. The Sport of half Mankind is Mifchief; and for a fingle Error they make Men Devils. If their Tales reach you disbelieve 'em.

Mrs. *Bev.* What Tales? By whom? Why told? I have heard nothing—or if I had, with all his Errors, my *Beverley*'s firm Faith admits no Doubt——It is my Safety, my Seat of Reft and Joy, while the Storm threatens round me. I'll not forfake it. (Stukely *fighs and looks down*) Why turn you, Sir, away? And why that Sigh?

Stu. I was attentive, Madam; and Sighs will

come

come we know not why. Perhaps I have been too bufy——If it fhould feem fo, impute my Zeal to Friendfhip, that meant to guard you againft evil Tongues. Your *Beverley* is wrong'd, flander'd moft vilely——My Life upon his Truth.

Mrs. *Bev.* And mine too. Who is't that doubts it? But no Matter——I am prepar'd, Sir——Yet why this Caution?——You are my Husband's Friend; I think you mine too: the common Friend of both. (*paufes*) I had been unconcern'd elfe.

Stu. For Heaven's Sake, Madam, be fo ftill! I meant to guard you *againft* Sufpicion, not to alarm it.

Mrs. *Bev.* Nor have you, Sir. Who told you of Sufpicion? I have a Heart it cannot reach.

Stu. Then I am happy—I wou'd fay more—but am prevented.

Enter Charlotte.

Mrs. *Bev.* Who was it *Charlotte?*

Char. What a Heart has that *Jarvis!* — A Creditor, Sifter. But the good old Man has taken him away——Don't diftrefs his Wife! Don't diftrefs his Sifter! I cou'd hear him fay. 'Tis cruel to diftrefs the afflicted——And when he faw me at the Door, he begg'd Pardon that his Friend had knock'd fo loud.

Stu. I wifh I had known of this. Was it a large Demand, Madam?

Char. I heard not that; but Vifits fuch as thefe, we muft expect often.—Why fo diftrefs'd, Sifter? This is no new Affliction.

Mrs. *Bev.* No, *Charlotte*; but I am faint with watching——quite funk and fpiritlefs—— Will

C   you

you excuse me, Sir? I'll to my Chamber, and try to rest a little.

Stu. Good Thoughts go with you, Madam.

(*Exit Mrs. Bev.*

My Bait is taken then. (*Afide.*) Poor Mrs. *Beverley*! How my Heart grieves to see her thus!

Char. Cure her, and be a Friend then.

Stu. How cure her, Madam?

Char. Reclaim my Brother.

Stu. Ay; give him a new Creation; or breathe another Soul into him. I'll think on't, Madam. Advice I see is thankless.

Char. Useless I am sure it is, if thro' mistaken Friendship, or other Motives, you feed his Passion with your Purse, and sooth it by Example. Physicians to cure Fevers keep from the Patient's thirsty Lip the Cup that wou'd enflame him; You give it to his Hands—(*a Knocking.*) Hark! Sir— These are my Brother's desperate Symptoms—— Another Creditor.

Stu. One not so easily got rid of——What, *Lewson!*

Enter Lewson.

Lew. Madam, your Servant——Yours, Sir. I was enquiring for you at your Lodgings.

Stu. This Morning? You had Business then?

Lew. You'll call it by another Name, perhaps. Where's Mr. *Beverley*, Madam?

Char. We have sent to enquire for him.

Lew. Is he abroad then? He did not use to go out so early.

Char. No; nor to stay out so late.

Lew. Is that the Case. I am sorry for it. But Mr. *Stukely*, perhaps, may direct you to him.

Stu.

Stu. I have already, Sir.——But what was your Bufinefs with Me?

Lew. To congratulate you upon your late Succeffes at Play. Poor *Beverley!* But You are his Friend; and there's a Comfort in having fuccefsful Friends.

Stu. And what am I to underftand by this?

Lew. That *Beverley's* a poor Man, with a rich Friend—that's all.

Stu. Your Words wou'd mean fomething, I fuppofe. Another Time, Sir, I fhall defire an Explanation.

Lew. And why not now? I am no Dealer in long Sentences. A Minute or two will do for me.

Stu. But not for Me, Sir. I am flow of Apprehenfion, and muft have Time and Privacy. A Lady's Prefence engages my Attention——Another Morning I may be found at Home.

Lew. Another Morning then, I'll wait upon you.

Stu. I fhall expect you, Sir. Madam, your Servant.   (*Exit* Stu.

Char. What mean you by this?

Lew. To hint to him that I know him.

Char. How know him? Mere Doubt and Suppofition!

Lew. I fhall have Proof foon.

Char. And what then? Wou'd you rifk your Life to be his Punifher.

Lew. My Life, Madam! Don't be afraid. And yet I am happy in your Concern for me. But let it content you that I know this *Stukely*——'Twou'd be as eafy to make him honeft as brave.

Char. And what do you intend to do?

C 2   *Lew*

Lew. Nothing, 'till I have Proof. Yet my Suspicions are well grounded——But methinks, Madam, I am acting here without Authority. Cou'd I have leave to call Mr. *Beverley* Brother, his Concerns would be my own. Why will you make my Services appear officious?

Char. You know my Reasons, and shou'd not press me. But I am cold, you say; and cold I will be, while a poor Sister's destitute——My Heart bleeds for her! and 'till I see her Sorrows moderated, Love has no Joys for me.

Lew. Can I be less a Friend by being a Brother? I wou'd not say an unkind Thing——But the Pillar of your House is shaken. Prop it with another, and it shall stand firm again——You must comply.

Char And will——when I have Peace within myself. But let us change the Subject.——Your Business here this Morning is with my Sister. Misfortunes press too hard upon her: Yet till to Day she has borne 'em nobly.

Lew. Where is she?

Char. Gone to her Chamber——Her Spirits fail'd her.

Lew. I hear her coming——Let what has pass'd with *Stukely* be a Secret—She has already too much to trouble her.

Enter Mrs. Beverley,

Mrs. *Bev.* Good Morning, Sir; I heard your Voice, and as I thought, enquiring for Me —— Where's Mr. *Stukely, Charlotte?*

Char. This Moment gone——You have been in Tears, Sister; but here's a Friend shall comfort you.

Lew.

Lew. Or if I add to your Diftreffes, I'll beg your Pardon, Madam. The Sale of your Houfe and Furniture was finifh'd Yefterday.

Mrs. *Bev.* I know it, Sir. I know too your generous Reafon for putting me in Mind of it. But you have obliged me too much already.

Lew. There are Trifles, Madam, which I know you have fet a Value on: Thofe I have purchas'd, and will deliver. I have a Friend too that efteems you——He has bought largely; and will call nothing his, till he has feen you. If a Vifit to him would not be painful, he has begg'd it may be this Morning.

Mrs. *Bev.* Not painful in the leaft. My Pain is from the Kindnefs of my Friends. Why am I to be oblig'd beyond the Power of Return?

Lew. You fhall repay us at your own Time. I have a Coach waiting at the Door——Shall we have your Company, Madam? (*To* Char.

Char. No. My Brother may return foon; I'll ftay and receive him.

Mrs. *Bev.* He may want a Comforter, per-haps. But don't upbraid him, *Charlotte.* We fhan't be abfent long——Come, Sir, fince I muft be fo oblig'd

Lew. 'Tis I that am oblig'd. An Hour or lefs will be fufficient for us. We fhall find you at Home, Madam? (*To* Char.

(*Exit* Lew. & *Mrs.* Bev.

Char. Certainly. I have but little Inclination to appear abroad——O! this Brother! this Bro-ther! To what Wretchednefs has he reduc'd us.

(*Exit* Char.

SCENE

S C E N E *changes to* Stukely's *Lodgings.*

Enter Stukely.

Stu. That *Lewfon* fufpects me, 'tis too plain.
Yet why fhou'd he fufpect me?——I appear the
Friend of *Beverley* as much as he.—But I am
rich it feems—and fo I am ; Thanks to another's
Folly and my own Wifdom. To what Ufe is
Wifdom, but to take Advantage of the weak?
This *Beverley*'s my Fool ; I cheat him, and he
calls me Friend——But more Bufinefs muft be
done yet. His Wife's Jewels are unfold ; fo is
the Reverfion of his Uncle's Eftate. I muft have
thefe too——And then there's a Treafure above
all——I love his Wife——Before fhe knew this
Beverley I lov'd her ; but like a cringing Fool,
bow'd at a Diftance, while he ftept in and won
her——Never, never will I forgive him for't.
My Pride, as well as Love, is wounded by this
Conqueft. I muft have Vengeance. Thofe Hints,
this Morning, were well thrown in——Already
they have faften'd on her. If Jealoufy fhou'd
weaken her Affections, Want may corrupt her
Virtue——My Hate rejoyces in the Hope——
Thefe Jewels may do much. He fhall demand
'em of her ; which, when mine, fhall be con-
verted to fpecial Purpofes——What now, *Bates?*

Enter Bates.

Bates. Is it a Wonder then to fee me? The
Forces are in readinefs, and only wait for Orders.
Where's *Beverley?*

Stu. At laft Night's Rendezvous, waiting for
Me. Is *Dawfon* with you?

Bates. Drefs'd like a Nobleman ; with Money
in

in his Pocket, and a Set of Dice that shall deceive the Devil.

Stu. That Fellow has a Head to undo a Nation. But for the rest, they are such low-manner'd, ill-looking Dogs, I wonder *Beverley* has not suspected 'em.

Bates. No Matter for Manners and Looks. Do You supply 'em with Money and they are Gentlemen by Profession———The Passion of Gaming casts such a Mist before the Eyes, that the Nobleman shall be surrounded with Sharpers, and imagine himself in the best Company.

Stu. There's that *Williams* too———It was He, I suppose, that call'd at *Beverley's* with the Note this Morning. What Directions did you give him?

Bates. To knock loud, and be clamorous. Did not you see him?

Stu. No. The Fool sneak'd off with *Jarvis.* Had he appear'd within Doors, as directed, the Note had been discharg'd. I waited there on Purpose. I want the Women to think well of me; for *Lewson's* grown suspicious; he told me so himself.

Bates. What Answer did you make him?

Stu. A short one———That I wou'd see him soon, for farther Explanation.

Bates. We must take care of him. But what have we to do with *Beverley?* *Dawson* and the rest are wondering at you.

Stu. Why let 'em wonder. I have Designs above their narrow Reach. They see me lend him Money; and they stare at me. But they are Fools. I want him to believe me beggar'd by him.

Bates.

Bates. And what then?

Stu. Ay, there's the Queſtion; but no Matter. At Night you may know more. He waits for me at *Wilſon*'s. I told the Women where to find him.

Bates. To what Purpoſe?

Stu. To ſave Suſpicion. It look'd friendly; and they thank'd me. Old *Jarvis* was diſpatch'd to him.

Bates. And may intreat him Home.

Stu. No; he expects Money from me: But I'll have none. His Wife's Jewels muſt go——— Women are eaſy Creatures, and refuſe nothing where they love———Follow to *Wilſon*'s; but be ſure he ſees you not. You are a Man of Character, you know; of Prudence and Diſcretion. Wait for me in an outer Room; I ſhall have Buſineſs for you preſently. Come, Sir———

Let drudging Fools by Honeſty grow great.
The ſhorter Road to Riches is Deceit. (Exeunt.

End of the firſt A C T.

ACT

A C T II.

SCENE *a Gaming Houſe, with a Table, Box, Dice, &c.*

BEVERLEY *is diſcover'd ſitting.*

BEVERLEY.

WHY, what a World is this! The Slave that digs for Gold, receives his daily Pittance, and ſleeps contented; while thoſe, for whom he labours, convert their Good to Miſchief; making Abundance the Means of Want. O Shame! Shame!——Had Fortune given me but a little, that little had been ſtill my own. But Plenty leads to Waſte; and ſhallow Streams maintain their Currents, while ſwelling Rivers beat down their Banks, and leave their Channels empty. What had I to do with Play? I wanted nothing. My Wiſhes and my Means were equal. The Poor follow'd me with Bleſſings; Love ſcatter'd Roſes on my Pillow, and Morning wak'd me to Delight—— O, bitter Thought! that leads to what I was, by what I am! I wou'd forget both——— Who's there?

Enter a Waiter.

Wait. A Gentleman, Sir, enquires for you.

Bev. He might have us'd leſs Ceremony. *Stukely* I ſuppoſe?

Wait. No, Sir, a Stranger.

Bev. Well, ſhew him in.　　(*Exit* Waiter. A Meſſenger from *Stukely* then! From Him that has undone me!——Yet all in Friendſhip; and now he lends me from his Little, to bring back Fortune to me.

D　　　　　　　*Enter*

Enter Jarvis.

Jarvis! Why this Intrusion?————Your Absence had been kinder

Jar. I came in Duty, Sir. If it be troublesome————

Bev. It is————I wou'd be private————hid
even from myself. Who sent you hither?

Jar. One that wou'd persuade you Home
again. My Mistress is not well; her Tears
told me so.

Bev. Go with thy Duty there then————But
does she weep? I am to blame to let her weep.
Prithee begone; I have no Business for thee.

Jar. Yes, Sir; to lead you from this Place.
I am your Servant still. Your prosperous For-
tune bless'd my old Age. If That has left you,
I must not leave you.

Bev. Not leave me! Recall past Time then;
or through this Sea of Storms and Darkness,
shew me a Star to guide me————But what
can'st Thou?

Jar. The little that I can, I will. You have
been generous to me————I wou'd not offend
you, Sir————but————

Bev. No. Think'st thou I'd ruin Thee too!
I have enough of Shame already————My Wife!
my Wife! Wou'd'st thou believe it, *Jarvis?* I
have not seen her all this long Night————I,
who have lov'd her so, that every Hour of Absence seem'd as a Gap in Life. But other Bonds
have held me————O! I have play'd the Boy,
dropping my Counters in the Stream, and reaching to redeem 'em, have lost myself. Why wilt
Thou follow Misery? Or if thou wilt, go to thy
Mistress. She has no Guilt to sting her, and
therefore may be comforted.   *Jar.*

Jar. For Pity's Sake, Sir!———I have no Heart to fee this Change.

Bev. Nor I to bear it———How fpeaks the World of me, *Jarvis?*

Jar. As of a good Man dead. Of one, who walking in a Dream, fell down a Precipice. The World is forry for you.

Bev. Ay, and pities me. Says it not fo? But I was born to Infamy———I'll tell thee what it fays. It calls me Villain; a treacherous Husband; a cruel Father; a falfe Brother; one loft to Nature and her Charities. Or to fay all in one fhort Word, it calls me---Gamefter. Go to thy Miftrefs———I'll fee her prefently.

Jar. And why not now? Rude People prefs upon her; loud, bawling Creditors; Wretches, who know no Pity———I met one at the Door; he wou'd have feen my Miftrefs. I wanted Means of prefent Payment, fo promis'd it To-morrow. But others may be preffing; and fhe has Grief enough already. Your Abfence hangs too heavy on her.

Bev. Tell her I'll come then. I have a Moment's Bufinefs. But what haft Thou to do with My Diftreffes? Thy Honefty has left thee poor; and Age wants Comfort. Keep what thou haft for Cordials; left between thee and the Grave, Mifery fteal in. I have a Friend fhall counfel me ———This is that Friend.

Enter Stukely.

Stu. How fares it, *Beverley?* Honeft Mr. *Jarvis,* well met; I hop'd to find you here. That Viper *Williams!* Was it not He that troubled you this Morning?

Jar. My Miftrefs heard him then?———I am forry that fhe heard him.   *Bev.*

Bev. And *Jarvis* promis'd Payment.

Stu. That muſt not be. Tell him I'll ſatisfy him.

Jar. Will you, Sir? Heaven will reward you for't.

Bev. Generous *Stukely!* Friendſhip like yours, had it Ability like Will, wou'd more than ballance the Wrongs of Fortune.

Stu. You think too kindly of me--Make haſte to *Williams*; his Clamours may be rude elſe. (*to* Jar.

Jar. And my Maſter will go Home again---Alas! Sir, we know of Hearts there breaking for his Abſence. (*Exit.*

Bev. Wou'd I were dead!

Stu. Or turn'd Hermit; counting a String of Beads in a dark Cave; or under a weeping Willow, praying for Mercy on the Wicked. Ha! ha! ha!---Prithee be a Man, and leave dying to Diſeaſe and old Age. Fortune may be ours again; at leaſt we'll try for't.

Bev. No; it has fool'd us on too far.

Stu. Ay, ruin'd us; and therefore we'll ſit down contented. Theſe are the Deſpondings of Men without Money; but let the ſhining Ore chink in the Pocket, and Folly turns to Wiſdom. We are Fortune's Children---True, ſhe's a fickle Mother; but ſhall We droop becauſe She's peeviſh?--No; ſhe has Smiles in Store. And theſe her frowns are meant to brighten 'em.

Bev. Is this a Time for Levity? But You are ſingle in the Ruin, and therefore may talk lightly of it. With Me 'tis complicated Miſery.

Stu. You cenſure me unjuſtly------I but aſſum'd theſe Spirits to cheer my Friend. Heaven knows he wants a Comforter.

Bev. What new Misfortune?

Stu.

Stu. I wou'd have brought you Money; but Lenders want Securities. What's to be done? All that was mine is yours already.

Bev. And there's the double Weight that finks me. I have undone my Friend too; one, who to fave a drowning Wretch, reach'd out his Hand, and perifh'd with him.

Stu. Have better Thoughts.

Bev. Whence are they to proceed?——I have nothing left.

Stu. (*Sighing*) Then we're indeed undone. What Nothing? No Moveables? Nor ufelefs Trinkets? Bawbles lock d up in Cafkets to ftarve their Owners?——I have ventur'd deeply for you.

Bev. Therefore this Heart-ake; for I am loft beyond all Hope.

Stu. No; Means may be found to fave us. *Jarvis* is rich. Who made him fo? This is no Time for Ceremony.

Bev. And is it for Difhonefty? The good old Man! Shall I rob Him too? My Friend wou'd grieve for't. No; let the little that he has, buy Food and Cloathing for him.

Stu. Good Morning then.   (*Going.*

Bev. So hafty! Why, then good Morning.

Stu. And when we meet again, upbraid me. Say it was I that tempted you. Tell *Lewfon* fo; and tell him I have wrong'd you——He has Sufpicions of me, and will thank you.

Bev. No; we have been Companions in a rafh Voyage, and the fame Storm has wreck'd us both. Mine fhall be Self-Upbraidings.

Stu. And will they feed us? You deal unkindly by me. I have fold and borrow'd for you, while Land or Credit lafted; and now, when Fortune

fhou'd

ſhou'd be try'd, and my Heart whiſpers me Succeſs, I am deſerted; turn'd looſe to Beggary,
while You have Hoards.

Bev. What Hoards? Name 'em, and take 'em.

Stu. Jewels.

Bev. And ſhall this thriftleſs Hand ſeize Them
too? My poor, poor Wife! Muſt ſhe loſe all? I
wou'd not wound her ſo.

Stu. Nor I, but from Neceſſity.   One Effort
more, and Fortune may grow kind.   I have un-
uſual Hopes.

Bev. Think of ſome other Means then.

Stu. I have; and you rejected 'em.

Bev. Prythee let me be a Man.

Stu. Ay, and your Friend a poor one.   But I
have done.   And for theſe Trinkets of a Woman,
why, let her keep 'em to deck out Pride with,
and ſhew a laughing World that ſhe has Finery to
ſtarve in.

Bev. No; ſhe ſhall yield up all.   My Friend
demands it.   But need he have talk'd lightly of
her?   The Jewels that She values are Truth and
Innocence————Thoſe will adorn her ever; and
for the reſt, ſhe wore 'em for a Husband's Pride,
and to his Wants will give 'em.   Alas! you know
her not.   Where ſhall we meet?

Stu. No Matter.   I have chang'd my Mind.
leave me to a Priſon; 'tis the Reward of Friendſhip.

Bev. Periſh Mankind firſt—Leave you to a Priſon! No; fallen as you ſee me, I'm not that
Wretch. Nor wou'd I change this Heart, o'ercharg'd
as 'tis with Folly and Misfortune, for one moſt
prudent and moſt happy, if callous to a Friend's
Diſtreſſes.

Stu.

Stu. You are too warm.

Bev. In fuch a Caufe, not to be warm is to be frozen. Farewel. I'll meet you at your Lodgings.

Stu. Reflect a little. The Jewels may be loft. Better not hazard 'em———I was too prefling.

Bev. And I ungrateful. Reflection takes up Time. I have no Leifure for't. Within an Hour expect me. (*Exit.*

Stu. The thoughtlefs, fhallow Prodigal! We fhall have Sport at Night then———But hold—The Jewels are not ours yet———The Lady may refufe 'em———The Husband may relent too——— 'Tis more than probable———I'll write a Note to *Beverley,* and the Contents fhall fpur him to demand 'em———But am I grown this Rogue thro' Avarice? No; I have warmer Motives, Love and Revenge———Ruin the Husband, and the Wife's Virtue may be bid for? 'Tis of uncertain Value, and finks, or rifes in the Purchafe, as Want, or Wealth, or Paffion governs. The Poor part cheaply with it; rich Dames, tho' pleas'd with felling, will have high Prices for't. Your Lovefick Girls give it for Oaths and Lying. But tender Wives, who boaft of Honour and Affections, keep it againft a Famine———Why, let the Famine come then; I am in hafte to purchafe.

Enter Bates.

Look to your Men, *Bates;* there's Money ftirring. We meet To-night upon this Spot. Haften, and tell 'em fo. *Beverley* calls upon me at my Lodgings, and we return together. Haften, I fay, the Rogues will fcatter elfe.

Bates. Not 'till their Leader bids 'em.

Stu. Come on then. Give 'em the Word and

follow

follow me; I muſt advife with you————This
is a Day of Bufinefs.   (*Exeunt*

S C E N E *changes to* Beverley's *Lodgings.*

Enter Beverley *and* Charlotte.

Char. Your Looks are chang'd too; there's
Wildneſs in 'em. My wretched Siſter! How
will it grieve her to fee you thus!

Bev. No, no---a little Reſt will eafe me. And
for your *Lewfon's* Kindneſs to her, it has my
Thanks; I have no more to give him.

Char. Yes; a Siſter and her Fortune. I trifle
with him and he complains.---My Looks, he
fays, are cold upon him. He thinks too————

Bev. That I have loſt your Fortune---He dares
not think fo.

Char. Nor does he---You are too quick at
gueffing. He cares not if you had. That Care is
mine---I lent it you to husband, and now I claim it.

Bev. You have Sufpicions then.

Char. Cure 'em, and give it me.

Bev. To ftop a Siſter's Chiding.

Char. To vindicate her Brother.

Bev. How if he needs no Vindication?

Char. I would fain hope fo.

Bev. Ay, wou'd and cannot. Leave it to
Time then; 'twill fatisfy all Doubts.

Char. Mine are already fatisfy'd.

Bev. 'Tis well. And when the Subject is renew'd, fpeak to me like a Siſter, and I will anfwer
like a Brother.

Char. To tell me I'm a Beggar.---Why, tell it
now. I that can bear the Ruin of thofe dearer to
me, the Ruin of a Siſter and her Infant, can bear
That too.

                                        Bev.

Bev. No more of this — you wring my Heart.

Cha. Wou'd that the Mifery were all your own! But Innocence muft fuffer — Unthinking Rioter! whofe Home was Heaven to him; an Angel dwelt there, and a little Cherub, that crown'd his Days with Bleffings — How has he loft this Heaven, to league with Devils!

Bev. Forbear, I fay; Reproaches come too late; they fearch, but cure not: And for the Fortune you demand, we'll talk To-morrow on't; our Tempers may be milder.

Cha. Or if 'tis gone, why farewell all. I claim'd it for a Sifter. She holds my Heart in hers; and every Pang fhe feels tears it in Pieces — But I'll upbraid no more. What Heaven permits, perhaps, it may ordain; and Sorrow then is finful. Yet that the Hufband! Father! Brother! fhould be its Inftrument of Vengeance! —— 'Tis grievous to know that.

Bev. If you're my Sifter, fpare the Remembrance — it wounds too deeply. To-morrow fhall clear all; and when the worft is known, it may be better than your Fears. Comfort my Wife; and for the Pains of Abfence, I'll make Atonement. The World may yet go well with us.

Cha. See where fhe comes! — Look chearfully upon her — Afflictions fuch as hers are prying, and lend thofe Eyes that read the Soul.

Enter Mrs. Beverley *and* Lewfon.

Mrs. Bev. My Life!

Bev. My Love! How fares it? I have been a truant Hufband.

E

Mrs.

Mrs. Bev. But we meet now, and that heals all — Doubts and Alarms I have had; but in this dear Embrace I bury and forget 'em — My Friend here [*pointing to* Lewson] has been indeed a Friend. *Charlotte,* 'tis you must thank him : Your Brother's Thanks and mine are of too little Value.

Bev. Yet what we have we'll pay. I thank you, Sir, and am oblig'd. I wou'd say more, but that your Goodness to the Wife, upbraids the Husband's Follies. Had I been wise, She had not trepass'd on your Bounty.

Lew. Nor has she trespass'd. The little I have done, Acceptance over-pays.

Cha. So Friendship thinks ———

Mrs. Bev. And doubles Obligations by striving to conceal 'em — We'll talk another Time on't. — You are too thoughtful, Love.

Bev. No, I have Reason for these Thoughts.

Cha. And hatred for the Cause — Wou'd you had that too!

Bev. I have — The Cause was Avarice.

Cha. And who the Tempter?

Bev. A ruin'd Friend — ruin'd by too much Kindness.

Lew. Ay, worse than ruin'd; stabb'd in his Fame, mortally stabb'd — Riches can't cure him.

Bev. Or if they cou'd, those I have drain'd him of. Something of this he hinted in the Morning — That *Lewson* had Suspicions of him — Why these Suspicions?   [*angrily.*

Lew. At School we knew this *Stukely.* A cunning plodding Boy he was, sordid and cruel. Slow at his Task, but quick at Shifts and Tricking. He schem'd out Mischief, that others might

be

be punifh'd; and wou'd tell his Tale with fo much
Art, that for the Lafh he merited, Rewards and
Praife were given him. Shew me a Boy with
fuch a Mind, and Time that ripens Manhood in
him, fhall ripen Vice too — I'll prove him, and
lay him open t'you — 'Till then be warn'd — I
know him, and therefore fhun him.

Bev. As I wou'd thofe that wrong him —You
are too bufy, Sir.

Mrs. Bev. No, not too bufy — Miftaken perhaps — That had been milder.

Lew. No matter, Madam. I can bear this,
and praife the Heart that prompts it — Pity fuch
Friendfhip fhou'd be fo plac'd!

Bev. Again, Sir! But I'll bear too — You
wrong him, *Lewfon*, and will be forry for't.

Cha. Ay, when 'tis prov'd he wrongs him.
The World is full of Hypocrites.

Bev. And *Stukely* one — fo you'd infer I think
— I'll hear no more of this — my Heart akes for
him — I have undone him.

Lew. The World fays otherwife

Bev. The World is falfe then — have Bufinefs
with you, Love. [*to* Mrs. Bev.] We'll leave 'em
to their Rancour. [*going.*

Cha. No. We fhall find Room within for't —
Come this way, Sir. [*to* Lewfon.

Lew. Another Time my Friend will thank me;
that Time is haftening too. [*Ex. Lew. and* Char.

Bev. They hurt me beyond bearing — Is *Stukely*
falfe? Then Honefty has left us! 'Twere finning
againft Heav'n to think fo.

Mrs. Bev. I never doubted him.

E 2

Bev.

Bev. No; You are Charity. Meeknefs and ever-during Patience live in that Heart, and Love that knows no Change — Why did I ruin you?

Mrs. Bev. You have not ruin'd me. I have no Wants when You are prefent, nor Wifhes in your Abfence but to be bleft with your Return. Be but refign'd to what has happen'd, and I am rich beyond the Dreams of Avarice.

Bev. My generous Girl! — But Memory will be bufy; ftill crouding on my Thoughts, to four the Prefent by the Paft. I have another Pang too.

Mrs. Bev. Tell it, and let me cure it.

Bev. That Friend —— that generous Friend, whofe Fame they have traduc'd — I have undone Him too. While he had Means he lent me largely; and now a Prifon muft be his Portion.

Mrs. Bev. No; I hope otherwife.

Bev. To hope muft be to act. The charitable Wifh feeds not the Hungry — Something muft be done.

Mrs. Bev. What?

Bev. In Bitternefs of Heart he told me, juft now he told me, I had undone him. Cou'd I hear that, and think of Happinefs? No; I have difclaim'd it, while He is miferable.

Mrs. Bev. The World may mend with us, and then we may be grateful. There's Comfort in that Hope.

Bev. Ay; 'tis the fick Man's Cordial, his pro-mis'd Cure; while in preparing it the Patient dies. ——What now?

Enter

Enter Lucy.

Lucy. A Letter, Sir.   [*delivers it and Ex.*
Bev. The Hand is *Stukely*'s.

[*opens and reads it to himself.*

Mrs. Bev. And brings good News —— at leaft
I'll hope fo —— What fays he, Love?

Bev. Why this —— too much for Patience.
Yet he directs me to conceal it from you.   [*reads.*

" Let your Hafte to fee me be the only Proof
" of your Efteem for me. I have deter-
" min'd, fince we parted, to bid Adieu to
" *England*; chufing rather to forfake my
" Country than to owe my Freedom in it
" to the Means we talk'd of. Keep this a
" Secret at Home, and haften to the ruin'd
                                        " *R. Stukely.*"

Ruin'd by Friendfhip! I muft relieve or follow
him.

Mrs. Bev. Follow him, did you fay? Then I
am loft indeed!

Bev. O this infernal Vice! how has it funk me!
A Vice, whofe higheft Joy was poor to my do-
meftic Happinefs. Yet how have I purfu'd it!
turn'd all my Comforts to bittereft Pangs! and all
thy Smiles to Tears. Damn'd, damn'd Infatua-
tion!

Mrs. Bev. Be cool, my Life! What are the
Means the Letter talks of? Have you —— have I
thofe Means? Tell me, and eafe me. I have no
Life while you are wretched.

Bev. No, no; it muft not be. 'Tis I alone
have finn'd; 'tis I alone muft fuffer. You fhall
                                        referve

referve thofe Means to keep my Child and his wrong'd Mother from Want and Wretchednefs.

Mrs. *Bev.* What Means?

Bev, I came to rob you of 'em—but cannot—dare not — Thofe Jewels are your fole Support — I fhou'd be more than Monfter to requeft 'em.

Mrs. *Bev.* My Jewels! Trifles, not worth the fpeaking of, if weigh'd againft a Hufband's Peace; but let 'em purchafe That, and the World's Wealth is of lefs Value.

Bev. Amazing Goodnefs! How little do I feem before fuch Virtues!

Mrs. *Bev.* No more, my Love. I kept 'em 'till Occafion call'd to ufe 'em; now is the Occafion, and I'll refign 'em chearfully.

Bev. Why we'll be rich in Love then. But this Excefs of Kindnefs melts me. Yet for a Friend one wou'd do much —— He has deny'd Me nothing.

Mrs. *Bev.* Come to my Clofet —— But let him manage wifely. We have no more to give him.

Bev. Where learn'd my Love this Excellence? —'Tis Heaven's own teaching: That Heaven, which to an Angel's Form has given a Mind more lovely. I am unworthy of you, but will deferve you better.

Henceforth my Follies and Neglects fhall ceafe,
And all to come be Penitence and Peace;
Vice fhall no more attract me with her Charms,
Nor Pleafure reach me, but in thefe dear Arms.
[Exeunt.

End of the Second ACT.

ACT

A C T III.

S C E N E Stukely's *Lodgings.*

Enter Stukely *and* Bates.

Stu. SO runs the World, *Bates.* Fools are the natural Prey of Knaves; Nature defign'd them fo, when fhe made Lambs for Wolves. The Laws that Fear and Policy have fram'd, Nature difclaims: She knows but two; and thofe are Force and Cunning. The nobler Law is Force; but then there's Danger in't; while Cunning, like a fkillful Miner, works fafely and unfeen.

Bat. And therefore wifely. Force muft have Nerves and Sinews; Cunning wants neither. The Dwarf that has it fhall trip the Giant's Heels up.

Stu. And bind him to the Ground. Why, we'll erect a Shrine for Nature, and be her Oracles. Confcience is Weaknefs; Fear made it, and Fear maintains it. The Dread of Shame, inward Reproaches, and fictitious Burnings fwell out the Phantom. Nature knows none of this; Her Laws are Freedom.

Bat. Sound Doctrine, and well deliver'd!

Stu. We are fincere too, and practice what we teach. Let the grave Pedant fay as much. —— But now to Bufinefs. The Jewels are difpos'd of; and *Beverly* again worth Money. He waits to count his Gold out, and then comes hither. If my Defign fucceeds, this Night we finith with him. Go to your Lodgings and be bufy — You underftand Couveyances, and can make Ruin fure.

Bat.

Bat. Better ſtop here. The Sale of this Reverſion may be talk'd of—There's Danger in't.

Stu. No, 'tis the Mark I aim at. We'll thrive and laugh. You are the Purchaſer, and there's the Payment. [*giving a Pocket Book.*] He thinks you rich; and ſo you ſhall be. Enquire for Titles, and deal hardly; 'twill look like Honeſty.

Bat. How if he ſuſpects us?

Stu. Leave it to me. I ſtudy Hearts, and when to work upon 'em. Go to your Lodgings; and if we come, be buſy over Papers. Talk of a thoughtleſs Age, of Gaming and Extravagance; you have a Face for't.

Bat. A Feeling too that wou'd avoid it. We puſh too far; but I have caution'd you. If it ends ill, you'll think of me—and ſo adieu.

[*Exit.* Bates.

Stu. This Fellow ſins by halves; his Fears are Conſcience to him. I'll turn theſe Fears to Uſe. Rogues that dread Shame, will ſtill be greater Rogues to hide their Guilt——This ſhall be thought of. *Lewſon* grows troubleſome——We muſt get rid of him.—He knows too much. I have a Tale for *Beverley*; Part of it Truth too—He ſhall call *Lewſon* to Account—If it ſucceeds, 'tis well; if not, we muſt try other Means—But here he comes—I muſt diſſemble.

Enter Beverley.

Look to the Door there! [*in a ſeeming Fright*]—My Friend!——I thought of other Viſitors.

Bev. No: Theſe ſhall guard you from 'em—[*offering Notes*] Take 'em, and uſe 'em cautiouſly—The World deals hardly by us.

Stu.

Stu. And fhall I leave you deftitute ? No Your Wants are greateft. Another Climate may treat me kinder. The Shelter of To-night takes me from this.

Bev. Let thefe be your Support then — Yet is there need of Parting ? I may have Means again ; we'll fhare 'em, and live wifely.

Stu. No. I fhou'd tempt you on. Habit is Nature in me ; Ruin can't cure it. Even now I wou'd be gaming. Taught by Experience as I am, and knowing this poor Sum is all that's left us, I am for venturing ftill — And fay I am to blame — Yet will this little fupply our Wants? No ; we muft put it out to Ufury. Whether 'tis Madnefs in me, or fome refiftlefs Impulfe of good Fortune, I yet am Ignorant ; but ——

Bev. Take it, and fucceed then. I'll try no more.

Stu, 'Tis furely Impulfe ; it pleads fo ftrongly — But you are cold — We'll e'en part here then. And for this laft Referve keep it for better ufes ; I'll have none on't. I thank you tho', and will feek Fortune fingly — One Thing I had forgot —

Bev. What is it ?

Stu. Perhaps, 'twere beft forgotten. But I am open in my Nature, and zealous for the Honour of my Friend — *Lewfon* fpeaks freely of you.

Bev. Of You I know he does.

Stu. I can forgive him for't ; but for my Friend I'm angry.

Bev. What fays he of Me ?

Stu. That *Charlotte*'s Fortune is embezzled — He talks on't loudly.

Bev. He fhall be filenc'd then — How heard you of it ?

Stu.

Stu. From many. He queſtion'd *Bates* about it. You muſt account with Him, he ſays.

Bev. Or He with Me — and ſoon too.

Stu. Speak mildly to him. Cautions are beſt.

Bev. I'll think on't — But whither go you?

Stu. From Poverty and Priſons — No matter whither. If Fortune changes you may hear from me.

Bev. May theſe be proſperous then. [*offering the Notes, which he refuſes*] Nay, they are yours — I have ſworn it, and will have nothing — take 'em and uſe 'em.

Stu. Singly I will not. My Cares are for my Friend; for his loſt Fortune, and ruin'd Family. All ſeparate Intereſts I diſclaim. Together we have fall'n: together we muſt riſe. My Heart, my Honour and Affections, all will have it ſo.

Bev. I am weary of being fool'd.

Stu. And ſo am I — Here let us part then — Theſe Bodings of Good-fortune ſhall all be ſtifled; I'll call 'em Folly, and forget 'em — This one Embrace, and then farewel. [*offering to Embrace.*

Bev. No; Stay a Moment — How my poor Heart's diſtracted! I have theſe Bodings too; but whether caught from You, or prompted by my good or evil Genius, I know not — The Trial ſhall determine — And yet, my Wife ————

Stu. Ay, ay, ſhe'll chide.

Bev. No; My Chidings are all here.

[*pointing to his Heart.*

Stu. I'll not perſwade you.

Bev. I am perſwaded; by Reaſon too; the ſtrongeſt Reaſon; Neceſſity. Oh! cou'd I but regain the Height I have fallen from, Heaven ſhou'd

thou'd forſake me in my lateſt Hour, if I again
mix'd in theſe Scenes, or ſacrific'd the Huſband's
Peace, his Joy and beſt Affections to Avarice and
Infamy!

Stu. I have reſolv'd like You; and ſince our
Motives are ſo honeſt, why ſhou'd we fear Succeſs?

Bev. Come on then—where ſhall we meet?

Stu. At *Wilſon's* — Yet if it hurts you, leave
me: I have miſled you often.

Bev. We have miſled each other — But come!
— Fortune is fickle, and may be tir'd with plaguing
us — There let us reſt our Hopes.

Stu. Yet think a little ——

Bev. I cannot — thinking but diſtracts me.

When Deſperation leads all Thoughts are vain;
Reaſon wou'd loſe, what Raſhneſs may obtain.

[Exeunt.

SCENE *changes to* Beverley's *Lodgings.*

Enter Mrs. Beverley *and* Charlotte.

Cha. 'Twas all a Scheme, a mean one; unworthy
of my Brother.

Mrs. Bev. No, I am ſure it was not — *Stukely*
is honeſt too; I know he is — This Madneſs has
undone 'em both.

Cha. My Brother irrecoverably — You are too
ſpiritleſs a Wife — A mournful Tale, mixt with
a few kind Words, will ſteal away your Soul. The
World's too ſubtle for ſuch Goodneſs. Had I been
by, he ſhou'd have aſk'd your Life ſooner than
thoſe Jewels.

Mrs.

Mrs. Bev. He fhou'd have had it then. [*warmly*]
I live but to oblige him. She who can love, and is
belov'd like Me, will do as much. Men have done
more for Miftreffes, and Women for a bafe Delu-
der. And fhall a Wife do lefs? Your Chidings
hurt me, *Charlotte*.

Cha. And come too late; they might have fav'd
you elfe. How cou'd he ufe fo?

Mrs. Bev. 'Twas Friendfhip did it. His Heart
was breaking for a Friend.

Cha. The Friend that has betray'd him.

Mrs. Bev. Prithee don't think fo.

Cha. To-morrow he Accounts with Me.

Mrs. Bev. And fairly --- I will not doubt it.

Cha. Unlefs a Friend has wanted --- I have no
Patience --- Sifter! Sifter! we are bound to curfe
this Friend.

Mrs. Bev. My *Beverley* fpeaks nobly of him.

Cha. And *Lewfon* truly --- But I difpleafe you
with this Talk --- To-morrow will inftruct us.

Mrs. Bev. Stay till it comes then --- I wou'd
not think fo hardly.

Cha. Nor I, but from Conviction --- Yet we
have Hope of better Days. My Uncle is infirm,
and of an Age that threatens hourly --- Or if
he lives, you never have offended him; and for
Diftreffes fo unmerited he will have Pity.

Mrs. Bev. I know it, and am chearful. We
have no more to lofe; and for what's gone, if it
brings Prudence Home, the Purchafe was well
made.

Cha. My *Lewfon* will be kind too. While he
and I have Life and Means, You fhall divide with
us --- And fee, he's here.

Enter

Enter Lewfon.

We were juft fpeaking of you.

Lew. 'Tis beft to interrupt you then. Few Characters will bear a Scrutiny; and where the Bad
out-weighs the Good, he's fafeft that's leaft talk'd
of. What fay you, Madam?   [*To Charlotte.*

Cha. That I hate Scandal, tho' a Woman ——
therefore talk feldom of you.

Mrs. *Bev.* Or, with more Truth, that, tho' a
Woman, fhe loves to Praife --- Therefore talks always of you.   I'll leave you to decide it.

[*Exit. Mrs.* Bev.

Lew. How good and amiable! I came to talk in
private with you; of Matters that concern you.

Cha. What Matters?

Lew. Firft anfwer me fincerely to what I afk.

Cha. I will--- But you alarm me.

Lew. I am too grave, perhaps; but be affur'd
of this, I have no News that troubles Me, and
therefore fhou'd not You.

Cha. I am eafy then --- Propofe your Queftion.

Lew. 'Tis now a tedious Twelve-month, fince
with an open and kind Heart you faid you lov'd me.

Cha. So tedious, did you fay?

Lew. And when in Confequence of fuch fweet
Words, I prefs'd for Marriage, you gave a volun-
tary Promife that you wou'd live for Me.

Cha. You think me chang'd then?   [*angrily.*

Lew. I did not fay fo.   A thoufand times I
have prefs'd for the Performance of this Promife;
but private Cares, a Brother's and a Sifter's Ruin,
were Reafons for delaying it.

Cha.

Cha. I had no other Reafons --- Where will this end ?

Lew. It fhall end prefently.

Cha. Go on, Sir.

Lew. A Promife, fuch as this, given freely, not extorted, The World thinks binding ; but I think otherwife.

Cha. And wou'd releafe me from it ?

Lew. You are too impatient, Madam.

Cha. Cool, Sir --- quite cool --- Pray go on.

Lew. Time and a near Acquaintance with my Faults may have brought Change --- if it be fo; or for a Moment, if you have wifh'd this Promife were unmade, here I acquit you of it --- This is my Queftion then; and with fuch Plainnefs as I afk it, I fhall entreat an Anfwer. Have you repented of this Promife ?

Cha. Stay, Sir. The Man that can Sufpect me, fhall Find me chang'd --- Why am I doubted ?

Lew. My Doubts are of myfelf. I have my Faults, and You have Obfervation. If from my Temper, my Words or Actions, you have conceiv'd a Thought againft me, or even a Wifh for Separation, all that has pafs'd is Nothing.

Cha. You ftartle me --- But tell me --- I muft be anfwer'd firft. Is it from Honour you fpeak this? or do you wifh me chang'd ?

Lew. Heaven knows I do not. Life and my *Charlotte* are fo connected, that to lofe one, were Lofs of both. Yet for a Promife, tho' given in Love, and meant for binding ; if Time, or Accident, or Reafon fhou'd change Opinion —— with Me that Promife has no Force.

Cha.

Cha. Why, now I'll anſwer you. Your Doubts are Prophecies--- I am really chang'd.

Lew. Indeed!

Cha. I cou'd torment you now, as you have Me; but 'tis not in my Nature---That I am chang'd I own; for what at firſt was Inclination, is now grown Reaſon in me; and from that Reaſon, had I the World! nay, were I poorer than the pooreſt, and you too wanting Bread; with but a Hovel to invite me to--- I wou'd be yours, and happy.

Lew. My kindeſt *Charlottte!* [*taking her Hand*] Thanks are too poor for this---and Words too weak! But if we love ſo, why ſhou'd our Union be delay'd?

Cha. For happier Times. The preſent are too wretched.

Lew. I may have Reaſons that preſs it now.

Cha. What Reaſons?

Lew. The ſtrongeſt Reaſons; unanſwerable ones.

Cha. Be quick and name 'em.

Lew. No, Madam; I am bound in Honour to make Conditions firſt — I am bound by Inclination too. This ſweet Profuſion of kind Words pains while it pleaſes. I dread the loſing you.

Cha. Aſtoniſhment! What mean you?

Lew. Firſt promiſe, that To-morrow, or next Day, you will be mine for ever.

Cha. I do---tho' Miſery ſhou'd ſucceed.

Lew. Thus then I ſeize you! And with you every Joy on this ſide Heaven!

Cha. And thus I ſeal my Promiſe. [*embracing him*] Now, Sir, your Secret?

Lew.

Lew. Your Fortune's loft.

Cha. My Fortune loft!---I'll ftudy to be humble then. But was my Promife claim'd for this? How nobly generous! Where learnt you this fad News?

Lew. From *Bates*, *Stukely's* prime Agent. I have oblig'd him, and he's grateful — He told it me in Friendfhip, to warn me from my *Charlotte*.

Cha. 'Twas honeft in him, and I'll efteem him for't.

Lew. He knows much more than he has told.

Cha. For Me it is enough. And for your gene-rous Love, I thank you from my Soul. If you'd oblige me more, give me a little Time.

Lew. Why Time? It robs us of our Happinefs.

Cha. I have a Tafk to learn firft. The little Pride this Fortune gave me muft be fubdu'd. Once we were equal; and might have met oblig-ing and oblig'd. But now 'tis otherwife; and for a Life of Obligations, I have not learnt to bear it.

Lew. Mine is that Life. You are too noble.

Cha. Leave me to think on't.

Lew. To-morrow then you'll fix my Happi-nefs?

Cha. All that I can, I will.

Lew. It muft be fo, we live but for each other. Keep what you know a Secret; and when we meet To-morrow, more may be known.---Fare-well. [*Exit.* Lewfon.

Cha. My poor, poor Sifter! how wou'd this wound her! But I'll conceal it, and fpeak Com-fort to her. [*Exit.*

SCENE

Scene changes to a Room in the Gaming-Houfe.

Enter Beverley *and* Stukely.

Bev. Whither wou'd you lead me ? *(Angrily.*

Stu. Where we may vent our Curfes.

Bev. Ay, on yourfelf, and thofe damn'd Coun-fels that have deftroy'd me. A thoufand Fiends were in that Bofom, and all let loofe to tempt me——I had refifted elfe.

Stu. Go on, Sir ——I have deferv'd this from you.

Bev. And Curfes everlafting——Time is too fcanty for 'em——

Stu. What have I done ?

Bev. What the Arch-Devil of old did ——— footh'd with falfe Hopes, for certain Ruin.

Stu. Myfelf unhurt; nay, pleas'd at your De-ftruction—So your Words mean. Why; tell it to the World. I am too poor to find a Friend in't.

Bev. A Friend ! what's he ? I had a Friend.

Stu. And have one ftill.

Bev. Ay; I'll tell you of this Friend. He found me happieft of the Happy. Fortune and Honour crown'd me ; and Love and Peace liv'd in my Heart. One Spark of Folly lurk'd there; That too he found ; and by deceitful Breath blew it to Flames that have confum'd me. This Friend were You to Me.

Stu. A little more perhaps—The Friend who gave his All to fave you ; and not fucceeding, chofe Ruin with you. But no matter, I have undone you, and am a Villain.

Bev. No; I think not———The Villains are within.

G   *Stu.*

Stu. What Villains?

Bev. Dawſon and the reſt——We have been Dupes to Sharpers.

Stu. How know you this? I have had Doubts as well as you; yet ſtill as Fortune chang'd I bluſh'd at my own Thoughts—But You have Proofs, perhaps.

Bev. Ay, damn'd ones. Repeated Loſſes — Night after Night, and no Reverſe—Chance has no Hand in this.

Stu. I think more charitably; yet I am peeviſh in my Nature, and apt to doubt——The World ſpeaks fairly of this *Dawſon,* ſo does it of the reſt. We have watch'd 'em cloſely too. But 'tis a Right uſurp'd by Loſers, to think the Winners Knaves — We'll have more Manhood in us.

Bev. I know not what to think. This Night has ſtung me to the quick—Blaſted my Reputation too——I have bound my Honour to theſe Vipers; play'd meanly upon Credit, 'till I tir'd 'em; and now they ſhun me to rifle one another. What's to be done?

Stu. Nothing. My Counſels have been fatal.

Bev. By Heaven I'll not ſurvive this Shame— Traitor! 'tis you have brought it on me. *(taking hold of him.)* Shew me the Means to ſave me, or I'll commit a Murder here, and next upon myſelf.

Stu. Why do it then, and rid me of Ingratitude.

Bev. Prithee forgive this Language—I ſpeak I know not what—Rage and Deſpair are in my Heart, and hurry me to Madneſs. My Home is Horror to me——I'll not return to't. Speak
quickly;

quickly; tell me, if in this Wreck of Fortune, one Hope remains ? Name it, and be my Oracle.

Stu. To vent your Curfes on—You have beftow'd 'em liberally. Take your own Counfel: and fhou'd a defperate Hope prefent itfelf, 'twill fuit your defperate Fortune. I'll not advife you.

Bev. What Hope ? By Heaven I'll catch at it, however defperate. I am fo funk in Mifery, it cannot lay me lower.

Stu. You have an Uncle.

Bev. Ay. What of Him ?

Stu. Old Men live long by Temperance; while their Heirs ftarve on Expectation.

Bev. What mean you ?

Stu. That the Reverfion of his Eftate is yours; and will bring Money to pay Debts with—Nay more, it may retrieve what's paft.

Bev. Or leave my Child a Beggar.

Stu. And what's his Father ? A difhonourable one; engag'd for Sums he cannot pay——That fhou'd be thought of.

Bev. It is my Shame——the Poifon that enflames me. Where fhall we go? To whom? I am impatient 'till all's loft.

Stu. All may be yours again—Your Man is *Bates*——He has large Funds at his Command, and will deal juftly by you.

Bev. I am refolv'd——Tell 'em within we'll meet 'em prefently; and with full Purfes too— Come, follow me.

Stu. No. I'll have no hand in this; nor do I counfel it—Ufe your Difcretion, and act from that. You'll find me at my Lodgings.

Bev.

Bev. Succeed what will, this Night I'll dare
the worſt.
'Tis loſs of Fear, to be compleatly curs'd.
(*Exit* Bev.

Stu. Why, loſe it then for ever—Fear is the
Mind's worſt Evil; and 'tis a friendly Office to
drive it from the Boſom—Thus far has Fortune
crown'd me—Yet *Beverley* is rich; rich in his
Wife's beſt Treaſure, her Honour and Affections. I wou'd ſupplant him there too. But 'tis
the Curſe of thinking Minds to raiſe up Difficulties.
Fools only conquer Women. Fearleſs of Dangers which they ſee not, they preſs on boldly,
and by perſiſting, proſper. Yet may a Tale of
Art do much — *Charlotte* is ſometimes abſent.
The Seeds of Jealouſy are ſown already. If I
miſtake not, they have taken Root too. Now
is the Time to ripen 'em, and reap the Harveſt.
The ſofteſt of her Sex, if wrong'd in Love, or
thinking that ſhe's wrong'd, becomes a Tygreſs
ın Revenge——I'll inſtantly to *Beverley*'s — No
Matter for the Danger—When Beauty leads us
on, 'tis Indiſcretion to reflect, and Cowardice to
doubt. (*Exit.*

Scene changes to Beverley's *Lodgings.*

Enter Mrs. Beverley *and* Lucy.
Mrs. *Bev.* Did *Charlotte* tell you any Thing?
Lu. No, Madam.
Mrs. *Bev.* She look'd confus'd methought; ſaid
ſhe had Buſineſs with her *Lewſon*; which, when
I preſs'd to know, Tears only were her Anſwer.
Lu. She ſeem'd in haſte too—Yet her Return
may bring you Comfort.

Mrs.

Mrs. *Bev.* No, my kind Girl; I was not born
for't—But why do I diſtreſs thee? Thy ſympa-
thizing Heart bleeds for the Ills of others—What
Pity that thy Miſtreſs can't reward thee! But
there's a Power above, that ſees, and will remember all. Prithee ſooth me with the Song
thou ſung'ſt laſt Night. It ſuits this Change
of Fortune; and there's a Melancholy in't that
pleaſes me.

Lu. I fear it hurts you, Madam—Your Goodneſs too draws Tears from me—But I'll dry 'em,
and obey you.

S O N G.

When Damon *languiſh'd at my Feet,*
   And I believ'd him true,
The Moments of Delight how ſweet!
   But ah! how ſwift they flew!
The ſunny Hill, the flow'ry Vale,
   The Garden and the Grove,
Have echo'd to his ardent Tale,
   And Vows of endleſs Love.

       2.
The Conqueſt gain'd, he left his Prize,
   He left her to complain;
To talk of Joy with weeping Eyes,
   And meaſure Time by Pain.
But Heav'n will take the Mourner's Part,
   In pity to Deſpair;
And the laſt Sigh that rends the Heart,
   Shall waft the Spirit there.

Mrs. *Bev.* I thank thee, *Lucy*——I thank
Heaven too my Griefs are none of theſe. Yet
Stukely deals in Hints—He talks of Rumours
          —I'll

—I'll urge him to fpeak plainly—Hark! there's fome one entering.

Lu. Perhaps my Mafter, Madam.   *(Exit.*

Mrs. *Bev.* Let him be well too, and I am fatify'd.   *(Goes to the Door, and liftens.)*   No; 'tis another's Voice; his had been Mufic to me. Who is it *Lucy*?

        Re-enter Lucy *with* Stukely.

Lu. Mr. *Stukely*, Madam.   *(Exit.*

Stu. To meet you thus alone, Madam, was what I wifh'd. Unfeafonable Vifits, when Friendfhip warrants 'em, need no Excufe —Therefore I make none.

Mrs. *Bev.* What mean you, Sir? And where's your Friend?

Stu. Men may have Secrets, Madam, which their beft Friends are not admitted to. We parted in the Morning, not foon to meet again.

Mrs. *Bev.* You mean to leave us then? To leave your Country too? I am no Stranger to your Reafons, and pity your Misfortunes.

Stu. Your Pity has undone you. Cou'd *Beverley* do this? That Letter was a falfe one; a mean Contrivance to rob you of your Jewels— I wrote it not.

Mrs. *Bev.* Impoffible! whence came it then?

Stu. Wrong'd as I am, Madam, I muft fpeak plainly——

Mrs. *Bev.* Do fo, and eafe me. Your Hints have troubled me. Reports, you fay, are ftirring——Reports of whom? You wifh'd me not to credit 'em. What, Sir, are thefe Reports?

Stu. I thought 'em Slander, Madam; and caution'd you in Friendfhip; left from officious

                2   Tongues

Tongues the Tale had reach'd you, with double
Aggravation.

Mrs. *Bev.* Proceed, Sir.

Stu. It is a Debt due to my Fame, due to
an injur'd Wife too——We both are injur'd.

Mrs. *Bev.* How injur'd? And who has injur'd us?

Stu. My Friend, your Husband.

Mrs. *Bev.* You wou'd resent for both then?
But know, Sir, My Injuries are my own, and do
not need a Champion.

Stu. Be not too hasty, Madam. I come not
in Resentment, but for Acquittance——You
thought me poor; and to the feign'd Distresses
of a Friend gave up your Jewels.

Mrs. *Bev.* I gave 'em to a Husband,

Stu. Who gave 'em to a ——

Mrs. *Bev.* What? Whom did he give 'em to?

Stu. A Mistress.

Mrs. *Bev.* No; on my Life he did not.

Stu. Himself confess'd it, with Curses on her
Avarice.

Mrs. *Bev.* I'll not believe it——He has no
Mistress——or if he has, why is it told to Me?

Stu. To guard you against Insults. He told
me, that to move you to Compliance, he forg'd
that Letter; pretending I was ruin'd; ruin'd by
Him too. The Fraud succeeded; and what a
trusting Wife bestow'd in Pity, was lavish'd on
a Wanton.

Mrs. *Bev.* Then I am lost indeed; and my
Afflictions are too powerful for me—His Follies
I have borne without upbraiding, and saw the
Approach of Poverty without a Tear—my Affec-
tions

tions, my ftrong Affections fupported me through
every Trial.

Stu. Be patient, Madam.

Mrs. *Bev.* Patient ! The barbarous, ungrateful
Man ! And does he think that the Tendernefs of
my Heart is his beft Security for wounding it ?
But he fhall find that Injuries fuch as thefe, can
arm my Weaknefs for Vengeance and Redrefs.

Stu. Ha ! then I may fucceed——   (*Afide.*
Redrefs is in your Power.

Mrs. *Bev.* What Redrefs ?

Stu. Forgive me, Madam, if in **my** Zeal to
ferve you, I hazard your Difpleafure.——Think.
of your wretched State.   Already Want fur-
rounds you.   Is it in Patience to bear That ? To
fee your helplefs little one robb'd of his Birth-
right ? A Sifter too, with unavailing Tears, la-
menting her loft Fortune ? No Comfort left you,
but ineffectual Pity from the Few, out-weigh'd
by Infults from the Many ?

Mrs. *Bev.* Am I fo loft a Creature ? Well,
Sir, my Redrefs ?

Stu. To be refolv'd is to fecure it. The marriage Vow, once violated, is in the Sight of
Heaven diffolv'd——Start not, but hear me ! 'Tis
now the Summer of your Youth ; Time has not
cropt the Rofes from your Cheek, tho' Sorrow
long has wafh'd 'em——Then ufe your Beauty
wifely ; and freed by Injuries, fly from the
crueleft of Men, for Shelter with the kindeft.

Mrs. *Bev.* And who is He ?

Stu. A Friend to the Unfortunate ; a bold one
too ; who while the Storm is burfting on your
Brow, and Lightening flafhing from your Eyes,
dares tell you that he loves you.   Mrs.

Mrs. *Bev.* Wou'd that thefe Eyes had Heaven's own Lightening! that with a Look, thus I might blaft thee! Am I then fallen fo low? Has Poverty fo humbled me, that I fhou'd liften to a hellifh Offer, and fell my Soul for Bread? O Villain! Villain!——— But now I know thee, and thank thee for the Knowledge.

Stu. If you are wife, you fhall have Caufe to thank me.

Mrs. *Bev.* An injur'd Hufband too fhall thank thee.

Stu. Yet know, proud Woman, I have a Heart as ftubborn as your own; as haughty and imperious; and as it loves, fo can it hate.

Mrs. *Bev.* Mean defpicable Villain! I fcorn thee and thy Threats.. Was it for this that *Beverley* was falfe? That his too credulous Wife fhou'd in Defpair and Vengeance give up her Honour to a Wretch? But he fhall know it, and Vengeance fhall be his.

Stu. Why fend him for Defiance then. Tell him I love his Wife; but that a worthlefs Hufband forbids our Union. I'll make a Widow of you, and court you honourably.

Mrs. *Bev.* O Coward! Coward! thy Soul will fhrink at him. Yet in the Thought of what may happen, I feel a Woman's Fears. Keep thy own Secret, and begone. Who's there?

Enter Lucy.

Your Abfence, Sir, wou'd pleafe me.

Stu. I'll not offend you, Madam.

(*Ex.* Stu. *with* Lucy.

H   Mrs.

Mrs. *Bev.* Why opens not the Earth to fwallow fuch a Monfter? Be Confcience then his Punifher, 'till Heaven in Mercy gives him Penitence, or dooms him in his Juftice.

Re enter Lucy.

Come to my Chamber, *Lucy*; I have a Tale to tell thee, fhall make thee weep for thy poor Miftrefs.

Yet Heav'n the guiltlefs Sufferer regards,
And whom it moft afflicts, it moft rewards.

(Exeunt.

End of the T H I R D A C T.

A C T

ACT IV.

SCENE Beverley's *Lodgings.*

Enter Mrs. Beverley, Charlotte, *and* Lewfon.

Char. THE fmooth-tongu'd Hypocrite!

Lew. But we have found him, and will requite him—Be chearful, Madam; (*to Mrs.* Bev.) and for the Infults of this Ruffian, you fhall have ample Retribution.

Mrs. Bev. But not by Violence— Remember you have fworn it; I had been filent elfe.

Lew. You need not doubt me; I fhall be cool as Patience.

Mrs. Bev. See him To-morrow then.

Lew. And why not now? By Heaven the verieft Worm that crawls is made of braver Spirit than this *Stukely*—Yet for my Promife, I'll deal gently with him—I mean to watch his Looks— From thofe, and from his Anfwers to my Charge, much may be learnt. Next I'll to *Bates*, and fift him to the Bottom. If I fail there, the Gang is numerous, and for a Bribe will each betray the other—Good Night; I'll lofe no Time.

(*Ex.* Lewfon.

Mrs. Bev. Thefe boifterous Spirits! how they wound me! But Reafoning is in vain. Come, *Charlotte*; we'll to our ufual Watch. The Night grows late.

Cha.

Cha. I am fearful of Events; yet pleas'd——
To-morrow may relive us.　　　　　(*Going.*

Enter Jarvis.

Cha. How now, good *Jarvis?*

Jar. I have heard ill News, Madam.

Mrs. Bev. What News? Speak quickly.

Jar. Men are not what they seem. I fear me
Mr. *Stukely* is dishonest.

Char. We know it, *Jarvis.* But what's your
News?

Jar. That there's an Action against my Master,
at his Friend's Suit.

Mrs. Bev. O Villain! Villain! 'twas this he
threaten'd then. Run to that Den of Robbers,
Wilfon's——Your Master may be there. Entreat
him Home, good *Jarvis.* Say I have Business
with him—But tell him not of *Stukely*— It may
provoke him to Revenge— Haste! haste! good
Jarvis.　　　　　(*Exit* Jarvis.

Cha. This Minister of Hell! O I cou'd tear
him Piece-meal!———

Mrs. Bev. I am sick of such a World—Yet
Heaven is just; and in its own good Time, will
hurl Destruction on such Monsters.　(*Exeunt.*

SCENE changes to Stukely's Lodgings.

Enter Stukely and Bates meeting.

Bates. Where have you been?

Stu. Fooling my Time away— Playing my
Tricks, like a tame Monkey, to entertain a Wo-
man---No Matter where—I have been vext and
disappointed. Tell me of *Beverly*—How bore
he his last Shock?　　　　　8　　　　　*Bat.*

Bat. Like one (fo *Dawfon* fays) whofe Senfes had been numb'd with Mifery. When all was loft, he fixt his Eyes upon the Ground, and ftood fome Time, with folded Arms, ftupid and motionlefs. Then fnatching his Sword, that hung againft the Wainfcot, he fat him down; and with a Look of fixt Attention, drew Figures on the Floor—At laft he ftarted up, look'd wild, and trembled; and like a Woman, feiz'd with her Sex's Fits, laugh'd out aloud, while the Tears trickled down his Face—fo left the Room.

Stu. Why, this was Madnefs.

Bat. The Madnefs of Defpair.

Stu. We muft confine him then. A Prifon wou'd do well. (*a Knocking at the Door*) Hark! that Knocking may be his. Go that Way down;
(*Ex.* Bates.

Who's there?

Enter Lewfon.

Lew. An Enemy—an open and avow'd one.

Stu. Why am I thus broke in upon? This Houfe is mine, Sir; and fhou'd protect me from Infult and Ill-manners.

Lew. Guilt has no Place of Sanctuary; where-ever found, 'tis Virtue's lawful Game. The Fox's Hold, and Tyger's Den are no Security againft the Hunter.

Stu. Your Bufinefs, Sir?

Lew. To tell you that I know you—Why this Confufion? That Look of Guilt and Terror?—Is *Beverley* awake? Or has his Wife told Tales? The Man that dares like You, fhou'd have a Soul to juftify his Deeds, and Courage to confront Ac-
cufers.

cufers.   Not with a Coward's Fear to fhrink beneath Reproof.

Stu. Who waits there ?

(*Aloud, and in Confufion.*

Lew. By Heaven he dies that interrupts us.
(*fhutting the Door.*)   You fhou'd have weigh'd
your Strength, Sir; and then, inftead of climbing
to high Fortune, the World had mark'd you for
what you are, a little pau'try Villain.

Stu. You think I fear you.

Lew. I know you fear me.   This is to prove
it. (*pulls him by the Sleeve.*)   You wanted Privacy ! A Lady's Prefence took up your Attention !
Now we are alone, Sir.   Why, what a Wretch !
(*flings him from him.*)   The vileft Infect in Creation will turn when trampled on ; yet has this
Thing undone a Man— by Cunning and mean
Arts undone him.   But we have found you, Sir.;
trac'd you thro' all your Labyrinths.   If you
wou'd fave yourfelf, fall to Confeffion.   No
Mercy will be fhewn elfe.

Stu. Firft prove me what you think me—
'Till then your Threatenings are in vain—And
for this Infult, Vengeance may yet be mine.

Lew. Infamous Coward ! why, take it now
then— (*draws, and* Stukely *retires.*) Alas! I pity
thee— Yet that a Wretch like this fhou'd overcome a *Beverley* ! it fills me with Aftonifhment !
—A Wretch, fo mean of Soul, that even Defperation cannot animate him to look upon an Enemy— You fhou'd not thus have foar'd, Sir, unlefs, like others of your black Profeffion, you had
a Sword to keep the Fools in Awe, your Villany
has ruined.

Stu.

Stu. Villany ! 'Twere beſt to curb this Licence of your Tongue ; for know, Sir, while there are Laws, this Outrage on my Reputation will not be borne with.

Lew. Laws ! dar'ſt Thou ſeek Shelter from the Laws ? Thoſe Laws, which thou and thy infernal Crew live in the conſtant Violation of ? Talk'ſt thou of Reputation too ? when under Friendſhip's ſacred Name, thou haſt betray'd, robb'd, and deſtroy'd ?

Stu. Ay, rail at Gaming; 'tis a rich Topic, and affords noble Declamation— Go, preach a-gainſt it in the City : You'll find a Congregation in every Tavern. If they ſhou'd laugh at you, fly to my Lord, and ſermonize it there. He'll thank you and reform.

Lew. And will Example ſanctify a Vice? No, Wretch; the Cuſtom of my Lord, or of the Cit that apes him, cannot excuſe a Breach of Law, or make the Gameſter's Calling reputable.

Stu. Rail on, I ſay— But is this Zeal for beg-gar'd *Beverley ?* Is it for Him that I am treated thus ? No; he and his Wife might both have groan'd in Priſon, had but the Siſter's Fortune eſcap'd the Wreck, to have rewarded the diſin-tereſted Love of honeſt Mr. *Lewſon.*

Lew. How I deteſt thee for the Thought ! But thou art loſt to every human Feeling. Yet let me tell thee, and may it wring thy Heart ! that tho' my Friend is ruin'd by thy Snares, thou haſt unknowingly been kind to Me.

Stu. Have I ? It was indeed unknowingly.

Lew. Thou haſt aſſiſted me in Love ; given me the Merit that I wanted ; ſince but for Thee,

my

my *Charlotte* had not known 'twas her dear felf I figh'd for, and not her Fortune.

Stu. Thank me, and take her then.

Lew. And as a Brother to poor *Beverley*, I will purfue the Robber that has ftript him, and fnatch him from his Gripe.

Stu. Then know, imprudent Man, he *is* within my Gripe; and fhou'd my Friendfhip for him be flander'd once again, the Hand that has fupply'd him, fhall fall and crufh him.

Lew. Why, now there's Spirit in thee! This is indeed to be a Villain! But I fhall reach thee yet—Fly where thou wilt, my Vengeance fhall purfue thee—And *Beverley* fhall yet be fav'd, be fav'd from Thee, thou Monfter; nor owe his Refcue to his Wife's Difhonour. (*Exit.*

Stu. (*paufing*) Then Ruin has enclos'd me. Curfe on my coward Heart! I wou'd be bravely villanous; but 'tis my Nature to fhrink at Danger, and he has found me. Yet Fear brings Caution, and That Security—More Mifchief muft be done to hide the paft—Look to yourfelf, officious *Lewfon*—there may be Danger ftirring—How now, *Bates?*

Enter Bates.

Bat. What is the Matter? 'Twas *Lewfon* and not *Beverley* that left you—I heard him loud—You feem alarm'd too.

Stu. Ay, and with Reafon---We are difcover'd.

Bat. I fear'd as much, and therefore caution'd you——But You were peremptory.

Stu. Thus Fools talk ever; fpending their idle Breath on what is paft, and trembling at the future.

ture. We muſt be active. *Beverley*, at worſt, is but ſuſpicious ; but *Lewſon*'s Genius, and his Hate to Me, will lay all open. Means muſt be found to ſtop him.

Bat. What Means ?

Stu. Diſpatch him--- Nay, ſtart not—— Deſperate Occaſions call for deſperate Deeds——We live but by his Death.

Bat. You cannot mean it ?

Stu. I do, by Heaven.

Bat. Good Night then.   (*Going.*

Stu. Stay. I muſt be heard, then anſwer'd. Perhaps the Motion was too ſudden ; and human Weakneſs ſtarts at Murder, tho' ſtrong Neceſſity compels it. I have thought long of this ; and my firſt Feelings were like yours ; a fooliſh Conſcience aw'd me, which ſoon I conquer'd. The Man that wou'd undo me, Nature cries out, undo. Brutes know their Foes by Inſtinct ; and where ſuperior Force is given, they uſe it for Deſtruction. Shall Man do leſs ? *Lewſon* purſues us to our Ruin ; and ſhall we, with the Means to cruſh him, fly from our Hunter, or turn and tear him ? 'Tis Folly even to heſitate.

Bat. He has oblig'd me, and I dare not.

Stu. Why, live to Shame then, to Beggary and Puniſhment. You wou'd be privy to the Deed, yet want the Soul to act it. Nay more ; had my Deſigns been levell'd at his Fortune, you had ſtept in the foremoſt—— And what is Life without its Comforts ? Thoſe you wou'd rob him of ; and by a lingring Death, add Cruelty to Murder. Henceforth adieu to half-made Villains—There's Danger in 'em. What you have got is your's ;

I   keep

keep it, and hide with it— I'll deal my future
Bounty to thofe who merit it.

Bat. What's the Reward?

Stu. Equal Divifion of our Gains. I fwear
it, and will be juft.

Bat. Think of the Means then.

Stu. He's gone to *Beverley*'s—Wait for him in
the Street—'Tis a dark Night, and fit for Mischief. A Dagger would be ufeful.

Bat. He fleeps no more.

Stu. Confider the Reward! When the Deed's
done, I have farther Bufinefs with you. Send
Dawfon to me.

Bat. Think it already done—and fo farewel.
(Exit.

Stu. Why, farewel *Lewfon* then; and farewel
to my Fears—This Night fecures me. I'll wait
the Event within.   *(Exit.*

Scene changes to the Street. Stage darken'd.

Enter Beverley.

Bev. How like an Out-caft do I wander?
Loaded with every Curfe, that drives the Soul to
Defperation——The Midnight Robber, as he
walks his Rounds, fees by the glimmering Lamp
my frantic Looks, and dreads to meet me.——
Whither am I going?——My Home lies there;
all that is dear on Earth it holds too; yet are
the Gates of Death more welcome to me—I'll
enter it no more—Who paffes there? 'Tis *Lewfon*
—He meets me in a gloomy Hour; and Memory
tells me he has been meddling with my Fame.

Enter

Enter Lewſon.

Lew. Beverley! Well met. I have been buſy in your Affairs.

Bev. So I have heard, Sir; and now muſt thank you as I ought.

Lew. To-morrow I may deſerve your Thanks. Late as it is, I go to *Bates.* Diſcoveries are making that an arch Villain trembles at.

Bev. Diſcoveries are made, Sir, that You ſhall tremble at. Where is this boaſted Spirit? this high Demeanour, that was to call me to Account? You ſay I have wrong'd my Siſter——Now ſay as much. But firſt be ready for Defence, as I am for Reſentment.　(*Draws.*

Lew. What mean you? I underſtand you not.

Bev. The Coward's ſtale Acquittance. Who, when he ſpreads foul Calumny abroad, and dreads juſt Vengeance on him, cries out, What mean you, I underſtand you not.

Lew. Coward, and Calumny! Whence are thoſe Words? But I forgive, and pity you.

Bev. Your Pity had been kinder to my Fame. But you have traduc'd it; told a vile Story to the public Ear, that I have wrong'd my Siſter.

Lew. 'Tis falſe. Shew me the Man that dares accuſe me.

Bev. I thought you brave, and of a Soul ſuperior to low Malice; but I have found you, and will have Vengeance. This is no Place for Argument.

Lew. Nor ſhall it be for Violence. Imprudent Man! who in Revenge for fancy'd Injuries, wou'd pierce the Heart that loves him. But honeſt Friendſhip acts from itſelf, unmov'd by

　Slander,

Slander or Ingratitude. The Life you thirst for, shall be employ'd to serve you.

Bev. 'Tis thus you wou'd compound then—First do a Wrong beyond Forgiveness, and to re-dress it, load me with Kindness unsolicited. I'll not receive it. Your Zeal is troublesome.

Lew. No Matter. It shall be useful.

Bev. It will not be accepted.

Lew. It must. You know me not.

Bev. Yes; for the Slanderer of my Fame. Who under shew of Friendship, arraigns me of In-justice. Buzzing in every Ear foul Breach of Trust, and Family Dishonour.

Lew. Have I done this? Who told you so?

Bev. The World—'Tis talk'd of every where. It pleas'd you to add Threats too. You were to call me to Account——Why, do it now then; I shall be proud of such an Arbiter.

Lew. Put up your Sword, and know me bet-ter. I never injur'd you. The base Suggestion comes from *Stukely*; I see him and his Aims.

Bev. What Aims? I'll not conceal it; 'twas *Stukely* that accus'd you.

Lew. To rid him of an Enemy——Perhaps of two——He fears Discovery, and frames a Tale of Falsehood, to ground Revenge and Mur-der on.

Bev. I must have Proof of this.

Lew. Wait till To-morrow then.

Bev. I will.

Lew. Good Night—I go to serve you—For-get what's past as I do; and chear your Family with Smiles. To-morrow may confirm 'em, and make all happy.   (*Exit.*

Bev.

Bev. (Pauſing.) How vile, and how abſurd is Man! His boaſted Honour is but another Name for Pride; which eaſier bears the Conſcioufneſs of Guilt, than the World's juſt Reproofs. But 'tis the Faſhion of the Times; and in defence of Falſehood and falſe Honour, Men die Martyrs. I knew not that my Nature was ſo bad.   *(ſtands muſing.*

    Enter Bates *and* Jarvis.

Jar. This Way the Noiſe was— and yonder's my poor Maſter.

Bat. I heard him at high Words with *Lewſon.* The Cauſe I know not.

Jar. I heard him too.   Misfortunes vex him.

Bat. Go to him, and lead him Home—But he comes this Way——I'll not be ſeen by him.
                             Ex. Bates.

Bev. (ſtarting) What Fellow's that? *(feeing* Jarvis) Art thou a Murderer, Friend? Come, lead the Way; I have a Hand as miſchievous as thine; a Heart as deſperate too——*Jarvis!*— To Bed, old Man, the Cold will chill thee.

Jar. Why are you wandering at this late Hour?—Your Sword drawn too!—For Heav'n's Sake ſheath it, Sir— the Sight diſtracts me.

Bev, Whoſe Voice was that?   *(wildly.*

Jar. 'Twas mine, Sir.   Let me intreat you to give the Sword to Me.

Bev. Ay, take it—quickly take it—Perhaps I am not ſo curs'd, but Heav'n may have ſent thee at this Moment to ſnatch me from Perdition.

Jar. Then I am bleſs'd.

Bev. Continue ſo, and leave me. My Sorrows are contagious. No one is bleſt that's near me.   *Jar.*

Jar. I came to feek you, Sir.

Bev. And now thou haft found me, leave me
---My Thoughts are wild and will not be difturb'd.

Jar. Such Thoughts are beft difturb'd.

Bev. I tell thee that they will not——Who fent
thee hither?

Jar. My weeping Miftrefs.

Bev. Am I fo meek a Hufband then? that a
commanding Wife prefcribes my Hours, and
fends to chide me for my Abfence?— Tell her,
I'll not return.

Jar. Thofe Words wou'd kill her.

Bev. Kill her! Wou'd they not be kind then?
But fhe fhall live to curfe me—I have deferv'd it
of her. Does fhe not hate me, *Jarvis?*

Jar. Alas, Sir! Forget your Griefs, and
let me lead you to her. The Streets are dangerous.

Bev. Be wife, and leave me then. The Night's
black Horrors are fuited to my Thoughts———
Thefe Stones fhall be my Refting-place. (*lies
down.*) Here fhall my Soul brood o'er its Miferies; 'till with the Fiends of Hell, and Guilty of
the Earth, I ftart and tremble at the Morning's
Light.

Jar. For Pity's Sake, Sir!—Upon my Knees I
beg you to quit this Place, and thefe fad Thoughts.
Let Patience, not Defpair, poffefs you— Rife, I
befeech you—There's not a Moment of your Abfence, that my poor Miftrefs does not groan for.

Bev. Have I undone her, and is fhe ftill fo
kind? (*ftarting up*) It is too much----My Brain
can't hold it--- O, *Jarvis!* how defperate is that
Wretch's State, which only Death or Madnefs
can relieve. *Jar.*

Jar. Appeafe his Mind, good Heaven! and give him Refignation! Alas, Sir, cou'd Beings in the other World perceive the Events of this, how wou'd your Parents bleffed Spirits grieve for you, even in Heaven!--- Let me conjure you by their honour'd Memories; by the fweet Innocence of your yet helplefs Child, and by the ceafelefs Sorrows of my poor Miftrefs, to rouze your Manhood, and ftruggle with thefe Griefs.

Bev. Thou virtuous, good old Man! thy Tears and thy Entreaties have reach'd my Heart, thro' all its Miferies. O! had I liften'd to thy honeft Warnings, no earthly Bleffing had been wanting to me!--- I was fo happy, that even a Wifh for more than I poffefs'd, was arrogant Prefumption. But I have warr'd againft the Power that blefs'd me, and now am fentenc'd to the Hell I merit.

Jar. Be but refign'd, Sir, and Happinefs may yet be yours.

Bev. Prithee be honeft, and do not flatter Mifery.

Jar. I do not, Sir--- Hark! I hear Voices---- Come this Way; we may reach Home unnotic'd.

Bev. Well, lead me then--- Un-notic'd did'ft thou fay? Alas! I dread no Looks, but of thofe Wretches I have made at Home.   (*Exeunt*,

S C E N E *changes to* Stukely's.

Enter Stukely *and* Dawfon.

Stu. Come hither *Dawfon.* My Limbs are on the Rack, and my Soul fhivers in me, 'till this Night's Bufinefs be complete. Tell me thy
Thoughts :

Thoughts : Is *Bates* determin'd, or does he waver ?

Daw. At first he seem'd irresolute ; wish'd the Employment had been mine ; and mutter'd Curses on his Coward Hand, that trembled at the Deed.

Stu. And did he leave you so ?

Daw. No. We walk'd together ; and shelter'd by the Darkness, saw *Beverley* and *Lewson* in warm Debate. But soon they cool'd ; and then I left 'em to hasten hither ; but not 'till 'twas resolv'd *Lewson* shou'd die.

Stu. Thy Words have given me Life—That Quarrel too was fortunate ; for if my Hopes deceive me not, it promises a Grave to *Beverley*.

Daw. You misconceive me. *Lewson* and he were Friends.

Stu. But my prolific Brain shall make 'em Enemies. If *Lewson* falls, he falls by *Beverley*. An upright Jury shall decree it. Ask me no Questions, but do as I direct. This Writ *(takes out a Pocket Book)* for some Days past, I have treasur'd here, 'till a convenient Time call'd for its Use. That Time is come. Take it, and give it to an Officer. It must be serv'd this Instant.   *(Gives a Paper.*

Daw. On *Beverley ?*

Bev. Look at it. 'Tis for the Sums that I have lent him.

Daw. Must he to Prison then ?

Stu. I ask'd Obedience ; not Replies. This Night a Jail must be his Lodging. 'Tis probable he's not gone Home yet. Wait at his Door, and see it executed.

2

Daw.

Daw. Upon a Beggar? He has no Means of Payment.

Stu. Dull and infenfible! If *Lewfon* dies, who was it kill'd him? Why, he that was feen quarreling with him; and I that knew of *Beverley*'s Intents, arrefted him in Friendfhip — A little late, perhaps ; but 'twas a virtuous Act, and Men will thank me for't. Now, Sir, you underftand me?

Daw. Moft perfectly --- And will about it.

Stu. Hafte then ; and when 'tis done, come back and tell me.

Daw. 'Till then farewel.   [*Exit.*

Stu. Now tell thy Tale, fond Wife ! And *Lewfon*, if again thou can'ft infult me, I'll kneel and own thee for my Mafter.

Not Avarice now, but Vengeance fires my Breaft,
And one fhort Hour muft make me curft or bleft.

Exit.

End of the Fourth A C T.

A C T   V.   Scene continues.

Enter Stukely, Bates, *and* Dawfon.

Bat. POOR *Lewfon !* — But I told you enough laft Night — The Thought of him is horrible to me.

Stu. In the Street, did you fay? And no one near him?

Bat. By his own Door ; he was leading me to his Houfe. I pretended Bufinefs with him, and

K   ftabb'd

ſtabb'd him to the Heart, while he was reaching at the Bell.

Stu. And did he fall ſo ſuddenly?

Bat. The Repetition pleaſes you, I ſee. I told you, he fell without a Groan.

Stu. What heard you of him this Morning?

Bat. That the Watch found him in their Rounds, and alarm'd the Servants. I mingled with the Croud juſt now, and ſaw him dead in his own Houſe.—The Sight terrify'd me.

Stu. Away with Terrors, 'till his Ghoſt riſe and accuſe us—We have no living Enemy to fear —unleſs 'tis *Beverley*; and him we have lodg'd ſafe in Priſon.

Bat. Muſt He be murder'd too?

Stu. No; I have a Scheme to make the Law his Murderer—At what Hour did *Lewſon* fall?

Bat. The Clock ſtruck Twelve as I turn'd to leave him. 'Twas a melancholy Bell, I thought, tolling for his Death.

Stu. The Time was lucky for us—*Beverley* was arreſted at One, you ſay?   [*to* Dawſon.

Daw. Exactly.

Stu. Good. We'll talk of this preſently —— The Women were with him, I think?

Daw. And old *Jarvis.* I wou'd have told you of 'em, laſt Night, but your Thoughts were too buſy. 'Tis well you have a Heart of Stone, the Tale wou'd melt it elſe.

Stu. Out with it then.

Daw. I trac'd him to his Lodgings; and pretended Pity for his Misfortunes, kept the Door open, while the Officers ſeiz'd him. 'Twas a damn'd Deed--- but no Matter--- I follow'd my Inſtructions.

                                        Stu.

Stu. And what said he?

Daw. He upbraided me with Treachery; call'd You a Villain; acknowledg'd the Sums you had lent him, and submitted to his Fortune.

Stu. And the Women ——

Daw. For a few Minutes Aftonifhment kept 'em silent --- They look'd wildly at one another, while the Tears stream'd down their Cheeks. But Rage and Fury soon gave 'em Words; and then, in the very Bitterness of Despair, they curs'd me, and the Monfter that had employ'd me.

Stu. And you bore it with Philofophy?

Draw. 'Till the Scene chang'd, and then I melted. I order'd the Officers to take away their Prifoner. The Women fhriek'd, and wou'd have follow'd him; but we forbad 'em. 'Twas then they fell upon their Knees, the Wife fainting, the Sifter raving, and both with all the Eloquence of Mifery endeavouring to foften us. I never felt Compaffion 'till that Moment; and had the Officers been mov'd like Me, we had left the Bufinefs undone, and fled with Curfes on ourfelves. But their Hearts were fteel'd by Cuftom. The Tears of Beauty and the Pangs of Affection were beneath their Pity. They tore him from their Arms, and lodg'd him in Prifon, with only *Jarvis* to comfort him.

Stu. There let him lie, 'till we have farther Bufinefs with him -- And for You, Sir, let me hear no more of your Compaffion --- A Fellow nurs'd in Villany, and employ'd from Childhood in the Bufinefs of Hell, fhou'd have no Dealings with Compaffion.

Daw. Say you fo, Sir? —— You fhou'd have nam'd the Devil that tempted me ——

K 2

Stu.

Stu. 'Tis falfe. I found you a Villain, and therefore employ'd you--- But no more of this--- We have embark'd too far in Mifchief to recede. *Lewfon* is dead, and we are all Principals in his Murder. Think of that--- There's Time enough for Pity, when ourfelves are out of Danger —— *Beverley* ftill lives, tho' in a Jail---His Ruin will fit heavy on him; and Difcoveries may be made to undo us all. Something muft be done, and fpeedily ——You faw him quarrelling with *Lewfon* in the Street laft Night? [*To* Bates.

Bat. I did; his Steward, *Jarvis*, faw him too.

Stu. And fhall atteft it. Here's Matter to work upon——An unwilling Evidence carries weight with him. Something of my Defign I have hinted t'you before——*Beverley* muft be the Author of this Murder; and we the Parties to convict him—But how to proceed will require Time and Thought --- Come along with Me; the Room within is fitter for Privacy --- But no Compaffion, Sir---[*to* Dawfon] We want Leifure for't——This Way. [*Exeunt.*

SCENE *changes to* Beverley's *Lodgings.*

Enter Mrs. Beverley *and* Charlotte.

Mrs. *Bev.* No News of *Lewfon* yet?

Char. None. He went out early, and knows not what has happen'd.

Mrs. *Bev.* The Clock ftrikes Eight·—I'll wait no longer.

Cba.

Cha. Stay but 'till *Jarvis* comes. He has sent twice to stop us 'till we see him.

Mrs. *Bev.* I have no Life in this Separation --- O! What a Night was last Night! I wou'd not pass another such to purchase Worlds by it —— My poor *Beverley* too! What must He have felt! The very Thought distracts me! —— To have him torn at Midnight from me! --- A loathsome Prison his Habitation! A cold damp Room his Lodging! The bleak Winds perhaps blowing upon his Pillow! No fond Wife to lull him to his Rest! and no Reflections but to wound and tear him! --- 'Tis too horrible --- I wanted Love for him, or they had not forc'd him from me. They shou'd have parted Soul and Body first --- I was too tame.

Cha. You must not Talk so. All that we cou'd we did; and *Jarvis* did the rest --- The faithful Creature will give him Comfort. Why does he delay coming?

Mrs. *Bev.* And there's another Fear. His poor Master may be claiming the last kind Office from him --- His Heart perhaps is breaking.

Cha. See where he comes --- His Looks are chearful too.

Enter Jarvis.

Mrs. *Bev.* Are Tears then chearful? Alas, he weeps! Speak to him *Charlotte* —— I have no Tongue to ask him Questions.

Char. How does your Master, *Jarvis?*

Jar. I am old and foolish, Madam; and Tears will come before my Words --- But don't You

weep

weep. [*to Mrs.* Bev.] I have a Tale of Joy for you.

Mrs. Bev. What Tale? --- Say but he's well, and I have Joy enough.

Jar. His Mind too fhall be well --- all fhall be well --- I have News for him that fhall make his poor Heart bound again --- Fie upon old Age --- How childifh it makes me! I have a Tale of Joy for you, and my Tears drown it.

Cha. Shed 'em in Showers then, and make Hafte to tell it.

Mrs. Bev. What is it, *Jarvis?*

Jar. Yet why fhou'd I rejoice when a good Man dies? Your Uncle, Madam, dy'd Yefterday.

Mrs. Bev. My Uncle! --- O Heavens!

Cha. How heard you of his Death?

Jar. His Steward came Exprefs, Madam --- I met him in the Street, enquiring for your Lodgings --- I fhou'd not rejoice perhaps --- but he was old, and my poor Mafter a Prifoner --- Now he fhall live again --- O 'tis a brave Fortune! and 'twas Death to me to fee him a Prifoner.

Cha. Where left you the Steward?

Jar. I wou'd not bring him hither, to be a Witnefs of your Diftreffes; and befides, I wanted once before I die, to be the Meffenger of Joy t'you. My good Mafter will be a Man again.

Mrs. Bev. Hafte, hafte then; and let us fly to him --- we are delaying our own Happinefs.

Jar. I had forgot a Coach, Madam; and *Lucy* has order'd one.

Mrs. Bev. Where was the Need of that? The News has given me Wings.

Cha.

Cha. I have no Joy, 'till my poor Brother fhares it with me. How did he pafs the Night, *Jarvis?*

Jar. Why now, Madam, I can tell you. Like a Man dreaming of Death and Horrors. When they led him to his Cell --- For 'twas a poor Apartment for my Mafter --- He flung himfelf upon a wretched Bed, and lay fpeechlefs 'till Day-break. A Sigh now and then, and a few Tears that follow'd thofe Sighs, were all that told me he was alive. I fpoke to him, but he wou'd not hear me ; and when I perfifted, he rais'd his Hand at me, and knit his Brow fo ------ I thought he wou'd have ftruck me.

Mrs. *Bev.* O Miferable! But what faid he, *Jarvis?* Or was he filent all Night?

Jar. At Day-break he ftarted from the Bed, and looking wildly at me, afk'd who I was. I told him, and bid him be of Comfort --- Begone old Wretch, fays he --- I have fworn never to know Comfort --- My Wife! my Child! my Sifter! I have undone 'em all, and will know no Comfort --- Then letting go his Hold, and falling upon his Knees, he imprecated Curfes upon himfelf.

Mrs. *Bev.* This is too horrible! --- But you did not leave him fo?

Cha. No, I am fure he did not.

Jar. I had not the Heart, Madam. By Degrees I brought him to himfelf. A Shower of Tears came to his Relief; and then he call'd me his kindeft Friend, and begg'd Forgivenefs of me like a Child --- I was a Child too, when he begg'd Forgivenefs of me. My Heart throbb'd fo, I could not fpeak to him. He turn'd from me for a

Minute

Minute or two, and suppreffing a few bitter Sighs,
enquir'd after his wretched Family --- Wretched
was his Word, Madam --- Afk'd how you bore
the Mifery of laft Night --- If you had Goodnefs
enough to fee him in Prifon --- And then begg'd
me to haften to you. I told him he muft be
more himfelf firft --- He promis'd me he wou'd;
and bating a few fullen Intervals, he became
compos'd and eafy --- And then I left him; but
not without an Attendant --- A Servant in the Prifon, whom I hir'd to wait upon him --- 'Tis an
Hour fince we parted --- I was prevented in my
Hafte to be the Meffenger of Joy t'you.

Mrs. Bev. What a Tale is this? --- But we have
ftaid too long --- A Coach is needlefs.

Cha. Hark! I hear one at the Door.

Jar. And *Lucy* comes to tell us --- We'll away
this Moment.

Mrs. Bev. To comfort him or die with him.
[*Exeunt.*

SCENE *changes to* Stukely's *Lodgings.*

Enter Stukely, Bates *and* Dawfon.

Stu. Here's prefumptive Evidence at leaft ---
or if we want more, why, we muft fwear more.
But all unwillingly --- We gain Credit by Reluct-
ance --- I have told you how to proceed. *Beverley*
muft die --- We hunt him in View now, and
muft not flacken in the Chace. 'Tis either Death
for Him, or Shame and Punifhment for Us. Think
of that, and remember your Inftructions --- You,
Bates, muft to the Prifon immediately. I wou'd
be

be there but a few Minutes before you. And you, *Dawson*, must follow in a few Minutes after.. So here we divide————But answer me ; are you resolv'd upon this Business like Men ?

Bates. Like Villains rather---But you may depend upon us.

Stu. Like what we are then---You make no Answer, *Dawson*— Compassion, I suppose, has seiz'd you.

Daw. No ; I have disclaim'd it---My Answer is *Bates's*---You may depend upon me.

Stu. Consider the Reward ! Riches and Security ! I have sworn to divide with you to the last Shilling---So here we separate 'till we meet in Prison————Remember your Instructions and be Men. (*Exeunt.*

S C E N E *changes to a Prison.*

Beverley *is discover'd sitting. After a short Pause he starts up, and comes forward.*

Bev. Why, there's an End then. I have judg'd deliberately, and the Result is Death. How the Self-Murderer's Account may stand, I know not. But this I know—the Load of hateful Life oppresses me too much---The Horrors of my Soul are more than I can bear— (*Offers to kneel*) Father of Mercy !——I cannot pray---Despair has laid his iron Hand upon me, and seal'd me for Perdition---Conscience! Conscience! thy Clamours are too loud ————Here's that shall silence thee. (*Takes a Vial out of his Pocket, and looks at it.*) Thou art most friendly to the Miserable. Come then, thou Cordial for sick Minds————Come

L   to

to my Heart. (*Drinks.*) O, that the Grave wou'd bury Memory as well as Body! For if the Soul fees and feels the Sufferings of thofe dear Ones it leaves behind, the Everlafting has no Vengeance to torment it deeper————I'll think no m re on't————Reflection comes too late———— Once there was a Time for't—but now 'tis paft. ———— Who's there?

Enter Jarvis.

Jar. One that hop'd to fee you with better Looks————Why d'you turn fo from me? I have brought Comfort with me----And fee who comes to give it welcome.

Bev. My Wife and Sifter! Why, 'tis but one Pang then, and farewel World.   (*Afide.*

Enter Mrs. Beverley *and* Charlotte.

Mrs. *Bev.* Where is he? (*Runs and embraces him*) O I have him! I have him! And now they fhall never part us more---I have News, Love, to make you happy for ever.---But don't look coldly on me.

Char. How is it, Brother?

Mrs. *Bev.* Alas! he hears us not----Speak to me, Love. I have no Heart to fee you thus.

Bev. Nor I to bear the Senfe of fo much Shame————This is a fad Place.

Mrs. *Bev.* We come to take you from it. To tell you that the World goes well again. That Providence has feen our Sorrows, and fent the Means to heal 'em----Your Uncle dy'd Yefterday.

Bev. My Uncle!--- No, do not fay fo--- O! I am fick at Heart!

Mrs. *Bev.*

Mrs. *Bev.* Indeed! —— I meant to bring you Comfort.

Bev. Tell me he lives then——If you wou'd give me Comfort, tell me he lives.

Mrs *Bev.* And if I did———I have no Power to raife the Dead---He dy'd Yefterday.

Bev. And I am Heir to him?

Jar. To his whole Eftate, Sir---But bear it patiently---pray bear it patiently.

Bev. Well, well--- (*Paufing*) Why, Fame fays I am rich then?

Mrs. *Bev.* And truly fo---Why do you look fo wildly?

Bev. Do I? The News was unexpected. But has he left me all?

Jar. All, all, Sir---He cou'd not leave it from you.

Bev. I'm forry for it.

Cha. Sorry! Why forry?

Bev. Your Uncle's dead, *Charlotte.*

Char. Peace be with his Soul then---Is it fo terrible that an old Man fhould die?

Bev. He fhou'd have been immortal.

Mrs. *Bev.* Heaven knows I wifh'd not for his Death. 'Twas the Will of Providence that he fhou'd die---Why are you difturb'd fo?

Bev. Has Death no Terrors in it?

Mrs. *Bev.* Not an old Man's Death. Yet if it troubles ycu, I wifh him living.

Bev. And I, with all my Heart.

Char. Why, what's the Matter?

Bev. Nothing---How heard you of his Death?

Mrs. *Bev.* His Steward came Exprefs. Wou'd I had never known it!

　　　　　　　　　Bev.

Bev. Or had heard it one Day fooner——For I have a Tale to tell, fhall turn you into Stone; or if the Power of Speech remain, you fhall kneel down and curfe me.

Mrs. Bev. Alas! What Tale is this? And why are we to curfe you?——I'll blefs you for ever.

Bev. No; I have deferv'd no Bleffings. The World holds not fuch another Wretch. All this large Fortune, this fecond Bounty of Heaven, that might have heal'd our Sorrows, and fatisfy'd our utmoft Hopes, in a curs'd Hour I fold laft Night.

Char. Sold! How fold!

Mrs. Bev. Impoffible!——It cannot be!

Bev. That Devil *Stukely*, with all Hell to aid him, tempted me to the Deed. To pay falfe Debts of Honour, and to redeem paft Errors, I fold the Reverfion——Sold it for a fcanty Sum, and loft it among Villains.

Char. Why, farewel all then.

Bev. Liberty and Life——Come, kneel and curfe me.

Mrs. Bev. Then hear me Heaven! (*Kneels*) Look down with Mercy on his Sorrows! Give Softnefs to his Looks, and Quiet to his Heart! Take from his Memory the Senfe of what is paft, and cure him of Defpair! On Me! on Me! if Mifery muft be the Lot of either, multiply Misfortunes! I'll bear 'em patiently, fo He is happy! Thefe Hands fhall toil for his Support! Thefe Eyes be lifted up for hourly Bleffings on him! And every Duty of a fond and faithful Wife be doubly done to cheer and comfort him!———So hear me! So reward me! (*Rifes.*

Bev.

Bev. I wou'd kneel too, but that offended Heaven wou'd turn my Prayers into Curfes. What have I to afk for? I who have fhook Hands with Hope? Is it for Length of Days that I fhou'd kneel? No; My Time is limited. Or is it for this World's Bleffings upon You and Yours? To pour out my Heart in Wifhes for a ruin'd Wife, a Child and Sifter? O! no! For I have done a Deed to make Life horrible t'you.——

Mrs. *Bev.* Why horrible? Is Poverty fo horible?——The real Wants of Life are few. A little Induftry will fupply 'em all—And Chearfulnefs will follow——It is the Privilege of honeft Induftry, and we'll enjoy it fully.

Bev. Never, never——O, I have told you but in Part. The irrevocable Deed is done.

Mrs. *Bev.* What Deed?——And why do you look fo at me?

Bev. A Deed that dooms my Soul to Vengeance——That feals Your Mifery here, and Mine hereafter.

Mrs. *Bev.* No, no; You have a Heart too good for't——Alas! he raves, *Charlotte*——His Looks too terrify me —Speak Comfort to him— He can have done no Deed of Wickednefs.

Char. And yet I fear the worft——What is it, Brother?

Bev. A Deed of Horror.

Jar. Afk him no Queftions, Madam—This laft Misfortune has hurt his Brain. A little Time will give him Patience.

Enter Stukely.

Bev. Why is this Villain here?

Stu. To give you Liberty and Safety. There, Madam's

Madam's his Difcharge. (*Giving a Paper to Mrs.* Beverley) Let him fly this Moment. The Arreft laft Night was meant in Friendfhip; but came too late.

Char. What mean you, Sir?

Stu. The Arreft was too late, I fay; I wou'd have kept his Hands from Blood, but was too late.

Mrs. *Bev.* His Hands from Blood!-----Whofe Blood?----O, Wretch! Wretch!

Stu. From *Lewfon's* Blood.

Char. No, Villain! Yet what of *Lewfon*? Speak quickly.

Stu. You are ignorant then! I thought I heard the Murderer at Confeffion.

Char. What Murderer?----And who is murder'd? Not *Lewfon*?---Say he lives, and I'll kneel and worfhip you.

Stu. In Pity, fo I wou'd; but that the Tongues of all cry Murder. I came in Pity, not in Malice; to fave the Brother, not kill the Sifter. Your *Lewfon's* dead.

Char. O horrible!—Why who has kill'd him? And yet it cannot be. What Crime had He committed that he fhou'd die? Villain! he lives! he lives! and fhall revenge thefe Pangs.

Mrs. *Bev.* Patience, fweet *Charlotte!*

Char. O, tis too much for Patience!

Mrs. *Bev.* He comes in Pity, he fays. O! execrable Villain! The Friend is kill'd then, and this the Murderer?

Bev. Silence, I charge you----Proceed, Sir.

Stu. No. Juftice may ftop the Tale—and here's an Evidence.

Enter

Enter Bates.

Bates. The News, I fee has reach'd you. But take Comfort, Madam. (*To* Char.) There's one Without enquiring for you---Go to him and lofe no Time.

Char. O Mifery! Mifery!   (*Exit.*

Mrs. *Bev.* Follow her, *Jarvis.* If it be true that *Lewfon*'s dead, her Grief may kill her.

Bates. *Jarvis* muft ftay here, Madam. I have fome Queftions for him.

Stu. Rather let him fly. His Evidence may crufh his Mafter.

Bev. Why ay; this looks like Management.

Bates. He found you quarrelling with *Lewfon* in the Street laft Night.   (*To* Bev'

Mrs. *Bev.* No; I am fure he did not.

Jar. Or if I did----

Mrs. *Bev.* 'Tis falfe, old Man---They had no Quarrel; there was no Caufe for Quarrel.

Bev. Let him proceed, I fay---O! I am fick! fick!----Reach me a Chair.   (*He fits down.*

Mrs. *Bev.* You droop, and tremble, Love.--- Your Eyes are fixt too---Yet You are innocent. If *Lewfon*'s dead, You kill'd him not.

Enter Dawfon.

Stu. Who fent for *Dawfon?*

Bates. 'Twas I---We have a Witnefs too, you little think of---Without there!

Stu. What Witnefs?

Bates. A right one. Look at him.

Enter Lewfon *and* Charlotte.

Stu. *Lewfon!* O Villains! Villains!

                    (*To* Bates *and* Dawfon.
                    Mrs. *Bev.*

Mrs. Bev. Rifen from the Dead! Why, this is unexpected Happinefs!

Char. Or is't his Ghoft? (*To* Stukely) That Sight wou'd pleafe you, Sir.

Jar. What Riddle's this?

Bev. Be quick and tell it----My Minutes are but few.

Mrs. Bev. Alas! why fo? You fhall live long and happily

Lew. While Shame and Punifhment fhall rack that Viper (*Pointing to* Stukely) The Tale is fhort-- I was too bufy in his Secrets, and therefore doom'd to die. *Bates,* to prevent the Murder, undertook it---I kept aloof to give it Credit---

Char. And gave Me Pangs unutterable.

Lew. I felt 'em all, and wou'd have told you ---But Vengeance wanted ripening. The Villain's Scheme was but half executed. The Arreft by *Dawfon* follow'd the fuppos'd Murder---And now, depending on his once wicked Affociates, he comes to fix the Guilt on *Beverley.*

Mrs. Bev. O! execrable Wretch!

Bates. *Dawfon* and I are Witneffes of this.

Lew. And of a thoufand Frauds. His Fortune ruin'd by Sharpers and falfe Dice; and *Stukely* fole Contriver and Poffeffor of all.

Daw. Had he but ftopt on this Side Murder, we had been Villains ftill.

Mrs. Bev. Thus Heaven turns Evil into Good; and by permitting Sin, warns Men to Virtue.

Lew. Yet punifhes the Inftrument. So fhall our Laws; tho' not with Death. But Death were Mercy. Shame, Beggary, and Imprifonment,

ment, unpity'd Mifery, the Stings of Confcience, and the Curfes of Mankind fhall make Life hateful to him——till at laft, his own Hand end him——How does my Friend? (*To* Bev.

Bev. Why, well. Who's he that afks me?

Mrs. *Bev.* 'Tis *Lewfon*, Love——Why do you look fo at him?

Bev. They told me he was murder'd. (*Wildly.*

Mrs. *Bev.* Ay; but he lives to fave us.

Bev, Lend me your Hand----The Room turns round.

Mrs. *Bev.* O Heaven!

Lew. This Villain here, difturbs him. Remove him from his Sight —— And for your Lives, fee that you guard him.. (Stukely *is taken off by* Dawfon.*and* Bates.) How is it, Sir?

Bev. 'Tis here---and here. (*Pointing to his Head and Heart.*) And now it tears me!

Mrs. *Bev.* You feel convuls'd too---What is't difturbs you?

Lew. This fudden Turn of Joy perhaps---- He wants Reft too----Laft Night was dreadful to him. His Brain is giddy.

Char. Ay, never to be cur'd----Why, Brother!----O! I fear! I fear!

Mrs. *Bev.* Preferve him, Heaven!---My Love! my Life! look at me!----How his Eyes flame!

Bev. A Furnace rages in this Heart----I have been too hafty.

Mrs. *Bev.* Indeed!----O me! O me!---Help, *Jarvis*! Fly, fly for Help! Your Mafter dies elfe---Weep not but fly! (*Ex.* Jar.) What is this hafty Deed?----Yet do not anfwer me----My Fears have guefs'd it.

Bev

Bev. Call back the Meſſenger----'Tis not in Medicine's Power to help me.

Mrs. *Bev.* Is it then ſo?

Bev. Down, reſtleſs Flames!--- (*Laying his Hand on his Heart*) down to your native Hell--- There you ſhall rack me----O! for a Pauſe from Pain!

Mrs. *Bev.* Help *Charlotte!* Support him, Sir! (*To* Lewſon) This is a killing Sight!

Bev. That Pang was well---It has numb'd my Senſes.---Where's my Wife?----Can you forgive me, Love?

Mrs. *Bev.* Alas! for what?

Bev, (*Starting again*) And there's another Pang---Now all is quiet---Will you forgive me?

Mrs. *Bev.* I will---Tell me for what?

Bev. For meanly dying.

Mrs. *Bev.* No---do not ſay it.

Bev. As truly as my Soul muſt anſwer it--- Had *Jarvis* ſtaid this Morning, all had been well. But preſs'd by Shame---pent in a Priſon----tormented with my Pangs for You----driven to Deſpair and Madneſs---I took the Advantage of his Abſence, corrupted the poor Wretch he left to guard me, and------ſwallow'd Poiſon.

Mrs. *Bev.* O! fatal Deed!

Char. Dreadful and cruel!

Bev. Ay, moſt accurs'd---And now I go to my Account. This Reſt from Pain brings Death; yet 'tis Heaven's Kindneſs to me. I wiſh'd for Eaſe, a Moment's Eaſe, that cool Repentance and Contrition might ſoften Vengeance---Bend me, and let me kneel. (*They lift him from his Chair and ſupport him on his Knees*) I'll pray for You too.

Thou

Thou Power that mad'ft me, hear me! If for a
Life of Frailty, and this too hafty Deed of Death,
thy Juftice dooms me, here I acquit the Sentence.
But if, enthron'd in Mercy where thou fit'ft, thy
Pity has beheld me, fend me a Gleam of Hope;
that in thefe laft and bitter Moments my Soul
may tafte of Comfort! And for thefe Mourners
here, O! let their Lives be peaceful, and their
Deaths happy!----Now raife me,

(They lift him to the Chair.

Mrs. *Bev.* Reftore him, Heaven! Stretch forth
thy Arm omnipotent, and fnatch him from the
Grave!---O fave him! fave him!

Bev. Alas! that Prayer is fruitlefs. Already Death
has feiz'd me---Yet Heaven is gracious---I afk'd
for Hope, as the bright Prefage of Forgivenefs,
and like a Light, blazing thro' Darknefs, it came
and chear'd me---'Twas all I liv'd for, and now
I die.

Mrs. *Bev.* Not yet!---Not yet!---Stay but a
little and I'll die too.

Bev. No; live I charge you.----We have a
little One. Tho' I have left him, You will not
leave him.----To *Lewfon's* Kindnefs I bequeath
him---Is not this *Charlotte?* We have liv'd in
Love, tho' I have wrong'd you---Can you forgive
me, *Charlotte?*

Char. Forgive you!—O my poor Brother!

Bev. Lend me your Hand, Love—fo—raife
me---No---'twill not be---My Life is finifh'd---
O! for a few fhort Moments! to tell you how my
Heart bleeds for you---That even now, thus dying
as I am, dubious and fearful of Hereafter, my bofom Pang is for Your Miferies. Support her
Heaven!

Heaven! —— And now I go —— O, Mercy!
Mercy! (*Dies.*

Lew. Then all is over—— How is it, Madam?—— My poor *Charlotte* too!

Ente Jarvis.

Jar How does my Master, Madam? Here's
Help at Hand——Am I too late then?
(*Seeing* Beverley.

Char. Tears! Tears! Why fall you not?——
O wretched Sister! ——Speak to her, *Lewson*---
Her Grief is speechless.

Lew. Remove her from this Sight——Go to
her, *Jarvis*——Lead and support her. Sorrow
like Hers forbids Complaint——Words are for
lighter Griefs——Some miniftring Angel bring her
Peace! (*Jar. and* Char. *lead her off.*
And Thou, poor breathless Corps, may thy departed Soul have found the Reft it pray'd for! Save
but one Error, and this laft fatal Deed, thy Life
was lovely. Let frailer Minds take Warning;
and from Example learn, that Want of Prudence
is Want of Virtue.

Follies, if uncontroul'd, of every Kind,
Grow into Paffions, and fubdue the Mind ;
With Senfe and Reafon hold fuperior Strife,
And conquer Honour, Nature, Fame and Life.

F I N I S.

EXCERPTS
FROM
The World

THE

W O R L D.

NUMBER IX.

By *ADAM FITZ-ADAM.*

To be continued every THURSDAY.

THURSDAY, *March* the 1ſt, 1753.

"I AM that unfortunate man, madam," was the ſaying of a gentleman, who ſtopt and made a low bow to a lady in the park, as ſhe was calling to her dog by the name of cuckold.

WHAT a deal of good might be expected from theſe eſſays, if every man, who ſhould happen to read his own character in them, would as honeſtly acknowledge it as this gentleman! But it is the miſfortune of general ſatire, that few perſons will apply it to themſelves,

felves, while they have the comfort of thinking that it
will fit others as well. It is therefore, I am afraid, only
furnifhing bad people with fcandal againft their neighbours : for every man flatters himfelf, that he has the
art of playing the fool or knave fo very fecretly, that,
though he fees plainly how all elfe are employed, no
mortal can have the cunning to find out him.

T H U S a gentleman told me yefterday, " That he
" was very glad to fee a particular acquaintance of his
" expofed in the third number of the WORLD. The
" parfon who wrote that letter, continued he, was de-
" termined to fpeak plainly; for the character of my
" friend was fo ftrongly marked, that it was impoffible
" to miftake it." He then proceeded to inform me that
he had read Seneca, by obferving, " That there fhould
" be no mixture of feverity or reproof in the obligations
" we confer ; on the contrary, if there fhould be only
" occafion for the gentleft admonition, it ought to be
" deferred to another feafon ; for men, added he, are
" much more apt to remember injuries than benefits ;
" and it is enough if they forgive an obligation that
" has the nature of an offence."

M Y reader may, poffibly, be furprized, when I tell
him, that the man who could commit to memory thefe
maxims of Seneca, and who could rejoice to fee fuch
a character expofed as the curate's friend in my third paper, is an old batchelor with an eftate of three thoufand
pounds a year, and fifty thoufand in ready money ; who
never was known to lend a guinea in his life, without
making the borrower more miferable by the benefit than
he had been before by his wants. But it is the peculiar
talent of this gentleman to wound himfelf by proxy, or
(in the fportfman's phrafe) to knock himfelf down

by

by the recoiling of his own gun. I remember he told me fome time ago, after having harangued very learnedly upon the deteſtable ſin of Avarice, " That " the common people of a certain county in Eng- " land were the moſt covetous and brutal in the whole " world. I will give you an inſtance, ſays he. About " three years ago, by a very odd accident, I fell into a " well in that county, and was abſolutely within a few " minutes of periſhing, before I could prevail on an un- " conſcionable dog of a labourer, who happened to be " within hearing of my cries, to help me out for half a " crown. The fellow was ſo rapacious as to inſiſt upon " a crown for above a quarter of an hour; and I verily " believe he would not have abated me a ſingle farthing, " if he had not ſeen me at the laſt gaſp, and determined " to die rather than ſubmit to his extortion."

B u t to return to my ſubject. If there are objecti- ons to general ſatire, ſomething may alſo be ſaid againſt perſonal abuſe; which, though it is a kind of writing that requires a ſmaller portion of parts, and is ſure of having almoſt as many admirers as readers, is neverthelefs ſubject to great difficulties; it being abſolutely neceſſary that the author who undertakes it ſhould have no feeling of certain evils, common to humanity, which are known by the names of pain and ſhame. In other words, he muſt be infenſible to a good kicking, and have no me- mory of it afterwards. Now though a great many au- thors have found it an eaſy matter to arrive at this ex- cellence, with me the taſk would be attended with great labour and difficulty; as it is my misfortune to have con- tracted, either by the prejudice of education, or by ſome other means, an invincible averſion to pain and diſhonour. I am very ſenſible that I may hurt myſelf as a writer by
this

this confeſſion ; but it was never any pleaſure of mine to raiſe expectations with a deſign to diſappoint them: and though it ſhould loſe me the major part of my readers, I hereby declare, that I never will indulge them with any perſonal abuſe ; nor will I ſo much as attack any of thoſe fine gentlemen, or fine ladies, who have the honour of being ſingle in any one character, be it ever ſo ridiculous.

B u t if I had every requiſite for this kind of writing, there are certain people in town, whom it would be ingratitude in me to attack. The maſters of both theatres are my very good friends ; for which reaſon I forbear to ſay, that half the comedies in their catalogue ought to be damned for wickedneſs and indecency. But I not only keep this to myſelf, but have alſo been at great trouble and pains to ſuppreſs a paſſage bearing very hard againſt them in a book, which will ſpeedily be publiſhed, called the PROGRESS OF WIT. The author of this book, who, luckily for the theatres, happens to be a particular friend of mine, is a very great joker ; and, as I often tell him, does a vaſt deal of miſchief, without ſeeming to intend it. The paſſage which I prevailed with him to ſuppreſs, ſtood at the beginning of the thirteenth chapter of his book, and was exactly as follows.

" A s it was now clear to all people of faſhion that
" men had no ſouls, the buſineſs of life was pleaſure
" and amuſement ; and he that could beſt adminiſter
" to theſe two, was the moſt uſeful member of ſociety.
" From hence aroſe thoſe numerous places of reſort and
" recreation, which men of narrow and ſplenetic minds
" have called the peſts of the public. The moſt conſi-
" derable of which places, and which are at this day in
" the higheſt reputation, were the BAGNIO's and the
" THE-

" THEATRES. The BAGNIO's were conſtantly under
" the direction of diſcreet and venerable matrons, who
" had paſſed their youth in the practice of thoſe exer-
" ciſes, which they were now teaching to their daugh-
" ters ; while the management of the THEATRES was
" the province of the men. The natural connection
" between theſe houſes made it convenient that they
" ſhould be erected in the neighbourhood of each
" other ; and indeed the harmony ſubſiſting between
" them has inclined many people to think that the
" profits of both were divided equally by each. But
" I have always conſidered them as only playing into
" one another's hands, without any nearer affinity than
" that of the ſchools of Weſtminſter and Eton to the
" univerſities of Oxford and Cambridge. At the PLAY-
" HOUSE young gentlemen and ladies were inſtructed by
" an Etheridge, a Wycherley, a Congreve and a Van-
" brugh, in the rudiments of that ſcience which they
" were to perfect at the BAGNIO, under a Needham, a
" Haywood, a Haddock and a Roberts."

THUS much had my friend, in his PROGRESS OF
WIT, thought proper to obſerve upon the looſeneſs of
the ſtage. But as the whole paſſage is ſuppreſſed, the
managers will have nothing to fear from the publication
of that performance.

IT were to be wiſhed, indeed, that thoſe gentlemen
would have done entirely both with tragedy and comedy,
and reſolve at once to entertain the town only with
PANTOMIME. That greater advantages would accrue
from it, is beyond diſpute ; people of taſte and faſhion
having already given ſufficient proof that they think
it the higheſt entertainment the ſtage is capable of
affording : the moſt innocent, we are ſure it is ; for

where

where nothing is faid, and nothing meant, very little harm can be done. Mr. Garrick, perhaps, may ftart a few objections to this propofal; but with thofe univerfal talents, which he fo happily poffeffes, it is not to be doubted but he will, in time, be able to handle the wooden fword with as much dignity and dexterity as his brother Lun. He will alfo reap another advantage from this kind of acting; as he will have fewer enemies by being the fineft Harlequin of the age, than he has at prefent, by being the greateft Actor of any age or country.

To the PUBLIC.

WHEREAS fome gentlemen have doubted whether the fubfcription for the ufe of king THEODORE, *was really intended to be carried on, I am ordered to acquaint the Public, that Mr.* FITZ-ADAM *was not only in earneft in promoting fuch a contribution, but has already received fome noble benefactions for that purpofe; and he will take care to apply the fubfidy in the moft uncorrupt manner to the ufes for which it was defigned, and to the honour and dignity of the crown of* CORSICA.

ROBERT DODSLEY.

LONDON: Printed for R. DODSLEY in Pall-Mall, (where letters to the author are taken in) and fold by M. COOPER at the Globe in Pater-Nofter-Row. Price 2d.

THE

W O R L D.

NUMBER XLIII.

By *ADAM FITZ-ADAM.*

To be continued every THURSDAY.

THURSDAY, *October* the 25th, 1753.

I HAVE devoted to-day's paper to the miscellaneous productions of such of my correspondents as, in my own opinion, are either whimsical enough, or witty enough to be entertaining to my readers.

To Mr. FITZ-ADAM.

SIR,

I am an ENGLISHMAN and a PATRIOT, but neither a FREEHOLDER nor an INDEPENDENT WHIG. I am neither a CRAFTSMAN nor a FOOL, but a FREETHINKER and a PLAIN-DEALER ; a steady CHAMPION for virtue, and a sharp PROTESTER against vice.

I

I AM a daily INSPECTOR of my neighbour's actions, and take a MONTHLY REVIEW of my own; yet do not aſſume the title of CENSOR or GUARDIAN; being contented with the office of MONITOR, or REMEMBRANCER. My enemies nevertheleſs will call me a TATLER, a BUSY-BODY, an IMPERTINENT, &c.

I AM a great READER and a LOVER of polite literature. I am ſometimes an ADVENTURER abroad, ſometimes a RAMBLER at home, and rove like the BEE from MUSÆUM to MUSÆUM in queſt of knowledge and pleaſure.

I AM an OCCASIONAL WRITER too; in a fit of gaiety I am a HUMOURIST, in a fit of ſeriouſneſs a MORALIST; and when I am very angry indeed, I SCOURGE the age with all the ſpirit of a BUSBY.

To conclude, I am not an idle SPECTATOR, but a cloſe EXAMINER of what paſſes in the WORLD, and Mr. Fitz-Adam's

Admirer and humble ſervant,

PHILOCÓSMOS.

THIS letter puts me in mind of the following advertiſement in a late Daily Advertiſer. "Whereas Thomas "Turvey, ſnuff-man, who is lately removed from the "blackamoor's head in Piccadilly to the ſhop, late the "crown and dagger, three doors lower, and hopes for the "continuance of his friend's cuſtom"—And there it ends. I ſhould have been more obliged to my correſpondent, if after his WHEREAS that he was an ENGLISHMAN, a PATRIOT, a FREEHOLDER, &c. he had thought proper to inform me to what-purpoſe he was all this. But I have the pleaſure of hoping that his epiſtle is only an introductory diſcourſe to a larger work; and as ſuch I have given it to the public without addition or amendment.

SIR,

S I R,

IF it would not be medling with religion (a subject which you have declared against touching upon) I wish you would recommend it to all rectors, vicars and curates of parishes to omit in the prayer, commonly used in the pulpit before sermon, the petition for JEWS, TURKS and INFIDELS. For as the JEWS, since a late act of parliament, are justly detested by the whole nation; and as it is shrewdly suspected that a bill is now in agitation for naturalizing the TURKS, wife men are of opinion that it is no business of ours to be continually recommending such people in our prayers. Indeed, as for the INFIDELS, who are only our own people, I should make no scruple of praying for them, if I did not know that persons of fashion do not care to hear themselves named so very particularly in the face of a congregation. I have the honour of an acquaintance with a lady of very fine understanding, who assures me that the above-mentioned prayer is absolutely as terrible to her as being churched in public: for that she never hears the word INFIDEL mentioned from the pulpit, without fancying herself the stare of the whole rabble of believers.

As it is certainly the duty of a clergyman to avoid giving offence to his parishioners; and as our hatred to the JEWS, our alarms about the TURKS, and the modesty of persons of quality, are not to be overcome, I beg that you will not only insert this letter in the WORLD, but that you will also give it as your opinion that the petition should be omitted.

I am,

S I R,

Your most humble servant,

I. M.

MR.

Mr. Fitz-Adam,

Now the theatres are open, and the town is in nigh
expectation of feeing PANTOMIMES performed to the
greateft advantage, it would not be improper if you
were to give us a paper upon that fubject. Your pre-
deceffor the Spectator, and the Tatler before him ufed
frequently to animadvert upon theatrical entertainments;
but as thofe gentlemen happened to have no talents for
PANTOMIME, and were partial to fuch entertainments
as themfelves were able to produce, they treated the
nobler compofitions with unwarrantable freedom. Happy
is it for us, that we live in an age of TASTE, when the
dumb eloquence, and manual wit and humour of
HARLEQUIN is juftly preferred to the whining of tragedy, or the vulgarity of comedy. But it grieves me,
in an entertainment fo near perfection, to obferve certain
indelicacies and indecorums, which, though they never
fail of obtaining the approbation of the galleries, muft
be extremely offenfive to the politenefs of the boxes.
The indelicacies I mean, are, the frequent and figni-
ficant wriglings of HARLEQUIN's tail, and the affront
that PIEROT is apt to put upon the modefty of COLUM-
BINE, by fometimes fuppofing, in his fearches for her
lover, that fhe has hid him under her petticoats. That
fuch a fuppofition would be allowable in comedy, I am
very ready to own; the celebrated Mrs. Behn having
given us in reality what is here only fuppofed. In a
play of that delicate lady's, the wife to conceal her gallant from her hufband, not only hides him under her
petticoats, but, as Trulla did by Hudibrafs, ftraddles
over him, and holding her hufband in difcourfe, walks
backwards with her lover to the door, where with a
gentle love-kick fhe difmiffes him from his hiding place.

But

But that the chaste COLUMBINE should be suspected of such indelicacy, or that PIEROT should be so audacious as to attempt the examination of premises so sacred, is a solicism in PANTOMIME. Another impurity that gives me almost equal offence, is, HARLEQUIN's tapping the neck or bosom of his mistress, and then kissing his fingers. I am apprehensive that this behaviour is a little bordering upon wantonness; which in the character of HARLEQUIN, who is a foreigner, and a fine gentleman, and every thing agreeable, is as absurd, as it is immodest.

WHEN these reformations can be brought about, everybody must allow that a PANTOMIME will be a most rational and instructive entertainment: and it is to be hoped that none but principal performers will be suffered to have a part in it. How pleased would the town be this winter to read in one of the articles of news in the Public Advertiser, " We hear that at each of the theatres " royal there is an entire new PANTOMIME now actu- " ally in rehearsal, and that the principal parts are to " be performed by Mr. Garrick, Mr. Woodward, Mr. " Mossop, Mrs. Cibber and Mrs. Pritchard at Drury- " Lane ; and at Covent-Garden by Mr. Quin, Mr. Lun, " Mr. Barry, Miss Nossiter, &c. It is not to be doubted that a PANTOMIME so acted would run through the whole season to the politest as well as most crowded audiences. Indeed, I have often wondered at the good-humour of the town, that they can bear to see night after night so elegant an entertainment, with only one performer in it of real reputation.

IT was very well observed by a person of quality, " That if Mr. Addison, Doctor Swift and Mr. Pope " were alive, and were unitedly to write a PANTOMIME

" every

" every winter, provided Mr. Garrick and Mrs. Cibber
" were to do the principal parts, he verily believed
" there would not be a hundred people at any one rout
" in town, except it was of a funday." If it be from
no other confideration than this, I am for having PAN-
TOMIMES exhibited to the beft advantage; and though
we have no fuch WITS among us as his lordfhip was
pleafed to name, we are reckoned to have as good CAR-
PENTERS as any age has produced : and I take it, that the
moft ftriking beauties of PANTOMIMICAL compofition
are to be afcribed to the CARPENTER, more than to the
WIT. I am,

SIR,

Your conftant reader,

and moft humble fervant,

S. W.

LONDON: Printed for R. DODSLEY in Pall-Mall, (where
letters to the author are taken in) and fold by M. COOPER at the
Globe in Pater-Nofter-Row. Price 2 d.

THE
W O R L D.

N U M B E R LXXV.

By *A D A M F I T Z - A D A M.*

To be continued every T H U R S D A Y.

T H U R S D A Y, *June* the 6th, 1754.

I HAVE hinted more than once in the courfe of thefe papers, that the prefent age, notwithftanding the vices and follies with which it abounds, has the happinefs of ftanding as high in my opinion as any age whatfo-ever. But it has always been the fafhion to believe, that from the beginning of the world to the prefent day, men have been encreafing in wickednefs : and
> though

though we have the bible to turn to, which gives us the hiftory of mankind before the flood, and of the Jews after it, we have ftill the humility to retain this opinion, and to lament the amazing degeneracy of the prefent times. But the eye of a philofopher can penetrate into this falfe humility, and difcover it to be mere peevifhnefs and difcontent. The prefent times, like our wives and our other poffeffions, are OUR OWN, and therefore we have no relifh of them.

MANY of my readers may poffibly object to thefe encomiums on the times, imagining they may tend to make men fatisfied with what they are, inftead of inciting them to become what they ought to be. But it was always my opinion (and I believe it to be univerfally true) that men are more likely to be PRAISED into virtue, than to be RAILED out of vice. It is a maxim in everybody's mouth, that reputation once loft, is never to be recovered. He therefore to whom you give an ill name, will have little or no encouragement to endeavour at a good one, as knowing that if a character of infamy is once fixed, no change of behaviour can have power to redeem it. On the contrary, the man to whom you give a good name, 'hough he fhould have merited a bad one, will find in his commerce with the world the advantages of fuch a name, and from conviction of thofe advantages, will be fo folicitous to deferve it, as to become in reality the good man you have called him. People may reafon away the merit of fuch a perfon's behaviour if they pleafe, by afcribing it folely to felf-love; they may add too, if they chufe (and they have my hearty leave) that all virtue whatfoever has it's fource in that paffion: if

this

this be true (though the revealers of fuch truths cannot be complimented on their intention to promote virtue) can there be a ftronger argument for goodnefs,
than that it is neceffary to our happinefs? It is laid of
that fagacious infect, the bee, that he extracts honey
from poifon: and a mind, rightly turned, may draw
inftruction even from thefe gentlemen. But to return
to my fubject.

IF people, when they are railing againft the prefent
times, inftead of afferting in the grofs that they are
more wicked than the paft, would content themfelves
with pointing out what are really the vices that have
gathered head amongft us; if, for inftance, they were
to fay that luxury and gaming are at prefent at
a much higher pitch than formerly, I fhould be far
from contradicting them. Thefe are indeed the vices
of the times: but for the firft of them, I am afraid we
muft content ourfelves with complaints, inftead of offering at a remedy: for as luxury is always owing to too
much wealth, Providence in it's wifdom has fo ordered
it, that in due courfe of time it will deftroy itfelf. The
cure therefore of luxury is poverty; a remedy, which
though we do not care to prefcribe to ourfelves, we are
preparing at great pains and expence for thofe that are
to come after us. Of gaming I fhall only obferve, that,
like luxury, it will in time work out it's own cure; and
at the rate it goes on at prefent, one fhould imagine
that it cannot laft long.

I KNOW but of one evil more that feems to have gathered any degree of ftrength in thefe times, and that
is corruption: for as to extravagance and a love of pleafure, I include them in the article of luxury. And perhaps

haps the evil of corruption, as it is now practiced, may admit of palliation: for though it has been afferted by certain writers upon ethics, that it is unlawful to do evil that good may enfue, yet fomething may be faid in favour of a candidate for a feat in parliament, who if he fhould be tempted to commit the fmall evil of bribing a borough or a few particulars in a county, it is, no doubt, in order to effect fo great a good as the prefervation of the liberty, the property, the happinefs, the virtue, and the religion of a whole nation.

As to all other vices, I believe they will be found to exift amongft us pretty much in the fame degree as heretofore, forms only changing. Our grandfathers ufed to get drunk with ftrong beer and port; we get drunk with claret and champagne. They would lie abominably to conceal their wenching; we lie as abominably in boafting of ours. They ftole flyly in at the back-door of a bagnio; we march in boldly at the fore-door, and immediately fteal out flyly at the back-door. Our mothers were prudes; their daughters are coquetts. The firft dreffed like modeft women, and perhaps were wantons; the laft drefs like women of the town, and perhaps are virtuous. Thofe treated without hanging out a fign; thefe hang out the fign without intending to treat. To be ftill more particular, the abufe of power, the views of patriots, the flattery of dependants, and the promifes of great men, are I believe pretty much the fame now as in former ages. Vices that we have no relifh for, we part with for thofe we like; giving up avarice for prodigality, hypocrify for profligacy, and lewdnefs for play.

BUT

But as I have inftanced in this effay the particular vices of the times, it would be doing them injuftice if I neglected to obferve, that humanity, charity and the civilities of life never abounded fo much as now. I muft alfo repeat, what has already been taken notice of in thefe papers, that our virtues receive a luftre, and our vices a foftening, by manners and decorum.

There is a folly, indeed (for I will not call it a vice) with which the ladies of this age are particularly charged: it is, that not only their airs and their drefs, but even their faces are French. I wifh with all my heart that I could preferve my integrity, and vindicate my fair country women from this imputation: but I am forry to fay it, what by travelling abroad, and by French milleners, mantua-makers and hair-cutters at home, our politeft affemblies feem to be filled with foreigners. But how will it aftonifh many of my readers to be told, that while they are extolling the days of good queen Bess, they are complimenting that very reign in which thefe fafhions were originally introduced! But becaufe in a matter of fo much confequence no man's bare word fhould be taken, I fhall make good my affertion by publifhing an authentic letter, written by that fubtil minifter Sir William Cecil (afterwards lord Burleigh) to Sir Henry Norris, queen Elizabeth's ambaffador at the court of France. This letter was originally printed in the year fixteen hundred and fixty three among a collection of ftate letters called Scrinia Ceciliana, or Myfteries of Government, and is as follows.

" S i r,
" The queen's majefty would fain have a taylor that
" had fkill to make her apparel both after the French
" and

" and Italian manner: and fhe thinketh that you might
" ufe fome means to obtain fome one fuch there as
" ferveth that queen, without mentioning any manner
" of requeft in the queen's majefty's name. Firft to
" caufe my lady your wife to ufe fome fuch means to
" get one, as thereof knowledge might not come to
" the queen mother's ears, of whom the queen's ma-
" jefty thinketh thus; that if fhe did underftand that it
" were a matter wherein her majefty might be pleafured,
" fhe would offer to fend one to the queen's majefty:
" neverthelefs if it cannot be fo obtained by this indirect
" means, then her majefty would have you devife fome
" other good means to obtain one that were fkillful.

" *Yours in all truth,*

" W. Cecil."

I shall only obferve upon this letter (which I confefs to be a mafter-piece for fubtilty and contrivance)
that if by the introduction and increafe of French fafhions,
our religion and government are alfo in time to be
French (which many worthy patriots and elderly gentlewomen are in dreadful apprehenfion of) we ought no
doubt to throw off all regard to the memory of queen
Elizabeth, and to lament that her minifter was not im-
peached of high treafon, for advifing and encouraging fo
pernicious an attempt againft that Magna Charta of
drefs, the old Englifh Ruff and Fardingale.

L O N D O N: Printed for R. D O D S L E Y in Pall-Mall, (where
letters to the author are taken in) and fold by M. C O O P E R at the
Globe in Pater-Nofter-Row. Price 2 d.

THE

W O R L D.

NUMBER XCVI.

By *ADAM FITZ-ADAM.*

To be continued every THURSDAY.

THURSDAY, *October* the 31ſt, 1754.

 WAS not a little ſurpriſed the other day at receiving a letter by the penny-poſt, acquainting me that notwithſtanding all I had ſaid in a former paper concerning the general reformation that had taken place by means of theſe eſſays, there were people amongſt us who were taking pains to undo all I had done ; and that unleſs I exerted myſelf notably on a new occaſion, my labours for the good of mankind would fall ſhort of their effect. The writer of this letter proceeds to inform me, that he has lately obtained a ſight of a dramatic manuſcript (taken, as he ſuppoſes, from a ſtory in Machiavel) called BELPHEGOR, or the MARRIED DE-

VIL,

vil, which manufcript, he is credibly affured, is intended to be offered at one of the theatres this very feafon.
My correfpondent inveighs greatly againit the evu ten-
dency of this piece, of which he has fent me a fhort
tranfcript, entreating my publication of it, as a warning
to the managers againft confenting to it's exhibition.
The tranfcript, which confifts only of one fhort fcene,
together with the introduction, is exactly as follows.

BELPHEGOR, *a heathen devil, in the difguife of chriftian
flefh and blood, makes his entrance upon the ftage; where,
after a clap of thunder, and feveral flafhes of lightening,
another devil of a fmaller fize, dreffed like a lacquey, in a
flame-coloured livery, trimmed with black, and ftuck round
with fireworks, rifes from a trap door, delivers a letter
to* BELPHEGOR, *and, making a very low bow, defcends
in thunder and lightening as he rofe.* BELPHEGOR *then
comes forward and reads the letter, which contains thefe
words.*

  " FORASMUCH as our true and trufty devil and cou-
" fin, BELPHEGOR, hath, in obedience to our commands,
" fubmitted himfelf to the torments of the married ftate
" for one whole year upon earth, thereby to inftruct
" Us in the nature of wives, and to get remiffion of
" punifhments for all hufbands in thefe our realms;
" and We, well-knowing the many miferies he hath
" endured in this his ftate of flefh, and being gracioufly
" pleafed to releafe him from his bondage, have order-
" ed that the earth do open at fix in the evening of
" this prefent day, to re-admit him to our dominions.
" Given at our palace, &c.

" PLUTO."

BELPHEGOR *expreffes great joy at reading the letter,
and while he is thanking* PLUTO *for his clemency, and
congratulating*

congratulating himfelf that his deliverance is near at hand,
HARLEQUIN *enters at the back of the ftage, looking very
difconfolately, and bowing to* BELPHEGOR, *who, after fur-
veying him with wonder, exclaims as follows.*

BEL. Hey-day! Who, in the name of PROSERPINE,
have we here? Some other devil upon a frolic too, I
fuppofe! He looks plaguy difcontented. If thou art a
devil, fpeak to me. (*Harlequin fhakes his head*) A
Frenchman I prefume; but then he would have found
his tongue fooner. Are you married, friend?

HAR. A very miferable fellow, fir.

BEL. Why, ay; that founds a little like matrimony.
But who are you? For by the knave's look, and the
fool's coat, you fhould be fome extraordinary perfonage.

HAR. I could eat a little, fir.

BEL. Very likely, friend. But who are you, I fay?

HAR. A poor Harlequin, fir; married yefterday,
and now running away from my wife.

BEL. A Harlequin! What's that?

HAR. Were you never at the playhoufe, fir? A Harlequin is a man of wit without words; his bufinefs is
to convey moral fentiments with a nod of the head, or
a fhake of the nether parts—I'll fhew you after dinner,
if you pleafe, fir.

(BELPHEGOR *waves his hand, and a table rifes with
provifion and wine.*)

HAR. Sir, you moft humble fervant. If it was not
for hunger, now, I fhould beg leave to afk, fir, if you
are not the devil. (*Sits down and eats.*)

BEL. A devil that will do you no harm, friend.

HAR. But are you really the devil, fir?

BEL. Have you any objection, Mr. Harlequin?

HAR. None in the leaft, fir; it is not my way to
object to trifles. Sir, my humble duty to you. (*Drinks*)

Yes,

Yes, yes, fir, you muft be the devil, or fome fuch great perfon. And pray, fir, if one may make bold to afk, how go matters below, fir? I fuppofe you have a world of fine company there. But I am afraid, fir, the place is a little too fmoaky for the ladies.

BEL. To thofe who have not been ufed to town indeed————

HAR. To be fure, fir, the town is a very natural preparation. You live pretty much as we do, I fuppofe?

BEL. Pretty much fo, as to the pleafures of the place; rather lefs fcandal among us.

HAR. And more finning, perhaps?

BEL. Very little difference as to that: hypocrify we have none of: people of fafhion, you know, are above hypocrify; and we are chiefly people of fafhion.

HAR. No doubt, fir. A good many new-comers I reckon from England?

BEL. A good many, friend; we are particularly fond of the Englifh.

HAR. You have them of all profeffions, I prefume?

BEL. Lawyers we do not admit. They are good fort of people in general, and take great pains to come among us; but I don't know how it is, we are apt to be jealous of them I think————and fo they go a little lower down.

HAR. Divines of all religions, I fuppofe?

BEL. Rather of NO religion, friend: of thofe we have abundance; and very much refpected they are indeed.

HAR. Phyficians too no doubt?

BEL. And that's a little odd; for we have no deaths among us; and yet there is no country under Heaven, I believe, fo ftocked with phyficians as ours.

HAR. Any traders, pray?

BEL. A world of them, of the better fort. The induftry

duſtry and wealth of thoſe gentlemen will always ſecure them a warm place with Us.

HAR. Atheiſts I ſuppoſe in plenty?

BEL. Atheiſts! Not that I remember. We have abundance of fine gentlemen; but I never heard that they profeſſed atheiſm below.

HAR. And pray, ſir, do any of the players make you a viſit?

BEL. I never heard that they went anywhere elſe. They are a little unmanageable indeed; but we have them all, from Roſcius of Rome, to Joe Millar of Drury-lane: and a fine company they are. Beſides, we have all the wits that ever wrote; and then we have no licencer to be a check upon their fancies; though I don't remember that lewdneſs has been carried a degree farther than with You.

HAR. Very likely, ſir. But pray, ſir, if I may be indulged, who are your favourite ladies at preſent?

BEL. Why, indeed, among ſo large a number, it is hard to ſay which. The nuns of all nations are reckoned mighty good ſort of women; but a devil of true taſte will tell you that a thorough-bred Engliſh woman of quality will go beyond them.

HAR. You are pleaſed to compliment the Engliſh ladies, ſir. And what extraordinary buſineſs, if I may have leave to aſk, may have been the occaſion of this viſit?

BEL. Curioſity and a wife: the very two things that ſend you gentlemen upon a viſit to Us.

HAR. May be ſo. And pray, ſir, what ſtay do you intend to make?

BEL. Only this evening.

HAR. Can I do you any ſervice, ſir?

BEL.

BEL. Ay; you fhall make love to my wife.

HAR. Her ladyfhip is from hell too, I fuppofe?

BEL. Going thither as faft as fhe can, Mr. Harlequin——But I hear her coming; walk this way, and
I'll inftruct you.   *Exeunt.*

THUS ends the fcene; which my correfpondent inveighs againft with fo much bitternefs, that when I confider it throughout, I am almoft of opinion that (in the
fafhionable phrafe) he is *taking me in,* and that he has
defired my publication of it in order to excite curiofity,
and to get the piece talked of before it's appearance upon
the ftage. And indeed this method of PUFFING by
ABUSE is frequently the moft fuccefsful of any; for as
in thefe very reformed times a wicked book is fo rare to
be met with, people will be tempted to read it out of
mere curiofity.

I REMEMBER a very fceptical pamphlet, that was
nowhere to be feen but in the bookfeller's fhop, till the
author bethought himfelf of felecting the moft offenfive
paffages of it, and by printing them in the Daily Adver-
tifer, and calling upon the clergy to confute, and the
magiftrate to fupprefs fo pernicious a performance,
he carried it through three impreffions in lefs than
a fortnight. If my prefent correfpondent has adopted
this plan, I fhall take care to counterwork his defign,
by giving it as my opinion, that the above fcene (however it may be objected to by people of a particular turn)
is perfectly harmlefs.

L O N D O N: Printed for R. D O D S L E Y in Pall-Mall, (where
letters to the author are taken in) and fold by M C O O P E R at the
Globe in Pater-Nofter-Row. Price 2d.

THE

W O R L D.

NUMBER XCVII.

By *ADAM FITZ-ADAM.*

To be continued every THURSDAY.

THURSDAY, *November* the 7th, 1754.

 THE following letter is written with such an air of truth, that, though it comes from one of those unhappy creatures who have always a story to tell in palliation of their infamy, I cannot refuse giving it a place in this paper. If the artifice that undid this poor girl be a common one, it may possibly be less practiced by being more known. All I shall say farther is, that I have made no other alteration in the letter, than to correct false spellings and a few errors in the English.

To Mr. FITZ-ADAM.

SIR,

I AM the daughter of very honest and reputable parents in the north of England; but as an account of my family does in no way relate to my story, I shall avoid troubling you with any farther particulars on that head. At the age of seventeen I had leave from my father and mother to accompany a neighbouring family of some distinction to town, having lived in the strictest intimacy with the young ladies of that family ever since I was a child.

AT

AT our arrival in town, we were vifited by a great deal of company, and among the reft, by a young gentleman of fortune, who feldom paffed a day without feeing us. As this gentleman's family, and that of my friends had been long acquainted, his admiffion to us was without the leaft ceremony; and indeed he was looked upon by the young ladies and myfelf rather as a brother than a vifitor. I had often obferved, and I confefs, with a fecret fatisfaction, that his behaviour to Me, efpecially when alone, was fomewhat more particular than to any of my companions; and I could not help placing it to his favourable opinion of me, that he was continually contriving parties abroad to amufe and entertain us.

ONE afternoon, having been troubled with the head-ach in the morning, and having therefore excufed myfelf from dining and fupping out with the family where I lived, he called, as he had many times done, to afk us to the play. I expreffed my concern at the ladies being from home, but foolifhly fuffered myfelf to be perfuaded to go alone with him into the gallery, after having been laughed at for my objections, and told that I ought to have a better opinion of him than to think him capable of afking me to do an improper thing.

WHEN the play was over, we took coach to return home; but the coachman, having no doubt received his leffon, ftopped juft at the door of a tavern, telling us that one of the traces was broke, and that he could go no farther. I fuffered myfelf to be handed into the tavern, while another coach was called, which not being immediately to be had, my companion obferved to me fmilingly, that it was a happy accident, and as the family I lived with would not fup at home, I fhould be his gueft that evening; and without waiting for a reply, ordered fupper and a bottle of champaign. It was in vain that I remonftrated againft this propofal; he knew, he faid, that my friends would not return till twelve; and there could be no kind of harm in eating a bit of chicken, and drinking a glafs of wine where we were. I was frightened at the thoughts of what I was doing, but was indifcreet enough to confent. His behaviour to me all the time was the moft refpectful in the world. He took care to engage my attention by fome interefting difcourfe, affuring me, as often as I attempted to move, that it was quite early, and that till a coach could be had, it was to no purpofe to attempt going.

I VERY freely confefs, that being extremely heated at the playhoufe, I was tempted to drink a glafs or two of of wine more than I was accuſtomed to, which flurried me a good deal; and as my heart was by no means indifferent to Him who was entertaining me, the time paſſed away almoſt imperceptibly. However, recollecting myſelf at laſt, I inſiſted peremptorily upon going; when, ſeeing me in earneſt, he pulled out his watch, and, as if violently ſurpriſed, declared it was paſt two o'clock; adding, in the greateſt ſeeming conſternation, that it would be impoſſible for me to go home that night, and curſing his own folly for the miſchief he had brought upon me.

I will not attempt, Mr. Fitz-Adam, to deſcribe the confuſion I was in. Yet ſtill I inſiſted upon going home, which he endeavoured to diſuade me from, by ſaying, that he too well knew the temper of the gentleman at whoſe houſe I lived, to think of carrying me thither at ſo late an hour; that he would conduct me to a lady of his acquaintance, who ſhould wait on me home in the morning, and make an excuſe for my lying out. I anſwered him, that I would lie nowhere but at home; that I deteſted myſelf for going out with him, and that I would return immediately, let the hour be what it would. " Let us go firſt of all, replied he; to the la-
" dy's, where I will leave you but for a moment, and
" ſee if the family are ſitting up for you; for to knock
" at the door and be refuſed admittance would ruin
" your reputation in the opinion of all the neighbour-
" hood." I ſtill inſiſted upon going home; and a coach was accordingly called and procured; but inſtead of carrying me to my friends, it ſtopped at a houſe in another ſtreet. Here I was forced againſt my will to alight. The miſtreſs of it was up; a circumſtance which I ſhould have wondered at, if I had not been frightened almoſt to death, and incapable of thinking, ſpeaking, or knowing what I did.

The wretch, after having apologized to the lady for the diſtreſs he had brought me into, left me in great haſte, to bring me intelligence of what was doing at home. He returned in a ſhort time, and with the greateſt ſeeming concern in his countenance, told me, that he had learnt from one of the ſervants, that the family had ſupped at home; that they were exaſperated againſt me beyond forgiveneſs; that they concluded me undone; and that they had ſworn never to admit me within their doors again.

I was quite thunderſtruck at this intelligence, and accuſed the wretch who brought it me as the vileſt of
men.

men. He fell upon his knees, conjuring me not to think him capable of any defign in what was done, and vowing to facrifice his life and fortune to reinftate me in the good opinion of my friends. I was obliged now to put myfelf under his protection; but refufed going to bed, though preffed to it by the lady of the houfe, who called herfelf his relation. Early in the morning, taking the lady along with him, he pretended to go again to my friends; but returned to me with an account that they were quite outrageous againft me, and abfolutely determined never to fee me again. I wrote to them in the moft moving manner that my heart could dictate, and gave the letter to the care of this falfe friend. I wrote alfo to my parents letter after letter, but without receiving a fyllable from them in return; fo that I now looked upon myfelf as compleatly undone. The anxiety I fuffered threw me into a fever, during which time the wretch hardly ever ftirred from my bed-fide, vowing that his life depended upon my recovery. I was foon indeed reftored to my health, but never to my peace. My betrayer began now to talk to me of love; and I began foolifhly to regard him as one that had fuffered too much for what I could not impute to him as a crime. He faw, and took care hourly to improve, my too favourable opinion of him; and at length (for why fhould I dwell minutely on what I wifh forever to forget?) by a thoufand ftratagems on his fide, and by fatal inclination on my own, irrecoverably undid me.

FROM that very day his affections began to cool: and (will it be believed when I tell it?) he grew in a very little time to hate me to that degree, that in order to get rid of me, and to make our feparation my own act, he confeffed to me the whole fcheme he had laid to get me; fhewed me advertifements in the papers from my friends and parents, offering rewards for my difcovery; and returned me the letters I had written to them, every one of which he had detained.

I STOOD aftonifhed at his villany, and abhorred him in my foul. But alas! it was now too late for me to apply to friends. Ruminating one afternoon on my deplorable condition, I was furprifed at feeing an elderly lady enter my chamber. She made me an apology for her vifit, and very frankly told me, that from fome diftant hints which fhe had that day received from the miftrefs of the houfe, fhe apprehended I was fallen into bad hands; which, if true, fhe would be glad to affift me to the utmoft of her power. She fpoke this with fo

much

much affection and good-nature, that I made no fcruple of telling her my whole ftory, which fo extremely affected her, that fhe fhed tears while I fpoke, and often interrupted me with her exclamations againft the villany of men. At the conclufion fhe offered that moment to take me away, affuring me that her houfe, her purfe, and her finacereft friendfhip fhould always be mine. I would have fallen on my knees to thank her, but fhe prevented me ; and ordering a coach to be called, fhe conveyed me that very evening to her country houfe.

I STAYED there a week, and met with the moft kind and tender treatment from her. She compelled me to accept of fome changes of clothes and linen, and then brought me to her houfe in town ; where, in lefs than four-and-twenty hours, fhe told me, without the leaft ceremony, that I no doubt knew for what purpofe fhe had taken me, and that as I could have no pretenfions to modefty, fhe hoped my behaviour would be fuch as fhould give her no occafion to repent of her kindnefs to me. I defired to underftand her, and was informed (though not in plain words) that my benefactrefs was a bawd, and that fhe had taken me into her family for the moft infamous of purpofes. I trembled with amazement, and infifted on leaving the houfe that inftant. She told me, I was at full liberty to do fo ; but that firft I muft pay her for my lodging and clothes. She fpoke this with great eafe and carelelfnefs, and then left me to my-felf. I ran down ftairs with precipitation ; but alas ! fcarce was I out of the ftreet before I was ftopt and brought back by a bailiff who had a writ againft me. I requefted that I might have leave to write to the gentle-man from whom I had been taken : for bad as he was, I faid, he would not utterly defert me. I was permitted to write as I defired ; and the wretch indeed anfwered my letter : but it was only to tell me, that as I had thought proper to run away from him, he fhould have nothing farther to fay to me ; and that, in fhort, I muft either fubmit to conditions, or go immediately with the bailiff. Frightened at the horrors of a prifon, and hoping that my ftory might move compaffion in thofe to whom I was to be introduced, I confented to do as they would have me. But alas, fir ! I was miftaken : they liftened in-deed to my ftory ; but inftead of melting at my misfor-tunes, they adored me, they faid, for my invention. At length, having led the life of a proftitute for more than a month, I attempted to make a fecond efcape, and to fly to the hands of juftice for protection : but I was again caught, and carried to a fpunging-houfe ; where,

after

after remaining two days, a gentleman who had been
admitted to me at that vile woman's, came to see me in
my confinement, paid off the debt for which I was arreſted, and took me to be his miſtreſs.

But though the life I now lead is in ſome degree
more ſupportable than that which I have eſcaped from,
yet to one who hopes that ſhe has ſtill ſome remains of
principle left, it is terrible and ſhocking. My friends
know what I am, and what I have been, but they reject
and hate me: and I have not the leaſt glimmering of
hope ever to recover from the ſituation I am in, unleſs
my ſtory ſhould merit the compaſſion of Him to whom
I now ſend it, and find a place in the World. Vile as
I am, I would be otherwiſe if I might. I am not old
in wickedneſs, though I have gone ſuch lengths in it;
being now really and truly but juſt turned of eighteen,
and having left my father's houſe no more than fifteen
months ago, two of which months I lived in innocence
and reputation with the moſt worthy of families.

As to him who has brought upon me all this weight
of miſery, and who ſerenely and unconcernedly can reflect upon what he has done (for ſo I am ſure he does) I
have nothing to fear, and nothing to hope. I can therefore have but one inducement to deſire your publication
of this letter, which is, that my friends may know that I
have gained that credit with a ſtranger which they have
refuſed to give me, and that I am really and truly an
object of compaſſion.

I am, Sir,

(though loſt to myſelf)

Your moſt faithful humble ſervant.

LONDON: Printed for R. DODSLEY in Pall-Mall, (where
letters to the author are taken in) and ſold by M. COOPER at the
Globe in Pater-Noſter-Row. Price 2d.

T H E

W O R L D.

NUMBER CLXXXIII.

By *ADAM FITZ-ADAM.*

To be continued every THURSDAY.

THURSDAY, *July* the 1ft, 1756.

I T was with great fatisfaction that I attended to the declaration of war againft France, having for above a twelve-month paft been fenfibly hurt in my own private property by the people of that nation. Yet injured as I was, I concealed my refentment while there was the leaft expectation of peace, that it might not be faid of me I had contributed, by any complaints of my own, to the involving my country in a hazardous and expenfive war.

EVERYBODY

EVERYBODY knows, that till within thefe two years, or thereabouts, it was a general fafhion for the ladies to wear hair upon their heads ; and I had piqued myfelf not a little on the thoughts that thefe my papers had been of confiderable fervice towards curling the faid hair.   I had indeed long ago difcovered, that very few ladies of condition could fpare time and attention enough from the various avocations of drefs, vifiting, affemblies, plays, operas, Ranelagh and Vauxhall, to read over a paper that contained no lefs than fix pages in folio ; but as the demand for the WORLD was ftill very confiderable, I contented myfelf with knowing that I was every week adorning their heads, though I could not be permitted to improve their underftandings; and it was a particular pleafure to me in all public affemblies, to think that the fineft faces there were indebted to the goodnefs of my paper for fetting them off. So long as the fafhion of hair continued (and to fay truth, I never fo much as dreamt that it was fo foon to change) I depended on the cuftom of the fair and polite ; but by the inftigation of French hair-cutters, whom the minifters of their monarch have fent to this metropolis in pure fpite to me, the ladies have been prevailed on to cut their hair clofe to their temples, to the great diminution of the fale of thefe papers.

IT was formerly a very agreeable amufement to me to look in at Mr. Dodfley's on a Thurfday morning, and obferve the great demand for thefe my lucubrations ; but though the fame demand continues among the men, I have frequently the mortification of hearing a fmart footman delivering a meffage in the fhop, " that his lady defires Mr. Dodfley will fend her " in no more WORLDS, for that fhe has cut off her " hair, and fhall have no occafion for them any longer.'

NOBODY

NOBODY will, I believe, make the leaft doubt that my principal view in this work was to amend the morals and improve the underftandings of my fellow-fubjects; but I will honeftly confefs, that ever fince the commencement of it, I have entertained fome diftant hopes of laying up a fortune fufficient to fupport me in my old age; and as money is at fo low an intereft, I intended making a fmall purchafe in fome retired and pleafant part of England, that I might have devoted my labours to the cultivation of land, after having weeded men's minds of whatever choaked the growth of virtue and good manners.   This I do not yet defpair of effecting, as I am not without hopes that while we are at open war with France, the ladies will conceive fuch a diflike to the fafhions of their enemies, as to let their hair grow again.   If this cannot fpeedily be brought about, I muft be forced to apply to the minifters for fome lucrative employment, in return for that indulgence and complaifance which I have at all times fhewn them.   It is impoffible for me to conceive that my merits have been overlooked, though they have hitherto been unrewarded; and I make no kind of doubt that I need only prefent myfelf at their levees, to be afked what poft I would chufe.   They do not want to be affured that I am as willing as able to affift them in all emergencies; or, which is ftill better, to vindicate their conduct againft all oppofers, to ftifle clamours in their birth, to convert fears to hopes, complaints to approbation, and faction to concord.

BUT as I do not at prefent recollect any particular poft of honour and profit that would better fuit me than another, and knowing that the abufers of an adminiftration are firft to be provided for, I am willing to accept of a

handfome

handfome fum of money, till fomething elfe may be done; or if a feat in parliament, with a proper qualifi-cation, be thought neceffary for me, I entirely acquiefce, as my eloquence in the houfe muft be of fignal fervice in all critical conjunctures. It would alfo be perfectly agreeable to me, if the government were to take off weekly twenty or thirty thoufand of my papers, and circulate them among their friends; or if they object to fuch an expence, and fhould difcover no inclination to oblige me in any of the particulars abovementioned, I humbly intreat, that in lieu of the depredations made upon me by the French hair-cutters, and in confidera-tion of my firm attachments to his Majefty's family and government, orders be immediately iffued from the lord Steward's office, the board of Green-cloth, or elfewhere, that henceforward all the tarts, pyes, paftry and confec-tionary of any kind whatfoever, appertaining to his Ma-jefty's houfehold, be conftantly baked upon thefe papers. This would be making me fufficient amends, and great-ly encourage me to continue this ufeful work till a per-fect library might be made of it, which otherwife muft have an end before a hundred volumes can be com-pleted.

THAT the miniftry may entertain juft notions of the efficacy of my good word, I fhall here prefent them with fome few of thofe offers, which are almoft daily made me by private perfons.

A LADY who has lately opened a new bagnio in Co-vent-garden, affures me in a letter, that if I will do her the favour to recommend her in the WORLD, I fhall not only have the run of her houfe, but every one of her young ladies fhall be obliged to take in my paper as long as it lafts. A grocer in the Strand has fent me

a

a pound of his beſt tea, and promiſes to wrap up every ounce he ſells, as alſo all his ſugars and ſpices, in theſe papers, if I will honour him ſo far as to make mention of him in any one of them. He adds in a poſtſcript, that his wife and five daughters, who do a great deal of work, make all their thread-papers of WORLDS.

BUT a more material offer ſtill, and which I have therefore reſerved for the laſt, is contained in the following letter.

To ADAM FITZ-ADAM,

ESTEEMED FRIEND,

THIS is to acquaint thee that we are makers of pins on the bridge called London bridge, and that we have each of us given a conſiderable portion of money for the good-will of the habitations wherein we make abode : but by an act of the legiſlature lately paſſed, the ſaid habitations are ſpeedily to be pulled down, and their dwellers to be forced to remove to other abodes. If thou art in the leaſt acquainted with traffic, thou canſt not be ignorant of the benefits that accrue from an old eſtabliſhed ſhop, in a ſtreet where the principal dealers in any particular commodity are known to dwell ; inaſmuch as when thou wanteſt a ſilken garment for thy wife, thou wouldſt repair to the habitations of Round court or Ludgate hill ; or if thy linen was rent, thou wouldſt doubtleſs reſort to Cheapſide or Cornhill : in like manner, if thy help-mate or thy maidens wanted pins, thou wouldſt not fail, if thou wert wiſe, to take thy walk to London bridge. But by the act above-named, thy friends are exiled from their dwellings, and compelled to ſojourn in a ſtrange ſtreet, where even their names are unknown. We therefore requeſt it of thee, if the rulers of the land behold thee with regard, that thou wilt apply thyſelf ſpeedily

to

to obtain a repeal of this act; wherein if thou fucceedeft, we will buy up thy weekly labours in reams, and ftick all our pins therein, fo that thy name fhall be known far and wide, and thy days profperous in the land.

If thou art a well-wifher to thyfelf, thou wilt ufe thy beft endeavours for the fervice of

Thy friends,

EPHRAIM MINNIKIN,
MALACHY SHORTWHITE,
OBADIAH MIDLING,
HEZEKIAH LONGPIN,
&c. &c.

AFTER duly deliberating upon this propofal, I am enclined to trouble the government no farther at prefent than to requeft the repeal of this act, which if they are fo kind as to grant me, my papers will again find their way to the drefling-rooms of the ladies, in fpite of the intrigues of France, and her emiffaries the hair-cutters.

LONDON: Printed for R. and J. DODSLEY in Pall-Mall, (where letters to the author are taken in) and fold by M. COOPER at the Globe in Pater-Nofter-Row.   Price 2d.

T H E

W O R L D.

N U M B E R CXCII.

By *A D A M F I T Z - A D A M.*

To be continued every THURSDAY.

THURSDAY, *September* the 2d, 1756.

I N all my refearches into the human heart (the ftudy of which has taken up my principal attention for thefe forty years paft) I have never been fo confounded and perplexed as at difcovering that while people are indulging themfelves openly and without difguife in the commiffion of almoft every vice that their natures encline them to, they fhould defire to conceal their virtues, as if they were really afhamed of them, and confidered them as fo many weaknefles in their conftitutions. I know a man at this very hour, who is in his heart the moft domeftic creature living, and whofe wife and children are the only delight of his life, yet who for fear of
being

being laughed at by his acquaintance, and to get a reputation in the world, is doing penance every evening at the tavern, and perpetually hinting to his companions that he has a miftrefs in private. I am acquainted with another, who being over-heard upon a fick bed to recommend himfelf to the care of Heaven in a fhort ejaculation, was fo afhamed at being told of it, that he pleaded lightheadednefs for his excufe, protefting that he could not poffibly have been in his right fenfes, and guilty of fuch a weaknefs. I know alfo a third, who from a ferious turn of mind, goes to church every funday in a part of the town where he is totally unknown, that he may recommend himfelf to his acquaintance by laughing at public worfhip, and ridiculing the parfons.

THERE are men who are fo fond of the reputation of an intrigue with a handfome married woman, that without the leaft paffion for the object of their purfuit, or perhaps the ability to gratify it if they had, are toafting her in all companies, purfuing her to every public place, and eternally buzzing in her ear, to convince the world that they are in poffeffion of a happinefs, which if offered to them, would only end in their difappointment and difgrace. And what is ftill more unaccountable, the lady, thus purfued, who poffibly prefers her hufband to all other men, fhall countenance by her behaviour the fufpicions entertained of her; and contenting herfelf with the fecret confcioufnefs of her innocence, fhall take pains to be thought infamous by the whole town.

THAT there are perfons of a different ftamp from thefe, I very readily allow; perfons who determine to pay themfelves by pleafure for the fcandal they have occafioned. But it is really my opinion, that if the mafk

were

were taken off, we fhould find more virtues and fewer
vices to exift amongft us, than are commonly imagined
by thofe who judge only from appearances.

A VERY ingenious French writer, fpeaking of the
force of cuftom and example, makes the following remarks upon his own countrymen.

" A MAN, fays he, of good fenfe and good nature
" fpeaks ill of the abfent, becaufe he would not be
" defpifed by thofe who are prefent. Another would
" be honeft, humane, and without pride, if he was
" not afraid of being ridiculous : and a third becomes
" really ridiculous, through fuch qualities as would
" make him a model of perfection, if he dared to exert
" them, and affume his juft merits. In a word, con-
" tinues he, our vices are artificial as well as our virtues,
" and the frivoloufnefs of our characters permits us to
" be but imperfectly what we are. Like the play-things
" we give our children, we are only a faint refemblance
" of what we would appear. Accordingly we are
" efteemed by other nations only as the petty toys and
" trifles of fociety. The firft law of our politenefs re-
" gards the women. A man of the higheft rank owes
" the utmoft complaifance to a woman of the very low-
" eft condition, and would blufh for fhame, and think
" himfelf ridiculous in the higheft degree, if he offered
" her any perfonal infult. And yet fuch a man may
" deceive and betray a woman of merit, and blacken
" her reputation, without the leaft apprehenfion either
" of blame or punifhment."

I HAVE quoted thefe remarks that I might do juftice
to the candour of the Frenchman who wrote them, and
at the fame time vindicate my countrymen (unaccountable as they are) from the unjuft imputation of being
more ridiculous and abfurd than the reft of mankind.

IN

IN France every married woman of condition intrigues openly; and it is thought the higheſt breach of French politeneſs for the huſband to interfere in any of her plea- ſures. A man may be called to an account for having ſeduced his friend's ſiſter or daughter, becauſe it may be preſumed he has carried his point by a promiſe of marriage; but with a married woman the caſe is quite different, as her gallant can only have applied to her inclinations, or gratifiedsthe longings of a lady, whom it had been infamy to have refuſed.

THERE is a ſtory of a Frenchman, which as I have only heard once, and the majority of my readers per- haps never, I ſhall beg leave to relate. A banker at Paris, who had a very handſome wife, invited an En- gliſh gentleman, with whom he had ſome money trans- actions, to take a dinner with him at his country-houſe. Soon after dinner the Frenchman was called out upon buſineſs, and his friend left alone with the lady, who to his great ſurpriſe, from being the eaſieſt and gayeſt woman imaginable, ſcarcely condeſcended to give an anſwer to any of his queſtions, and at laſt, ſtarting from her chair, and ſurveying him for ſome time with a look of indignation and contempt, ſhe gave him a hearty box on the ear, and ran furiouſly out of the room. While the Engliſhman was ſtroaking his face, and endeavour- ing to penetrate into this myſterious behaviour, the huſ- band returned; and finding his friend alone, and en- quiring into the reaſon, was told the whole ſtory. What, ſir, ſays he, did ſhe ſtrike you? How did you entertain her? With the common occurrences of the town, anſwered the Engliſhman, nothing more I aſſure you. And did you offer no rudeneſs to her, returned the other? No, upon my honour, replied the friend.

She

She has behaved as fhe ought then, faid the Frenchman: for to be alone with a fine woman, and to make no attempt upon her virtue is an affront to her beauty; and fhe has refented the indignity as became a woman of fpirit.

I AM prevented from returning to the fubject of this paper, by a letter which I have juft now received by the penny-poft, and which I fhall lay before my readers exactly as it was fent me.

Mr. FITZ-ADAM,

WALKING up St. James's ftreet the other day, I was ftopt by a very fmart young female, who begged my pardon for her boldnefs, and looking very innocently in my face, afked me if I did not know her. The manner of her accofting me, and the extreme prettinefs of her figure, made me look at her with attention; and I foon recollected that fhe had been a fervant girl of my wife's, who had taken her from the country, and after keeping her three years in her fervice, had difmiffed her about two months ago. "What, Nanny, faid I, is it you?
" I never faw any body fo fine in all my life." O fir!"
" fays fhe (with the moft innocent fmile imaginable, brideling her head, and curt'fying down to the ground)
" I have been debauched fince I lived with my miftrefs."
": Have you fo, Mrs. Nanny, faid I! And pray, child,
" who is it that has debauched you?" "O fir! fays fhe,
" one of the worthieft gentlemen in the world, and he
" has bought me a new negligee for every day in the
" week." The girl preffed me earneftly to go and look at her lodgings, which fhe affured me were hard by in Bury ftreet, and as fine as a duchefs's; but I declined her offer, knowing that any arguments of mine in favour of virtue and ftuff-gowns, would avail but little againft

pleafure

pleafure and filk negligeès. I therefore contented myfelf with expreffing my concern for the way of life fhe
had entered into, and bad her farewell.

BEING a man enclined to fpeculate a little, as often as
I think of the finery of this girl, and the reafon alledged
for it, I cannot help fancying, whenever I fall in company with a pretty woman, dreffed out beyond her vifi-
ble circumftances, patched, painted and ornamented to
the extent of the mode, that fhe is going to make me
her beft curt'fy, and to tell me, O fir! I have been
debauched fince I kept good company.

BUT though this excufe for finery was given me by a
woman, I believe it may with equal propriety be applied
to the men. Fine places, fine fortunes, fine houfes, and
fine things of all kinds, are too often purchafed at the
expence of honefty; and I feldom fee a plain country
gentleman turned courtier, and bowing in a fine coat at
the levees of great men, whofe looks do not tell me
that he is come to town to be debauched.

I COULD wifh, Mr. Fitz-Adam, that from thefe rude
hints, you would favour your readers with a fpeculation
upon this fubject, which would be highly entertaining
to all, and particularly obliging to,

SIR,

Your moft obedient fervant,

C. D.

LONDON: Printed for R. and J. DODSLEY in Pall-Mall,
(where Letters to the author are taken in) and fold by M. COOPER at
the Globe in Pater-Nofter-Row. Price 2 d.

THE LIST OF TITLES

31. **The Plays of John O'Keeffe.** Edited with an introduction by Frederick M. Link. *Four volumes.*

32. **The Plays of Mary Pix and Catherine Trotter.** Edited with an introduction by Edna L. Steeves. *Two volumes.*

33. **The Plays of Frederick Reynolds.** Edited with an introduction by Stanley W. Lindberg. *Two volumes.*

34. **The Plays of Edward Thompson.** Edited with an introduction by Catherine Neal Parke.

35. **The Plays of James Thomson.** Edited with an introduction by Percy G. Adams.